ASCETICISM IN
GRAECO-ROMAN

Asceticism deploys abstention, self-control and self-denial, to order oneself or a community in relation to the divine. Both its practices and the cultural ideals they expressed were important to pagans, Jews, Christians of different kinds, and Manichees. Richard Finn presents for the first time a combined study of the major ascetic traditions, which have previously been misunderstood by being studied separately. He examines how people abstained from food, drink, sexual relations, sleep and wealth; what they meant by their behaviour; and how they influenced others in the Graeco-Roman world. Against this background, the book charts the rise of monasticism in Egypt, Asia Minor, Syria and North Africa, assessing the crucial role played by the third-century exegete, Origen, and asks why monasticism developed so variously in different regions.

RICHARD FINN OP is a Dominican friar and currently Regent of Blackfriars Hall at Oxford University, where he is a member of the Theology Faculty and of the Classics Faculty. He most recently published *Almsgiving in the Later Roman Empire* in 2006.

KEY THEMES IN ANCIENT HISTORY

EDITORS

P. A. Cartledge
Clare College, Cambridge
P. D. A. Garnsey
Jesus College, Cambridge

Key Themes in Ancient History aims to provide readable, informed and original studies of various basic topics, designed in the first instance for students and teachers of Classics and Ancient History, but also for those engaged in related disciplines. Each volume is devoted to a general theme in Greek, Roman, or where appropriate, Graeco-Roman history, or to some salient aspect or aspects of it. Besides indicating the state of current research in the relevant area, authors seek to show how the theme is significant for our own as well as ancient culture and society. By providing books for courses that are oriented around themes it is hoped to encourage and stimulate promising new developments in teaching and research in ancient history.

Other books in the series

Death-ritual and social structure in classical antiquity, by Ian Morris
978 0 521 37465 1 (hardback) 978 0 521 37611 2 (paperback)

Literacy and orality in ancient Greece, by Rosalind Thomas
978 0 521 37346 3 (hardback) 978 0 521 37742 3 (paperback)

Slavery and society at Rome, by Keith Bradley
978 0 521 37287 9 (hardback) 978 0 521 37887 1 (paperback)

Law, violence, and community in classical Athens, by David Cohen
978 0 521 38167 3 (hardback) 978 0 521 38837 5 (paperback)

Public order in ancient Rome, by Wilfried Nippel
978 0 521 38327 1 (hardback) 978 0 521 38749 1 (paperback)

Friendship in the classical world, by David Konstan
978 0 521 45402 5 (hardback) 978 0 521 45998 3 (paperback)

Sport and society in ancient Greece, by Mark Golden
978 0 521 49698 8 (hardback) 978 0 521 49790 9 (paperback)

Food and society in classical antiquity, by Peter Garnsey
978 0 521 64182 1 (hardback) 978 0 521 64588 1 (paperback)

Banking and business in the Roman world, by Jean Andreau
978 0 521 38031 7 (hardback) 978 0 521 38932 7 (paperback)

Roman law in context, by David Johnston
978 0 521 63046 7 (hardback) 978 0 521 63961 3 (paperback)

Religions of the ancient Greeks, by Simon Price
978 0 521 38201 4 (hardback) 978 0 521 38867 2 (paperback)

Christianity and Roman society, by Gillian Clark
978 0 521 63310 9 (hardback) 978 0 521 63386 4 (paperback)

Trade in classical antiquity, by Neville Morley
978 0 521 63279 9 (hardback) 978 0 521 63416 8 (paperback)

Technology and culture in Greek and Roman antiquity, by Serafina Cuomo
978 0 521 81073 9 (hardback) 978 0 521 00903 4 (paperback)

Law and crime in the Roman world, by Jill Harries
978 0 521 82820 8 (hardback) 978 0 521 53532 8 (paperback)

The social history of Roman art, by Peter Stewart
978 0 521 81632 8 (hardback) 978 0 521 01659 9 (paperback)

Asceticism in the Graeco-Roman world, by Richard Finn OP
978 0 521 86281 3 (hardback) 978 0 521 68154 4 (paperback)

ASCETICISM IN THE GRAECO-ROMAN WORLD

RICHARD FINN OP

CAMBRIDGE
UNIVERSITY PRESS

CAMBRIDGE UNIVERSITY PRESS
Cambridge, New York, Melbourne, Madrid, Cape Town, Singapore, São Paulo, Delhi

Cambridge University Press
The Edinburgh Building, Cambridge CB2 8RU, UK

Published in the United States of America by Cambridge University Press, New York

www.cambridge.org
Information on this title: www.cambridge.org/9780521681544

© Richard Finn 2009

First published 2009

Printed in the United Kingdom at the University Press, Cambridge

A catalogue record for this publication is available from the British Library

Library of Congress Cataloguing in Publication data
Finn, R. D. (Richard Damian), 1963–
Asceticism in the Graeco-Roman world / Richard Finn.
p.   cm. – (Key themes in ancient history)
Includes bibliographical references and index.
ISBN 978-0-521-86281-3 (hardback)
1. Asceticism – History – Early church, ca. 30–600.   2. Ascetics – Rome.
3. Origen.   I. Title.   II. Series.
BV5023.F56   2009
204′.470937 – dc22   2009009367

ISBN 978-0-521-86281-3 hardback
ISBN 978-0-521-68154-4 paperback

For Anthony

Contents

Acknowledgements

My academic debts are many. It will be evident to the reader how far I have relied as a jack-of-all-trades upon the scholarship of others whose particular expertise exceeds my knowledge of their specialist field. They are, I hope, appropriately identified in the footnotes. Three people have generously commented on drafts of individual chapters and thereby much improved them: Jaś Elsner, Sr Margaret Atkins OSA, and, above all, Peter Garnsey. I am immensely grateful to them for their work and encouragement. I should also thank Timothy Radcliffe OP and Ros Hunt for their patience with me in a project that has meant taking the laptop on holiday with us more times than I care to remember. However, even their patience has been exceeded by that of Michael Sharp at Cambridge University Press who allowed me the necessary time to complete the work. I thank him and his colleagues at the Press for their work in its production.

Abbreviations

ANRW	*Aufstieg und Niedergang der römischen Welt* (Berlin: de Gruyter, 1972–)
CA	*Clemens Alexandrinus*, ed. O. Stählin, L. Früchtel, and U. Treu, 4 vols., GCS (Berlin: Akademie Verlag, 1970–85)
CHC2	*Cambridge History of Christianity*, vol. II, *Constantine to c. 600*, ed. A. Casiday and F. W. Norris (Cambridge University Press, 2007)
CHJ4	*Cambridge History of Judaism*, vol. IV, *The Late Roman-Rabbinic Period*, ed. S. T. Katz (Cambridge University Press, 2006)
CCSL	*Corpus Christianorum Series Latina* (Turnhout: Brepols, 1953–)
CSCO	Corpus Scriptorum Christianorum Orientalium (Paris: Secretariat du CSCO, 1903–)
CSEL	Corpus Scriptorum Ecclesiasticorum Latinorum (Vienna: Tempsky, 1865–)
DL	Diogenes Laertius, *Lives of Eminent Philosophers*, ed. M. Marcovitch, *Diogenes Laertivs, Vitae Philosophorum*, 2 vols. (Stuttgart and Leipzig: Teubner, 1999)
DSS	*The Dead Sea Scrolls, A New Translation*, ed. M. Wise, M. Abegg, and E. Cook (London: Harper Collins, 1996)
En. in Ps.	*Enarrationes in Psalmos*
FC	Fathers of the Church
GCS	Die griechischen christlichen Schriftsteller (Berlin: Akademie Verlag, 1897–)
HTR	*Harvard Theological Review*
JAAR	*Journal of the American Academy of Religion*
JAOS	*Journal of the American Oriental Society*
JECS	*Journal of Early Christian Studies*
JEH	*Journal of Ecclesiastical History*

JHS	*Journal of Hellenic Studies*
JRS	*Journal of Roman Studies*
JThS	*Journal of Theological Studies*
NHL	*The Nag Hammadi Library in English*, ed. J. M. Robinson, 4th revised edition (Leiden, New York, and Cologne: Brill, 1996)
NTA	*New Testament Apocrypha*, ed. W. Schneemelcher and R. McL. Wilson, 2 vols. (Cambridge and Louisville: James Clarke and Westminster Press, 1991–2)
Or.	*Oration*
OSA	Oeuvres de saint Augustin
OTP	*The Old Testament Pseudepigrapha*, ed. J. H. Charlesworth, 2 vols. (London: DLT, 1983–5)
PG	Patrologia Graeca, ed. J.-P. Migne (Paris, 1857–66)
Ph*DVM*	Philo, *De vita Mosis*, ed. R. Arnaldez, C. Mondésert, J. Pouilloux, and P. Savinel (Paris: Éditions du Cerf, 1967)
Ph*DVC*	Philo, *De vita contemplativa*, ed. F. Daumas and P. Miquel (Paris: Éditions du Cerf, 1963)
PL	Patrologia Latina, ed. J.-P. Migne
PO	Patrologia Orientalis (Paris: Firmin-Didot, 1903–)
RB	*Revue Bénédictine*
SBLSP	*Society of Biblical Literature Seminar Papers*
SC	Sources chrétiennes (Paris: Cerf, 1942–)
Serm.	*Sermon*
Sev	*Severan Culture*, ed S. Swain, S. Harrison, and J. Elsner (Cambridge University Press, 2007)
SP	*Studia Patristica*, ed. E. A. Livingstone (Louvain: Peeters Press)
TBS	*The Book of Steps: The Syriac Liber Graduum*, tr. Robert A. Kitchen and Martien Parmentier (Kalamazoo: Cistercian Publications, 2004)
TS	*Theological Studies*
VC	*Vigiliae Christianae*
ZAC	*Zeitschrift für antikes Christentum*
ZNW	*Zeitschrift für die Neutestamentliche Wissenschaft*

Introduction

The mid-fourth-century bishop Basil of Ancyra conceded in his treatise on virginity that goodness took many forms within the Church and that his readers could readily find works exalting different aspects of the good life. There were hymns on virginity, texts praising those who mortified the flesh by fasting and sleeping on the ground, and lengthy eulogies of those who sold their possessions for the sake of the Lord.[1] The existence of this growing body of literature justified the bishop's decision to restrict his theme to consecrated virginity and the godlike freedom which it won from all that was corruptible. Basil offers us a glimpse into the sustained promotion of different practices we commonly term 'ascetic' and neatly raises numerous questions about those practices. While the bishop associated different practices with different lives, to what extent were these practices common elements to one and the same life of renunciation? What beliefs gave meaning to these practices? Did the beliefs and practices known to Basil in the fourth century differ from those familiar to Christians in earlier centuries and what was their relationship to the rise of monasticism? While the bishop wrote only of their value within the life of the Church, to what extent were these practices and beliefs common to Christians, pagans, and Jews? And what might be meant by terming them 'ascetic'? These are the questions which this book aims to answer in its account of asceticism in the Graeco-Roman world.

The loose definition of asceticism which I shall use is that of voluntary abstention for religious reasons from food and drink, sleep, wealth, or sexual activity. Such abstention may be periodic or permanent. In matters of fasting it may involve abstention from particular items such as meat or

---

[1] Basil of Ancyra, *On True Purity of Virginity*, 1, PG 30, 669. I look further at this text in Chapter 5. For brevity's sake, in referring to texts of classical and Patristic literature, I note the book and chapter without page reference to the critical edition, except where I cite the Greek or Latin text. The most important editions are listed in the bibliography. Unless otherwise indicated, translations are my own.

wine, or a more comprehensive refusal to eat or drink for a given period. The key point, however, is that the understanding which informs a given pattern of religious abstention makes for a distinctive form of asceticism. The Graeco-Roman world contained many different forms of asceticism, with different meanings for those who practised them. It has been argued that 'virtually any cultural practice can have multiple social meanings'.[2] It is these meanings which I hope to elucidate.

Like his fourth-century predecessor, the twenty-first-century author must swiftly admit that much literature already exists in his chosen field. My readers can already find major studies on individual topics: the nature of asceticism, the figure of the holy man, consecrated virgins, and the rise of monasticism.[3] Indeed, one reason for the present book is to make this scholarship accessible to the non-specialist and integrate it into a single story. There is additional virtue, however, in a comprehensive study. Too narrow a spotlight may fail to illuminate significant connections between events. Histories of monasticism, and our understanding of why monasticism grew rapidly in the fourth century, have been impoverished through failure to recognize the powerful ascetic currents that already existed in the Christianity of the first three centuries after Christ. To miss connections can lead the historian to misconstrue the question: we need to ask not why Christianity took an ascetic turn, but why new forms of asceticism became fashionable.

Furthermore, monastic and other ancient hagiography is biased towards the individual holy man or woman at the centre of its story. This may lead us to think of asceticism as primarily marking out the individual over and against others, as essentially a tool in the construction of personal holiness. We may then overlook much that is important about the communal asceticism observed in the Early Church, including the degree to which different versions of Christianity partly defined themselves over and against each other through their divergent ascetic practices. Although this book will acknowledge the widespread (though patchy) influence on fourth- and fifth-century monasticism of Athanasius' *Life* of St Antony, the

---

[2] D. Boyarin, *Carnal Israel: Reading Sex In Talmudic Culture* (Berkeley, Los Angeles and Oxford: University of California Press, 1993), 94–5.

[3] E.g., V. L. Wimbush and R. Valantasis (eds.), *Asceticism* (Oxford and New York: Oxford University Press 1995); P. Brown, 'The Rise and Function of the Holy Man in Late Antiquity,' *JRS* 61 (1971), 80–101, and 'The Saint as Exemplar in Late Antiquity', *Representations* 2 (1983), 1–25; P. Cox, *Biography in Late Antiquity: A Quest for the Holy Man* (Berkeley: University of California Press, 1983); S. Elm, *'Virgins of God': The Making of Asceticism in Late Antiquity* (Oxford: Clarendon Press, 1994); M. Dunn, *The Emergence of Monasticism* (Oxford: Blackwell, 2000); D. Caner, *Wandering, Begging Monks: Spiritual Authority and the Promotion of Monasticism in Late Antiquity* (Berkeley, Los Angeles, London: University of California Press, 2002).

Egyptian hermit so often taken as the 'father of monks', it also counters the undue and often unrecognized influence of the *Life* over modern views of Christian asceticism. It is neither accidental nor helpful that 'studies of asceticism usually begin with the late third and early fourth centuries'.[4]

Presuppositions about the novelty of Christianity, and about ancient religion generally as comprising discrete bodies of believers and doctrines; the disciplinary divisions in universities which traditionally separated Theology from Classics, Church History from Ancient History; a tendency within academia to favour classical Athens and Augustan Rome over Late Antiquity; these factors have together contributed to the lack of books which examine Christian asceticism in the context of pagan and Jewish ascetic practices.[5] Yet the danger of misconstruing the story through missed connections applies not just to those internal to Christianity; it applies equally to connections between Christians, pagans, and Jews. The history of Early Christian asceticism will be shown to involve not least the concurrence of Jewish penitential practices that belong to humble prayer with pagan philosophical beliefs about the role of ascetic restraint in securing the contemplation of God, a coexistence which was only partly a confluence. Looking to the wider picture can also throw up surprising blind spots elsewhere. When you look at pagan sources for Christian asceticism, you notice that the great interest which ancient writers expressed in the ascetic lives of the philosophers is not necessarily matched by modern scholars, even those concerned with the ethical teachings of those philosophers: the select index to Brad Inwood's *Ethics and Human Action in Early Stoicism* has no entries for 'asceticism' or 'ascesis', 'food', 'sex', or 'marriage'.[6] A valid interest in the meta-ethics of Stoicism has led to a relative neglect of ethics as a certain purposive lifestyle.

Studies may also adopt definitions of asceticism which emphasize certain continuities of practice and belief at the expense of others. Thus, Susanna Elm in her excellent book *Virgins of God* defines asceticism as a 'discipline' based 'on distinct stoic-platonic notions'. She understands it as 'a systematic method to achieve self-control' through which the 'practitioner' is transformed 'into a pure vessel of the divine will', thereby enabling 'communication with the divine through some form of *unio mystica*'.[7] This definition acknowledges the interplay of practice and belief, and stresses

[4] James A. Francis, *Subversive Virtue: Asceticism and Authority in the Second-Century Pagan World* (Pennsylvania State University Press, 1995), xv.
[5] On religion in antiquity, see further below.
[6] B. Inwood, *Ethics and Human Action in Early Stoicism* (Oxford: Clarendon Press, 1985).
[7] Elm, *Virgins*, 13–14.

something of what one form of Christian asceticism in Late Antiquity owes to pagan philosophy (in part via the Hellenistic Judaism of Philo); but it obscures other significant continuities of belief and practice with Judaism, and does not do justice to the symbolic role played by consecrated virginity in the Early Church. It also has the odd (if interesting) result of excluding Augustinian monasticism from the Christian ascetic tradition. Niketas Siniossoglou, on the other hand, in a recent study of Theodoret which is influenced by the latter's praise for Syriac Christian solitaries, has described Christian ascetics as those who 'abandoned society in order to be ascetics' and further characterizes Christian asceticism as aiming at 'an annihilation of human nature and will as such'. He has argued on this basis against the 'dubious, yet widespread idea of a supposed continuity of Hellenic philosophical *paideia* within the realm of late antique asceticism'.[8] Yet this is to privilege another and contrasting form of Christian asceticism under the influence of Late Antique hagiography. It downplays the understanding of consecrated virginity explored by Elm, the role of the virgin as symbol of divine grace in the Church, and the concern of Egyptian monks to recover the human nature gravely damaged by the Fall with its original eagerness or zest for union with God.

Teresa Shaw adopts a wide definition of asceticism without reference to the philosophical tradition whereby asceticism is 'a way of life that requires daily discipline and intentionality in bodily behaviours'.[9] This leads to a focus on individuals 'who, by their physical renunciations, distinguish themselves from the wider Christian populace'. Yet, as she acknowledges, this is to privilege the *daily* ascetic practices of the few over the *periodic* ascetic practices of the many. Richard Valantasis in probing the Early Christian *Gospel of Thomas* depends upon an even broader anthropological definition of asceticism as comprising 'performances within a dominant social environment intended to inaugurate a new subjectivity, different social relations, and an alternative symbolic universe'.[10] Nonetheless, this definition still emphasizes the transformative role which ascetic behaviour

---

[8] Niketas Siniossoglou, *Plato and Theodoret: The Christian Appropriation of Platonic Philosophy and the Hellenic Intellectual Resistance* (Cambridge University Press, 2008), 31 and 129.

[9] T. M. Shaw, *The Burden Of The Flesh: Fasting And Sexuality In Early Christianity* (Minneapolis: Fortress Press, *c.* 1998), 6.

[10] R. Valantasis, 'Is the Gospel of Thomas ascetical? Revisiting an old problem with a new theory', *JECS* 7.1 (1999), 64. Cf. the same author's, 'Constructions of power in asceticism', *JAAR* 63 (1995), 797. There, Valantasis draws fruitfully on Foucault to analyze asceticism as involving 'technologies' of self-formation and governance, and on social semiotic theory to examine ascetic solidarity. Repeated consideration of 'the ascetic' nonetheless indicates the understanding of asceticism as the lifestyle of a particular individual.

may have for a minority group or individual to the exclusion of the roles it may play in maintaining the communal identity of a dominant group or its hierarchy.[11] It proves unhelpful, for example, in understanding the role of communal fasting in early rabbinic Judaism. No one definition has commanded general assent.[12]

To speak, as my title does, of the Graeco-Roman world is itself to employ a loaded and imprecise concept that requires clarification. This study has fuzzy edges which are geographical, chronological, and cultural. The book is concerned largely with the men and women who lived in the Roman empire from the first to the mid fifth century, but necessarily examines older Greek, Roman, and Jewish religious traditions because of their enduring significance for Hellenistic culture, and further describes one form of Christian asceticism that straddled the border between Rome and Persia. Within the empire, ruling urban elites from diverse ethnic groups observed Greek cults; they erected temples, shrines, and statues that displayed their loyalty to the Roman state; but they also in places retained and adapted traditional cults which differed significantly in practice from what was customary in Greek or Roman religion. Roman politics could significantly reshape older cults, as at Heliopolis (Baalbek), where the foundation of a colony under Augustus on the site of a much older city led to three Syrian deities being honoured as a triad identified with Jupiter, Venus, and Mercury.[13] The present book largely ignores the many native cults in the western provinces of the empire. They do not form a sufficiently close part of the religious thought-world which entered into the dominant culture to influence (and antagonize) Christians and Jews.

I have already noted the temptation in earlier studies to assume too neat a division between religions in the classical world. Recent scholarship has rightly stressed the danger in a simplistic use of the terms 'pagan', 'Christian', and 'Jew'. David Frankfurter has written that the use of the word 'pagan',

---

[11] For fasting and communal identity among Early Christians, cf. Chapter 3.

[12] Cf. Steven D. Fraade, 'Ascetical aspects of ancient Judaism', in A. Green (ed.), *Jewish Spirituality*, vol. I, *From the Bible Through the Middle Ages* (London: Routledge, 1986), 253: 'there is no scholarly consensus concerning how "asceticism" (and its related terms) should be defined . . . nor are the ways in which it is defined . . . consistently applied in the comparison of . . . religious traditions'. For further definitions and types of asceticism, cf. E. Diamond, *Holy Men and Hunger Artists: Fasting and Asceticism in Rabbinic Culture* (Oxford University Press, 2004), 3, and 8–12.

[13] On cults and loyalty to Rome, cf. S. Price, *Rituals and Power: The Roman Imperial Cult in Asia Minor* (Cambridge University Press, 1984). For a non-Greek cult in the East (Atargatis at Hierapolis), cf. J. L. Lightfoot, 'Pilgrims and ethnographers: in search of the Syrian goddess', in Jaś Elsner and Ian Rutherford (eds.), *Pilgrimage in Graeco-Roman and Early Christian Antiquity: Seeing the Gods* (Oxford University Press, 2005), 333–52; for Heliopolis, cf. Youssef Hajjar, *La Triade d'Héliopolis-Baalbek: iconographie, théologie, culte et sanctuaires* (University of Montreal, 1985), 177–280.

an 'ancient term of bias for the unconverted rustic, has inevitably led to
false contrasts between "pagans" and "Christians" and, despite contemporary scholars' earnest efforts to qualify their terminology, to the erroneous
reification of two essential religious "halves" in Late Antiquity.'[14] Reference
to two 'halves' suggests how far Judaism has remained a neglected 'third'
in the religious history of the Graeco-Roman world outside Palestine, but
Frankfurter's concern is with the risk of imagining there to be such a single
thing as paganism practised by 'pagans', especially when educated pagans
cannot be assumed to be polytheists in contrast to a simple Christian (and
Jewish) monotheism. When the emperor Decius in AD 249 or 250 decreed
that everyone in the empire should sacrifice to the gods, he may well have
intended to secure divine favour by the display of piety, but those who
sacrificed (to different gods) shared no single understanding of their worship. The pagan Maximus of Madauros could ask St Augustine in the fifth
century, 'Who is so insane as to deny the indubitable truth that there exists
one supreme god?'[15] The bishop of Hippo meanwhile had to rebuke those
who saw themselves as Catholics for 'visiting idols'.[16] Ordinary church
members, to the horror of their clergy, might have in common with pagans
the wearing of amulets, or recourse to magic.

Likewise, though we speak of Christian and Jew, we must not overlook 'the persistently complex dynamics of Jewish–Christian relations',
especially in the period before the fourth century.[17] Even to use a term
such as 'Jewish Christian' may cover a wide variety of ways of being Jewish *and* Christian. We must be alert to the different varieties of Judaism
and the many Christianities that flourished in the first few centuries after
the birth of Jesus alongside, and sometimes within, what would later be
recognized as an orthodox mainstream in each religion as they separated
out. The inadequacy of neatly dividing up the Graeco-Roman world into
Christians, Jews, and pagans, can be seen when we try to 'place' the various Gnostic texts found in the Nag Hammadi library, some of which
interpret the Old Testament to posit a plethora of emanations cascading
from the One God of the spiritual realm, and a disobedient demiurge
Yaltabaoth, who falsely sets himself up as God and creates the first man
in his own image.[18] The difficulty is not simply to decide what counts

---

[14] David Frankfurter, 'Beyond "Jewish Christianity": continuing religious sub-cultures of the second
and third centuries and their documents', in Annette Yoshiko Reed and Adam H. Becker (eds.), *The
Ways that Never Parted: Jews and Christians in Late Antiquity and the Early Middle Ages* (Tübingen:
Mohr Siebeck, 2003), 131.

[15] Augustine, *Ep.* 16.1.   [16] Augustine, *En. in Ps.*, 88.2.14.

[17] Reed and Becker, 'Introduction: Traditional Models and New Directions', in *The Ways that Never
Parted*, 22.

[18] *The Apocryphon of John*, 1–15.

as Christian belief, but lies in recognizing the complex nature of a person's religious identity. Manichaeism, for example, may be understood as a dualist religion distinct from Christianity. Yet its syncretistic adoption and re-interpretation of much Christian scripture allowed it to claim certain Christian figures, histories, and texts for itself within the Graeco-Roman world. This resulted in such mixed allegiance as that of the elderly fifth-century Manichee, Victorinus, who also served as subdeacon in a North African Catholic church![19]

Despite these warnings, I have nonetheless structured my book into chapters which divide pagan asceticism from Jewish and Christian asceticism. Terms which must be treated with caution need not be rejected for that reason. We cannot tell the story at all unless we use these labels to differentiate, generally speaking, those who practised traditional cults from those who saw themselves as members of Israel awaiting the Messiah, and those who saw themselves as followers of Jesus Christ. Chapter 1 begins the story, therefore, by examining (and rejecting) the claim of Porphyry, a Neoplatonist philosopher, to identify a single ascetic discipline or wisdom common to the sages of the ancient world. I distinguish the role played by periodic abstention in Graeco-Roman cults from the different forms of asceticism practised in the pagan philosophical schools. Cynic asceticism is not to be confused with Stoic, nor Neoplatonic, asceticism, though these share a common virtue of frugality. I also distinguish between the asceticism practised by the philosophers from the asceticism which may characterize them as holy men in literary texts.

Chapter 2 concerns Jewish asceticism. It looks first at how the Alexandrian exegete Philo drew on Neoplatonism to reinterpret traditional Jewish ascetic practices. Just as Porphyry's totalizing discourse hid the varieties of pagan asceticism, so Philo has obscured for us the different meanings of asceticism for groups in Hellenistic and later Rabbinic Judaism. I have placed these chapters on pagan and Jewish asceticism before those (Chapters 3 to 5) on Christian asceticism, because the Christian asceticism of the Graeco-Roman world is only fully explicable in terms of its debt to pagan and Jewish thought. In so doing, I do not wish to suggest that Judaism was superseded by Christianity, or that Christian asceticism did not influence Late Antique paganism.

I have also written at greater length on Christian asceticism. This is principally due to my wish to clarify the complex nature of Early Christian asceticism too long ill-served by accounts which unduly privilege the

---

[19] Augustine, *Ep.* 236.1.

Egyptian monks. Chapter 3 therefore examines the evidence for the various forms of communal asceticism practised by different Christians in the second and early third centuries up to the time of Origen. Chapter 4 then focuses on the ascetic theology of Origen, the most important exegete and thinker of the third century, and his profound influence on much Christian asceticism of the subsequent two hundred years, both for consecrated virgins in the cities and monks in the desert. It is to Origen in large part that we shall trace the growth of Christian asceticism as constructive of personal sanctity. Here, again, the story is one in which Neoplatonist ascetic ideas are deployed to reinterpret traditional practices, but now these ideas find broad acceptance among their practitioners. Chapter 5 is concerned first with the strands of monastic life that are largely independent of Origen's influence, especially the monasteries of Pachomius in Egypt, the holy men of the Syrian East, and North African clerical monasticism, to ask why they developed as they did. The chapter closes by reflecting on monasticism's impact on the wider Church. The reader who perseveres to the end will thus appreciate the different forms of asceticism practised in the Graeco-Roman world and their significance, the varied roles which these disciplines played for individuals and groups.

CHAPTER I

Pagan asceticism: cultic and contemplative purity

THE OLYMPICS OF THE SOUL

Shortly after the death of the Neoplatonist philosopher Plotinus (*c.* AD 205–70), his pupil and literary executor Porphyry (AD 234–*c.* 305) urged another member of the school, the wealthy Roman Castricius Firmus, to join him in renewed intellectual endeavour: they should together 'go stripped, without tunics, to the stadium, to compete in the Olympics of the soul'.[1] Porphyry understood the goal of philosophy as that contemplation in the soul of divine truth which was also an act of union with the divine. The athletic metaphor of his appeal to the dedicatee of *On Abstinence*, and through him to its readership, glorified both the goal and the philosopher who attained it; the image bestowed on the latter the prestige of victory in these most famous of all Greek games, and something of the victor's numinous power.[2] The metaphor further located this goal as the fruit of a strict training (in Greek *ascesis*) comparable to the diet, sexual abstinence, and exercises of the naked Olympic athlete.[3] It was an apt metaphor in as much as the philosopher had to divest his mind of the multiple concerns and passions which distracted it through its relationship to the body; such concentration could easily be envisaged as a stripping naked of the self, because Plato had long since characterized the body as clothing worn by the soul.[4] The figure was all the more apt in so far as the disciplined training which Porphyry thought would facilitate contemplation involved,

---

[1] Porphyry, *On Abstinence from Killing Animals*, 1.31.3, tr. G. Clark (London: Duckworth, 2000), 43. For the date of composition, cf. J. Bouffartigue (ed.), *Porphyre: De l'abstinence*, with introduction by J. Bouffartigue and M. Patillon (Paris: Les Belles Lettres, 1977–), vol. I, xviii–xix.

[2] L. Bruit Zaidman and P. Schmitt Pantel, *Religion in the Ancient Greek City*, tr. P. Cartledge (Cambridge University Press, 1992), 120.

[3] For the athlete's sexual abstinence, cf. M. Dillon, *Pilgrims and Pilgrimage in Ancient Greece* (London and New York: Routledge, 1997), 222. For the metaphor in Greek thought, cf. M. Foucault, *The Use of Pleasure: The History of Sexuality*, vol. II, tr. R. Hurley (Harmondsworth: Penguin, 1986), 72 and 119–20.

[4] Plato, *Cratylus*, 403b; *Gorgias*, 524d.

amongst other things, a daily practice of ascetic abstention in matters of diet, sexual activity, wealth, and wider social intercourse, all elements in a thoroughgoing detachment from the material and mortal.[5]

Porphyry's writings reveal much about this asceticism. It did not demand renunciation of all sexual activity, but a reduction towards the minimum which nature necessitated for the survival of the species.[6] Though Porphyry married, he advised Marcella (in a treatise masquerading as a letter) not to see herself as a woman or wife (in Greek *gyne*), just as he did not see her in this superficial way.[7] How much the philosopher ate was likewise to be reduced towards the minimum required for health, a level which liberated him from concern for the riches to fund more lavish fare and the slaves to prepare it.[8] The contemplative could thus refuse the wealth which was offered to him.[9] He was to practise a lifestyle marked by temperance and by frugality or simplicity (*to liton*).[10]

Detachment further involved an unspecified disengagement from civic life. The *Life of Pythagoras* presents the sage as exhorting people to avoid the twin desires characteristic of Graeco-Roman politics: love of honour and fame.[11] *On Abstinence* adduces the example of Pythagoras' followers. These had reportedly either sought the most deserted locations in which to live or had inhabited religious sanctuaries within the cities where they were undisturbed by mundane business. Porphyry then cites Plato's *The-atetus* (173c–174a) which describes the philosopher's lack of interest in public affairs.[12] What Porphyry urged above all, however, was complete and permanent abstention from meat in adoption of a vegetarian diet.[13] Such ascetic practices together made for a purity and holiness essential in the contemplative assimilation to God: 'inasmuch as the father of all is simpler and purer and more self-sufficient, being established far from the impact made by matter, the one who approaches him should be pure and holy (*katharos te kai hagnos*) in all respects, beginning with the body and culminating in the inner man, assigning to each of his parts, or altogether to what is his, the holiness (*hagneia*) that is natural to each.'[14]

To persuade the reader of *On Abstinence*, Porphyry marshalled a host of authorities and examples. From earlier Greek and Roman philosophy he drew explicitly on Plato and the Pythagorean tradition as mentioned above, on the Platonist Plutarch (pre AD 50–post 120), and on the Stoic Chrysippus (c. 280–207 BC) for arguments about the nature and purpose of different

---

[5] Porphyry, *On Abstinence*, 1.30.4–5 and 41.1.   [6] Ibid., 1.41.4.
[7] Porphyry, *Letter to Marcella*, 33.   [8] *On Abstinence*, 1.46–7.   [9] Ibid., 1.31.4.
[10] Ibid., 1.56.1, in Bouffartigue, *Porphyre*, vol. I, 88.   [11] *Life of Pythagoras*, 32.
[12] *On Abstinence*, 1.36.   [13] Ibid., II.3.1.   [14] Ibid., 1.57.3, tr. Clark, *On Abstinence*, 54.

animals,[15] as well as certain unnamed 'Platonists' whom he cited for their knowledge of demons.[16] He pointed out the advocacy by Epicurus (341–270 BC) of a frugal diet, and he signalled his dependence on Theophrastus (c. 371–287 BC), successor to Aristotle at the Lyceum, in the attack upon animal sacrifices.[17] The ancient poets Hesiod and Sophocles were quoted on the same topic.[18] To these explicit authorities Porphyry added arguments recognizable to the educated reader as drawn from the Stoics, in particular from the teachings of the Roman philosopher Musonius Rufus (pre AD 30–pre 102).[19] On the proper offerings to God, Porphyry cited a certain 'wise man' whom readers might identify as Apollonius of Tyana. This famed holy man of the first century AD was known to them as the purported author of a text *On the Sacrifices* and as a new Pythagoras through the *Life* by Philostratus in the first half of the third century AD.[20] Porphyry drew on the role of abstention from meat and sex in the construction of cultic purity to sanction the asceticism constructive of his contemplative purity of soul, as he does in his later *Letter to Marcella*.[21]

The ascetics to whom Porphyry pointed with admiration were not only found within the classical Greek tradition. The priests of ancient Egypt were praised for having 'practised simplicity (*litotēs*), restraint (*katastolē*), self-control (*enkrateia*), perseverance (*karteria*) and in everything justice and absence of greed'.[22] The philosopher approved their 'resistance to social contact' (*to dusepimikton*), when ritual purity kept them within the temple compounds; he lauded their dietary restrictions and periodic fasting, their avoidance of wine, their periodic abstention from all sexual activity and permanent abstention from homosexual acts.[23] There was a long description adapted from Josephus (AD 37/8 – ?) of the asceticism characteristic of the Jewish Essene communities which Porphyry presented as a philosophical school.[24] Here, too, the 'simplicity and frugality of their diet' were emphasized,[25] but also their rejection of private property, in which Porphyry saw contempt for wealth.[26] Such *ascesis* gave them the 'endurance' (*karteria*) to withstand the worst tortures.[27] Syrians and Brahmans provided further examples.[28]

[15] Ibid., III.18.3 and 20.1.   [16] Ibid., II.36.6.   [17] Ibid., I.48–50, II.5.1, 7.3, 11.3, 20.2, 26.1.
[18] Ibid., II.18.3 and 19.2.   [19] Cf. Bouffartigue, *Porphyre*, vol. I, 31–3.
[20] Porphyry, *On Abstinence*, II.34.2; cf. Clark, *On Abstinence*, 152, n. 291.
[21] Porphyry, *Letter to Marcella*, 28.   [22] *On Abstinence*, IV.6.4, tr. Clark, *On Abstinence*, 104.
[23] Ibid., IV.6.5, 6.8, and 7.6, tr. Clark, *On Abstinence*, 104–5.   [24] Ibid., IV.11.2.
[25] Ibid., IV.13.5 (ἡ λιτότης ἡ περὶ τὴν δίαιταν καὶ ὀλιγότης), in Bouffartigue, *Porphyre*, vol. III, 22, tr. Clark, *On Abstinence*, 110.
[26] Ibid., IV.11.5.   [27] Ibid., IV.13.6, tr. Clark, *On Abstinence*, 110.   [28] Ibid., IV.15–17.

To marshal these examples was in part a display of erudition. It demonstrated the elegant sophistication or *paideia* required of a serious writer which was also evident in allusion to Sophocles' *Electra* or Euripides' *Iphigenia at Aulis*.[29] However, it claimed these philosophical and religious figures as evidence for the singular wisdom of the ancients, a wisdom identified with Porphyry's understanding of ascetic practice and religious cult. That is why Porphyry cited Homer's *Iliad* (IX. 524) to vest the Pythagoreans and sages of Ancient Greece with the glory of epic heroes.[30] It is why he described the writings of past philosophers as the 'acts of the ancients',[31] why the Essenes are presented as the 'most venerable' of the Jewish philosophical schools,[32] and why the Egyptian priests are credited with 'a discipline (*ascesis*) of lifestyle which . . . has the dignity of antiquity'.[33] For similar reasons Porphyry cited an inscription from the sanctuary of Asclepius at Epidauros on purity as 'thinking holy thoughts'.[34] Porphyry's conflation of his own philosophical asceticism with the wisdom of the ancients largely explains why he says nothing about Christian forms of asceticism: in the eyes of many pagans Christianity remained a novel superstition. The Neoplatonist once remarked that Origen, through his Christianity, had sold himself and run his life aground on the rocks of a 'reckless and outlandish venture'.[35] A single, ancient, and ascetical wisdom, from which Christianity is excluded, is thus put forward as preserved and variously refracted among just these many witnesses.

Although Porphyry did not falsely ascribe to his cited sources views alien to them, he so edited them as to pass over in silence how they differed from, and disagreed with his own teachings.[36] *On Abstinence*, therefore, raises fundamental questions about asceticism in the Graeco-Roman world, about the realities behind Porphyry's rhetorical artifice: to what extent did different philosophical schools and religious groups in fact share ascetic practices, virtues, or ideals? Were similar practices commonly or variously understood? That is to say, what significance did they hold for the communities in which they were observed as well as for those who viewed them from across cultural boundaries? How influential in popular culture were the views and practices of a few highly educated philosophers? Furthermore, to the extent that Porphyry occluded the many divergences

---

[29] Ibid., 1.22.1.   [30] Ibid., 1.36.1.   [31] Ibid., III.18.1.

[32] Ibid., IV.11.2, tr. Clark, *On Abstinence*, 108.   [33] Ibid., IV.6.3, tr. Clark, *On Abstinence*, 104.

[34] Ibid., II.19.5, tr. Clark, *On Abstinence*, 62.

[35] Eusebius, *Church History*, VI.19.7. It is also possible, but cannot be proven, that Porphyry excluded Christian asceticism as a model of holiness with which he was competing in *On Abstinence*.

[36] Bouffartigue, *Porphyre*, vol. I, 18–19. This parallels the rhetorical strategy for which the later Christian Theodoret is berated by Siniossoglou in his *Plato and Theodoret*, 10–20 and passim.

in ascetic thought and practice across the Graeco-Roman world, were these divergences lessening or perceived as being of less importance in Late Antiquity?

I shall address these questions by first examining forms of ritual abstinence within pagan cultic practice, to show that an ascetic lifestyle of the kind advocated by Porphyry was, generally speaking, neither required for the successful performance of traditional cult, nor a common part of popular piety. The chapter then looks at the different forms of abstention which developed as ascetical practices in the philosophical movements or 'schools'. These gained their primary significance from the importance in Graeco-Roman thought of self-control or temperance (*sophrosyne*) understood in part as freedom from enslavement to pleasures and as independence from the uncertainties of fortune. We shall see that originally distinctive forms of asceticism in different schools had largely merged by Late Antiquity to form a characteristic marker of the philosophical life, in which the asceticism of a few manifested among the ruling elites a religious virtue of frugality. Philosophical asceticism was widely respected among the educated as a religious exercise.[37] This religious dimension of much Graeco-Roman philosophy is evident in an oration by the fourth-century philosopher Themistius for his dead father, Eugenius, himself an Aristotelian teacher. Philosophy checks Themistius' grief by teaching Eugenius' liberation from the body at death and entry into heaven. The language of cultic observance makes Eugenius a priest who initiates the pupil into the mysteries of Aristotle. Aristotle's work is said to have its 'inner sanctuary' where the student was 'filled with awe and anxiety' until the teacher 'would open the gateway of the temple, clothe the god's statue, and make it beautiful and clean on all sides. He would show the statue, now all sparkling and shining with a heavenly light, to the initiate.'[38] The true philosopher is thus a holy man or saint.

In approaching both topics, it is necessary to recognize both the vagaries of historical evidence and the frequent bias of historical interest. Knowledge of individual cults comes from widely differing periods and sources to raise the question of how far we may extrapolate from what happened at one time and place to practice in another place and period; we are better informed about classical Athens than other Greek cities; we know more about Rome, as her religious history was understood by writers (both

---

[37] Cf. Pierre Hadot, *Philosophy as a Way of Life: Spiritual Exercises from Socrates to Foucault*, ed. Arnold I. Davidson (Oxford: Blackwell, 1995), 56–9.

[38] Themistius, *Or.* 20, 233–5, tr. R. J. Penella, *The Private Orations of Themistius* (Berkeley, Los Angeles, and London: University of California Press, 2000), 52–3.

historians and antiquarians) of the imperial period onwards, than about the native cults of other Italian cities or of non-Greek cities in the provinces. Though cults may present ritual as a fixed tradition, 'traditions change in structure, details, and interpretation and such changes are not always fully recognized by those who live them'.[39] Similar problems bedevil our knowledge of the philosophers. Those who left no writings appear either as characters in dialogues and histories scripted by others or as authors of pseudonymous letters from the pens of much later pupils. Alexandrian writers of books which traced the *Successions of Philosophers* described Cynicism, for example, in ways which misrepresented its relationship to Socrates.[40] Historians of religion have argued for the relative stability over a long period of a single religious system common to the Greek city states from the classical period into Roman times, but this argument is open to question.[41]

LENTIL SOUP AND SACRED SPACE

It was reported in Late Antiquity that the Cynic philosopher Crates (c. 368–288 BC) had once taught his pupil Zeno of Citium (335–263 BC) a lesson. He had instructed the former merchant to carry a pot of lentil soup through the Kerameikos at Athens. When his embarrassed student tried to hide the pot, Crates smashed it with his staff, a public symbol of the Cynic's way of life, leaving Zeno to sprint away with the soup dripping down his legs.[42] Zeno's shame presumably arose from a taboo or social convention which prohibited him from bringing such prepared food into this public space, whether the Kerameikos is here the public cemetery at Athens or, more probably, the city's agora, a sacred space which served as both civic centre and market-place.[43] Crates, on the other hand, sought to free his pupil from what he regarded as foolish and craven subjection to human convention. The test set for Zeno was analogous to the notorious actions undertaken by Diogenes (c. 412/403–324/321 BC), the founder of Cynicism. For Diogenes had once dragged a jar of wine on a piece of rope through the Kerameikos after seeing someone ashamed to pick up a loaf of bread

---

[39] C. Bell, *Ritual Theory, Ritual Practice* (New York and Oxford: Oxford University Press, 1992), 118.

[40] D. Dudley, *A History of Cynicism; From Diogenes to the 6th Century AD*, 2nd edn (Bristol Classical Press, 1998), xv.

[41] S. Price, *Religions of the Ancient Greeks* (Cambridge University Press, 1999), 3–9.   [42] DL, VII.3.

[43] For frequent use of the term in this latter sense during the imperial period, cf. R. E. Wycherley, *The Athenian Agora*, vol. III, *Literary and Epigraphical Testimonia* (Princeton: American School of Classical Studies at Athens, 1957), 221–4. For the agora as a sacred space, cf. Zaidman and Schmitt Pantel, *Religion*, 55–6.

which had dropped to the ground; he had likewise flouted convention by eating in the agora and by masturbating there.[44] Crates' lesson, therefore, points (amongst other things) to the role that abstention from food and sexual activity could play in the construction of social spaces and categories within ancient Greek culture – public and private, sacred and profane, pure and impure.

Many shrines or sacred spaces in Ancient Greece were marked out by lustral basins or other vessels of water at the entrances which permitted the entrant to wash and thereby ensure ritual purity (*hagneia*).[45] Sexual intercourse, like death or birth, rendered someone impure and required such ritual cleansing.[46] Ritual purity might also demand a period of sexual abstention before entry into the shrine or contact with a cult statue. An inscription set up in the sanctuary of Athena at Pergamum after 133 BC declared that citizens 'and all other people who enter the temple of the female god shall be pure, having washed themselves clean from their own wife or their own husband for one day, or from another woman or another man for two days; similarly from a corpse or from a woman in labour for two days'.[47] At Heliopolis the men who carried the statue of Jupiter in procession first shaved their heads and abstained from sex for an unknown period.[48] It has been said that 'fasting had no part in the preparation of priests for sacrifice or for other liturgical functions in Latin and Greek city cults', but priests and priestesses might prepare to carry out sacrifices or other rituals by temporary abstention from certain foods as well as from sex.[49] At Cos priestesses of Demeter did not eat meat that had been slaughtered in a particular (now uncertain) manner. Nor were priests and priestesses there to eat offerings made in heroic or chthonic cult.[50] According to Iamblichus (*c.* AD 245–325) the priestess at Didyma uttered an oracle only after a three-day fast, while at Claros the priest or prophet spoke only after a one-day fast.[51] In Near-eastern cults like that of Cybele ritual purity required abstention from pork.[52] What was not normally required

[44] DL, VI.22, 35, 46, 58, 61, and 69.

[45] W. Burkert, *Greek Religion: Archaic and Classical*, tr. J. Raffan (Oxford: Blackwell, 1985), 77.

[46] R. Parker, *Miasma: Pollution and Purification in Early Greek Religion* (Oxford: Clarendon Press, 1983), 76.

[47] Tr. Price, *Religions of the Ancient Greeks*, 176.   [48] Hajjar, *La Triade*, 268–9.

[49] Veronika E. Grimm, *From Feasting to Fasting, The Evolution of a Sin: Attitudes to Food in Late Antiquity* (London and New York: Routledge, 1996), 41.

[50] Parker, *Miasma*, 52.

[51] Dillon, *Pilgrims*, 91–3. For Iamblichus' dates, cf. J. Dillon, 'Iamblichus of Chalcis', *ANRW* II.36.2 (1987), 863–909.

[52] J. L. Lightfoot (ed.), *Lucian: On the Syrian Goddess* (Oxford University Press, 2003), 512–13.

of priests or priestesses in Greek cult was the permanent renunciation of sexual relations.[53]

Temporary abstention marked the approach to the divine not only of priests but of pilgrims: suppliants in search of healing at a shrine of Asklepios might be required to abstain from sex and from certain foods over a number of days. At Pergamon, for example, the sick person who hoped for a healing vision of the god while sleeping in the shrine had first to observe certain rules of purity in abstaining from sex, goat meat, and cheese.[54] At Oropus, if Philostratus' *Life of Apollonius* is a credible source, the person seeking an oracle was required to fast from all food for one day and from wine for three days.[55] At Delos devotees of Atargatis abstained from fish for several days before participating in sacred banquets.[56] Concerns for purity also touched candidates for initiation into mystery cults. A chorus of initiates in Euripides' *The Cretans* tells of their abstention from meat ('living food') at the cave of Zeus Idaios on Mount Ida in Crete.[57] Livy (59 BC–AD 17) related in his *Histories* that initiation into the Bacchic mysteries at Rome before their suppression in 186 BC required an initiate to abstain from sex for ten days and seemingly to practise some form of fast broken by a meal on the tenth day.[58] From the late second century AD, readers of Apuleius' *Metamorphoses* learnt how the novel's protagonist Lucius, after his many misfortunes as an ass, had recovered his human form and been initiated into the cult of Isis at Cenchreae through rites preceded by a ten-day fast from meat and wine.[59] Whatever the reality behind these texts, the passages tell us what theatre-goers and readers in the Graeco-Roman world came to expect of participants in such rites.

Some forms of abstention were rites of mourning which mirrored the myths that governed particular festivals. Participants in the Eleusinian

[53] Andrew Fear, 'A journey to the end of the world', in Elsner and Rutherford (eds.), *Pilgrimage*, 320, asserts the existence of a 'celibate priesthood' in the Phoenician cult of Melqart (Herakles) at Cadiz. Silius Italicus describes them as 'castumque cubile' ('with chaste bedchamber'), in the *Punica*, III.28, ed. J. Delz, *Silius Italicus, Punica* (Stuttgart: Teubner, 1987), 55. It is not clear, however, that this implies more than periodic abstention, either for given rites or the limited duration of an individual's priesthood.

[54] Fred Naiden, '*Hiketai* and *Theoroi* at Epidauros', in Elsner and Rutherford (eds.), *Pilgrimage*, 79; Alexia Petsalis-Diomidis, 'The body in space: visual dynamics in Graeco-Roman healing pilgrimage', in Elsner and Rutherford (eds.), *Pilgrimage*, 202–3; Dillon, *Pilgrims*, 187.

[55] Philostratus, *Life of Apollonius*, II.37.   [56] Lightfoot, *Lucian*, 82–3.

[57] Euripides, *Cretans*, 19–20, ed. and tr. C. Collard, M. J. Cropp, and K. H. Lee, *Euripides, Selected Fragmentary Plays*, vol. 1 (Warminster: Aris and Phillips, 1995), 61; cf. Dillon, *Pilgrims*, 139.

[58] Livy, *Histories*, XXXIX.9–10.

[59] Apuleius, *Metamorphoses*, XI.23. For a commentary on this and the passage in Livy, cf. J. Gwyn Griffiths (ed.), *Apuleius of Madauros, The Isis-Book (Metamorphoses, Book XI)* (Leiden: Brill, 1975), 290–1.

mysteries at Athens imitated the mourning goddess Demeter by fasting and drinking the *kykeon*, a brew produced from barley meal, water, and penny-royal.[60] Married women who participated in the Athenian Thesmophoria fasted on the second day of Demeter's festival (itself named the *Nesteia* or Fast) while sitting on mats upon the ground within her sanctuaries to adopt the same posture as the grief-stricken goddess.[61] They also abstained from sexual relations for all three days of the festival.[62] How, though, should we 'read' this ritual prescription? Marcel Detienne has meticulously explored the complex mythic and ritual patterns that link this abstention from sex with the celebration of fertility and licensed obscenities at the winter festival of the Haloa; the festivals together affirm legitimate and fruitful marriage over which Demeter stood as tutelary deity.[63] Likewise, the fast which associates these women with Demeter's grief prepares for the celebration of her bounty as goddess of agriculture. In fact, both types of ritual abstinence gain significance from the women's role as symbols of the fertile field.[64]

The Thesmophoria was widely celebrated in the Greek cities, not just in Greece, but in Italy and Sicily. Around the mid third century BC, Greek festivals of Demeter gave rise to similar Roman festivals of Ceres, whose annual festival at the end of June included a nine-day period of sexual abstinence and fasting from bread and wine by its female participants or initiates.[65] In 191 BC, in response to portents, the Senate further decreed a day's fast to take place in October once every five years in honour of the goddess, but which appears to have been celebrated annually by the reign of Augustus.[66] Rome likewise adopted other rites from the Greek east which involved periodic fasting: by some point in the imperial period, the March ceremonies in honour of the Great Mother goddess Cybele included a nine-day fast from bread and other grain products, pomegranates, quinces, pork, fish, and perhaps wine.[67] Robert Turcan has described this as 'nine

---

[60] Dillon, *Pilgrims*, 61 and 65. Robert Parker, *Polytheism and Society at Athens* (Oxford University Press, 2005), 347 n.86 comments that 'sexual restrictions are plausible but unattested'.

[61] Parker, *Polytheism*, 272–4; M. Detienne, *The Gardens of Adonis: Spices in Greek Mythology* (Princeton University Press, 1994), 80; E. Simon, *Festivals of Attica: An Archaeological Commentary* (Madison, Wisc.: University of Wisconsin Press, 1983), 18.

[62] Detienne, *Gardens*, 79; Parker, *Polytheism*, 277–8.

[63] For the Haloa, cf. Simon, *Festivals*, 35–6.   [64] Parker, *Polytheism*, 280.

[65] Price, *Religions*, p.149; M. Beard, J. North, and S. Price, *Religions of Rome* (Cambridge University Press, 1998), vol. 1, 70–1; Detienne, *Gardens*, 77.

[66] Livy, *Histories*, XXXVI.37; R. Turcan, *The Gods of Ancient Rome: Religion in Everyday Life from Archaic to Imperial Times*, tr. A. Nevill (Edinburgh University Press, 2000), 79.

[67] Julian, *Or.* 5.16–17, 175b–177d.

days of penitence', but it would be misleading to read the meaning of Christian Lenten fasting across into this cultic practice.[68]

Strictly limited forms of abstention from food and sex served largely to demarcate sacred places and times, to mediate a safe entry into, or communication with, the sacred realm of the gods, and to sanction the social order where sex and food had their normal places within household and city. Abstention in this context often has as its correlate the orderly distribution of meats and feasting associated with the successful conclusion of sacrificial rites. These patterns of behaviour within a Greek religious system may be contrasted with the prolonged sexual renunciation of the Vestal Virgins at Rome (and perhaps of their counterparts at Alba Longa and Lavinium). Chosen for their exceptional role in childhood, these six unmarried women from the patrician elite were the only priestesses in ancient Roman cult, and they held this status for a minimum of thirty years, though it seems that most remained Vestals until death.[69] They lived together next to the temple of Vesta in the Forum, and there occupied an ambiguous position which transcended public and private spheres. At the religious and political heart of the city, the Vestals tended the flame at its sacred hearth, guarded a phallus symbolic of the nation's fecundity, and exercised important sacrificial duties in official cults. Despite their unmarried status they wore clothing appropriate for Roman matrons.[70] On their procession through Rome they were accompanied by the *fasces*, the rods and axe signifying a civic magistrate.[71] Their extraordinary abstention marked out a ritual purity which was assumed not only for the limited duration of particular rites, but enabled them to carry out the perpetual task of watching the flame. Virginity did not simply invest them with sacral status as individuals, but through the interplay of other factors (including the penalty which punished loss of virginity by burial alive) gave them a sacrality symbolic of the whole city or nation. Their ritual purity functioned as a guarantee of the city's preservation under divine protection.[72] We may sum up this section, however, by concluding that none of the abstention outlined here constituted an asceticism understood as a moral or spiritual training in the sense that Porphyry envisaged a discipline of soul and body for the good of the soul.

---

[68] R. Turcan, *The Cults of the Roman Empire*, tr. A. Nevill (Oxford: Blackwell, 1996), 44.
[69] Plutarch, *Numa*, 10; Turcan, *The Gods*, 56.
[70] Beard, North, and Price, *Religions*, vol. i, 51–4 and 194.   [71] Plutarch, *Numa*, 10.
[72] For a feminist critique, cf. D. Sawyer, *Women and Religion in the First Christian Centuries* (London and New York: Routledge, 1996), 127–9.

A DOG'S LIFE?

When Crates smashed Zeno's pot of soup, he was weaning his pupil from what he thought a foolish adherence to convention and good repute. He was to learn the 'shamelessness' (*anaideia*) which led to the Cynics being branded as 'dogs'. This was a basic part of the thoroughgoing training which sought to inure the Cynic to a haphazard fortune. Such *ascesis* in the wider sense included what we may recognize as ascetic practice in the narrower sense of a training in character through physical hardship and renunciation. A fundamental element of this training was voluntary poverty. Some time no earlier than the first or second century AD an anonymous Cynic propagandist composed a letter in which Crates supposedly advised the wealthy of the 'complete peace' enjoyed by Cynics, 'since we have been freed from every evil by Diogenes of Sinope, and although we possess nothing, we have everything, but you, though you have everything, really have nothing because of your rivalry, jealousy, fear, and conceit.'[73] It was widely held that Diogenes had persuaded Crates to throw his wealth into the sea.[74] Poverty and freedom from the constraints of social standing together ensured that the individual was not snared or deflected in other ways. Crates reputedly stated that ill-repute or obscurity (*adoxia*) and poverty (*penia*) were a homeland invincible to capture by chance forces.[75] Begging was more than a means of survival: it exposed the Cynic to contempt and tested the philosopher's ability to endure misfortune. Diogenes had famously gone through the motions of begging from a statue, and said that he did so in order to 'become practised in failure' or 'misfortune'.[76] Seeking alms, however, also asserted the claim to be a philosopher. As all things belong to God, and friends have all things in common, and since the wise man or philosopher is God's friend, the Cynic is only asking for what is properly his.[77]

The Cynic's chosen status as a homeless beggar was evident in his appearance: rough clothing, bare feet, staff, and sack or pouch in which to put what little he possessed.[78] By the first century AD, Diogenes and his supposed teacher Antisthenes could each be attributed with first adopting the

---

[73] Ps.-Crates, *Ep.* 7, tr. R. Hock, in A. Malherbe, *The Cynic Epistles: A Study Edition* (Missoula: Scholars Press, 1977), 59.

[74] DL, VI.87.   [75] Ibid., VI.93.

[76] Ibid., VI.49 (Μελετῶ . . . ἀποτυγχάνειν), ed. M. Marcovich, *Diogenes Laertius, Vitae Philosophorum*, 2 vols. (Stuttgart and Leipzig: Teubner, 1999), vol. I, 405.

[77] Ibid., VI.46 and 72; Ps.-Crates, *Ep.* 27, in Malherbe, *Cynic Epistles*, 76.

[78] M.-O. Goulet-Cazé, *L'Ascèse cynique: Un commentaire de Diogène Laërce* VI 70–1 (Paris: Vrin, 1986), 57.

cloak (which doubled as a blanket in which to sleep), the sack and staff, as their characteristic garb.[79] A character in Menander's play *The Groom* describes the Cynic Monimos of Syracuse as 'the dirty beggar'.[80] Lucian's comic dialogue *Philosophies for Sale* (itself modelled on Menippus' *Sale of Diogenes*) could easily sketch for its readers a portrait of Diogenes or the essential Cynic 'life' by describing the character as 'the unwashed one' with the sack and bare arms.[81] Diogenes was known to have lived for a time in a tub in the Metroon at Athens, though, like other beggars, he also inhabited temple porticoes.[82] Crates and his pupil Metrocles were reputed to have slept rough, the latter in temples during summer and at the baths during winter.[83] A Cynic likewise aimed to satisfy hunger with the beggar's basic fare. Metrocles lived on barley-bread and vegetables.[84] His teacher, who may not have begged himself, advocated lentil soup rather than stew, because the pursuit of richer fare was symptomatic of the desires that generated civic unrest.[85] A pseudonymous letter supposedly by a legendary Scythian prince, but which was probably written by a Cynic sympathiser in perhaps the third century BC, has its author describe how 'a Scythian cloak serves as my garment, the skin of my feet as my shoes, the whole earth as my resting place, milk, cheese, and meat as my favourite meal, hunger as my main course'.[86] A much later pseudonymous letter of Crates urged its implied readers, the youth of Athens, to 'wash with cold water, to drink only water, to eat nothing that has not been earned by toil, to wear a cloak, and to make it a habit to sleep on the ground'.[87]

How were the different ascetic traits to be understood? In the presentation of Diogenes the Cynic by Diogenes Laertius (fl. first half of the third century AD) they amount to a life marked by *euteleia*, a condition in which what was shabby, cheap, and plain, with potential for dishonour, could nonetheless also be understood as indicative of a virtuous frugality

---

[79] DL, VI.13 and 22. Since Xenophon (*c.* 430 BC – ?) presents Antisthenes as a householder with a bed in which to sleep, he was probably turned into a founding figure of Cynic asceticism at a later date, perhaps by the Stoics. Cf. Xenophon, *Symposium*, 38; Dudley, *History*, 2–4 and 6–7.

[80] ὁ προσαιτῶν καὶ ῥυπῶν; Menander, fr. 215, ed. A. Koerte and A. Thierfelder, *Menandri quae supersunt,* 2nd edn, 2 vols. (Leipzig: Teubner 1955–9), vol. II, 85.

[81] Lucian, *Philosophies for Sale*, 7 (τὸν αὐχμῶντα), ed. M. D. Macleod, *Luciani Opera*, 4 vols. (Oxford: Clarendon Press, 1972–87), vol. II, 29.

[82] DL, VI.22–3.

[83] Crates, no. 20, in G. Giannantoni (ed.), *Socraticorum reliquiae*, 2 vols. (Rome: Ateneo, 1983), vol. I, 713; Teles, *A Comparison of Poverty and Wealth*, ed. O. Hense, *Teletis Reliquiae*, 2nd edn (Tübingen, 1909), 41.

[84] Ibid.   [85] Crates, fr. 6 = no. 72 in Giannantoni, *Socraticorum reliquiae*, vol. I, 734.

[86] Ps.-Anacharsis, *Ep.* 5, tr. A. McGuire, in Malherbe, *Cynic Epistles*, 43. For the dating, cf. Malherbe, *Cynic Epistles*, 6–7.

[87] Ps.-Crates, *Ep.* 18, tr. Hock, in Malherbe, *Cynic Epistles*, 69.

or simplicity.[88] A similar characterization is found in a dialogue perhaps from the fourth century AD in which a Cynic defends his regimen as 'more economical' (*eutelesteron*) than that of the crowds.[89] Nor was this a late re-casting of Cynic life: Crates had composed a hymn to *Eutelia* as the 'sovereign mistress' honoured by those who care for justice.[90] Marie-Odile Goulet-Cazé, however, has argued convincingly that the Cynics' primary ethical concern was the freedom from pride and illusion (*atuphia*) which Clement of Alexandria (*c.* AD 150–215) identified as Antisthenes' ethical goal.[91] The aim was to live as the human being that one was, but this was understood to be a life in defiance of convention. Hence Diogenes mocked that, despite the crowds, he had come across all too few human beings.[92] He and his followers were said to 're-stamp' or 'deface' the 'coinage', that is, to regard as false the ethical values ascribed to many actions by their contemporaries, and to put their own value on them in accordance with their reasoning about nature.[93] Diogenes could be imagined by later Cynics as writing to his father how he lived 'not in conformity with popular opinion but according to nature, free under Zeus, and crediting the good to him and not to my neighbour'.[94] The dog's life was in fact the truly human one. This explains why Cynics generally decried marriage as an unnatural institution but did not include sexual abstention as a defining element of their ascetic lifestyle. The 'person insensitive to passion, who considers his own possessions to be sufficient for patient endurance (*hypomonē*), declines to marry and produce children'.[95] This rejection of marriage is echoed in Epictetus (mid first to second century AD) whose true Cynic declares himself to be without wife and children.[96] It lies behind Diogenes' supposed defence of incest.[97] In Cynic thought the shamelessness manifest in flouting conventions trumped the restraint of a sexual pleasure the capacity and desire for which were implanted by nature.[98] Crates was notorious in later centuries for having intercourse in public with Hipparchia, Metrocles' sister, whom he married at the bride's insistence.[99] The marriage was fruitful but unconventional: Hipparchia wore Cynic garb and attended

---

[88] DL, VI.21 and 37.   [89] Ps.-Lucian, *The Cynic*, 2.
[90] Crates, fr. 11 = no. 77, in Giannantoni (ed.), *Socraticorum reliquiae*, vol. I, 736.
[91] Goulet-Cazé, *L'Ascèse cynique*, 34; Clement of Alexandria, *Stromata* II.21.130.7, *CA*, vol. II, 184.
[92] DL, VI.60.   [93] Ibid., VI.71.
[94] Ps.-Diogenes, *Ep.* 7, tr. B. Fiore, in Malherbe, *Cynic Epistles*, 98 and 99. For the letter's likely composition in the first century BC, cf. Malherbe, *Cynic Epistles*, 17.
[95] Ps.-Diogenes, *Ep.* 47, tr. Fiore, in Malherbe, *Cynic Epistles*, 178–9. Cf. DL, VI.72.
[96] Epictetus, *On the Calling of the Cynic*, 45, in Arrian's *Discourses of Epictetus*, III.22.45.
[97] Dudley, *History*, 30.   [98] Foucault, *The Use of Pleasure*, 54–5.
[99] Crates, nos. 21–5, in Giannantoni, *Socraticorum reliquiae*, vol. I, 713–14.

dinner parties customarily restricted to men.[100] The Cynic poet Cercidas (fl. 225 BC) praised a carefree recourse to prostitutes, 'Aphrodite from the market-place'.[101] On the other hand, Crates' utopian island of Pera was imagined to be free from any 'glutton spell-bound by some prostitute's behind'.[102]

Physical asceticism was both an aspect of life re-ordered in accordance with correct values and a training in hardship which prepared the Cynic for inevitable sufferings thrown up by a properly human life.[103] Diogenes reportedly rolled his tub in hot sands and embraced icy statues to harden himself to extremes.[104] Asceticism reduced need to a minimum and made possible greater self-sufficiency (*autarkeia*). Propaganda recounted how Diogenes had encountered on the road the Olympic victor Cicermus whom he converted to the Cynic life. Diogenes exhorted the boxer to pursue what was really honourable and 'to be steadfast (*katerein*) under blows, not of puny men, but of the spirit, not through leather straps or fists, but through poverty, disrepute, lowly birth, and exile. For when you have learned to despise these things, you will live happily and will die in a tolerable way.' The alternative was 'endless suffering'.[105] The encounter repays close consideration. Life in accordance with true values authorizes plain speech to Cicermus, the Cynic's famous freedom of speech (*parrhesia*). The setting recalls the understanding of Cynicism as a 'short cut to virtue'[106] which avoided the lengthy education advocated by some philosophers and at once built up a person's endurance (*karteria*) in the prosecution of a genuinely free and fully human life. Diogenes, who was said to oppose courage to fortune as well as nature to custom,[107] emerges as the true Olympic victor. Cynic asceticism could also be understood as making for a virtuous virility. Hermes, in Lucian's *Philosophies for Sale*, advertizes Cynicism as a 'virile Life' (*bion andrikon*).[108] Cynics claimed that in their endurance of hardships they resembled the hero Heracles.[109] They saw in their asceticism the proper instrument for the formation of virtues traditionally held central to the moral worth of a Greek aristocratic male and ruler: self control with respect to sexual pleasures, food, and drink (*enkrateia*), endurance of

[100] DL, vi.88 and 96–7.
[101] Cercidas, fr. 5, ed. J. Powell, *Collectanea Alexandrina* (Oxford: Clarendon Press, 1925), 207: ἁ δ' ἐξ ἀγορᾶς Ἀφροδίτα.
[102] λίχνος πόρνης ἐπαγαλλόμενος πυγῇσιν. Crates, fr. 4 = no. 70 in Giannantoni, *Socraticorum reliquiae*, vol. 1, 732.
[103] Goulet-Cazé, *L'Ascèse cynique*, 81.   [104] DL, vi.23.
[105] Ps.-Diogenes, *Ep.* 31, tr. Fiore, in Malherbe, *Cynic Epistles*, 137.
[106] DL, vi.104 (σύντομον ἐπ' ἀρετὴν ὁδόν), in Marcovich, *Diogenes*, vol. 1, 443.
[107] DL, vi.38.   [108] Lucian, *Philosophies for Sale*, 7.   [109] DL, vi.71.

hardships (*kateria*), and frugality (*euteleia*). These were the qualities for which Xenophon praised the Spartan king Agesilaus and the philosopher Socrates.[110]

Cynicism, it has been claimed (wrongly), offered a 'debased' form of Socratic ethics which transformed Socrates' 'austerity to a fanatic asceticism'.[111] The Cynic way of life, and the mentality which informed it, indeed appeared reprehensible, if not obscene, to many in the Graeco-Roman world. Cicero warned that their 'whole way of thinking' was to be rejected as 'destructive of decency, without which nothing can be right, nothing upright'.[112] It was, in principle and intent, subversive of the social order to which nearly all others adhered, even those who sought to better their place within that order, though its very extremism effectively neutralized it as a political threat, and association with Heracles aided its toleration within the polis. If the place of the philosopher generally in the Roman empire was that of a 'licensed maverick', the Cynic could be accepted as the most maverick of them all.[113] The educated man practised temperance with respect to bodily and other pleasures but usually held that virtue did not require such a harsh rejection of traditional culture. Zeno, despite his lessons from Crates, had supposedly written to King Antigonus that 'a well-born nature which had received moderate training might easily come with the help of an ungrudging teacher to the perfect attainment of virtue'.[114] Diogenes, not surprisingly, had few immediate followers; they in turn gave rise to no widespread movement which practised entire the asceticism described above.[115] Rather, Cynicism became a recognized pattern or type of life reflected upon, approved of or disapproved, in whole or part, and used as a compass point in the placing of other figures and ideas, by a burgeoning philosophical literature.[116] Its *parrhesia* influenced writers who penned comic dialogues and satires, such as those pioneered by Menippus, and the diatribes or popular lectures traditionally associated with Bion and Teles.[117] Cynicism in this way offered authors and their readers a persona or perspective from which to flay opponents; its ascetic ideal and rejection

---

[110] Xenophon, *Agesilaus*, 5.2; *Memorabilia*, I.2.1, I.3.5, II.I.I–3.   [111] Dudley, *History*, xiii.

[112] Cicero, *On Duties*, I.148, ed. M. Winterbottom, *M. Tulli Ciceronis, De Officiis* (Oxford: Clarendon Press, 1994), 62: 'Cynicorum vero ratio tota est eicienda; est enim inimica verecundiae, sine qua nihil rectum esse potest, nihil honestum.'

[113] P. Brown, *Authority and the Sacred: Aspects of the Christianization of the Roman World* (Cambridge University Press, 1995), 38.

[114] DL, VII.8.   [115] Dudley, *History*, 40 and 95.

[116] M.-O. Goulet-Cazé, 'Le cynicisme à l'époque impériale', *ANRW* II.36.4 (1990), 2729.

[117] Scholars dispute the existence of diatribe as a distinct literary genre. Cf. F. G. Downing, *Cynics and Christian Origins* (Edinburgh: T&T Clark, 1992), 44–5.

of studies in logic and physics provided measures against which others fell short, convicted of folly, luxury, and vain learning. Lucian's *The Runaways* delights in turning this weapon against the Cynics themselves. Individuals might still lay claim to a Cynic identity while adopting more or less of its asceticism, or find themselves labelled as Cynics by others for some alleged resemblance to Cynicism, developments which generated disputes as to just who was the genuine follower of Diogenes.[118]

How widely or consistently Cynic asceticism was adopted in the imperial period is therefore unclear. It seems that Peregrinus publicly gave away his family wealth on adopting Cynic dress at Parium in the second century AD, though it is Lucian who staged the only extant version of the event, and his satirical account with its accusation of dishonesty and love of fame (*the* Cynic vice) is not to be trusted.[119] Peregrinus' subsequent *ascesis* under Athagobulus, his public masturbation and thrashing, stands in clear imitation of Diogenes' shamelessness, but may be Lucian's gleeful invention.[120] There is little other evidence for Cynic 'shamelessness' in the first and second centuries AD.[121] Aulus Gellius (a wealthy Roman writer in the second century) judged Peregrinus, whom he encountered inhabiting a hut outside Athens, 'a serious man committed to his calling', which tells against Lucian's account.[122]

Seneca (4 BC/AD 1–AD 65) described the Cynic Demetrius as accompanying him 'half-naked' (*seminudus*) at Rome under Caligula, and as lying down 'naked' without so much as a blanket, 'not so much a teacher of the truth as a witness to it'. The ascetic was to be admired for refusing a handsome offer of money from the emperor.[123] Seneca's accounts suggest that Demetrius had adopted the Cynic's cloak, the symbolic dress of a beggar, but does not allow us to ascertain whether he in fact begged; Demetrius features essentially, like Diogenes, as a model for Seneca's more circumspect asceticism. Philostratus, on the other hand, related how Demetrius had delivered a stinging attack on the morals of those attending the opening ceremonies for Nero's new baths, and had been exiled as a result.[124] Philostratus probably invented Demetrius' admiration for Apollonius, and may possibly have fabricated the episode at the baths, but it is plausible that Demetrius' asceticism served its original Cynic purpose of validating his freedom to make caustic speeches of the kind Philostratus ascribed to him, while he may well have exceeded his allotted license in the unstable

---

[118] Downing, *Cynics*, 27–8.   [119] Lucian, *Peregrinus*, 15.
[120] Ibid., 17.   [121] Downing, *Cynics*, 51.
[122] Aulus Gellius, *Attic Nights*, XII.11.1, ed. R. Marache and Y. Julien, *Aulu-Gelle, Les Nuits attiques*, 4 vols. (Paris: Les Belles Lettres, 1967–98), vol. III, 52: 'virum gravem atque constantem'.
[123] Seneca, *Moral Letters*, 20.9, 62.3; *De Beneficiis*, VII.11.   [124] Philostratus, *Life of Apollonius*, IV.42.

political arena of Neronian Rome.[125] Demetrius won notoriety on return to Rome by his defence of Publius Egnatius Celer, before renewed exile with other philosophers under the Emperor Vespasian.[126] This history is too complex to justify the generalization that 'ascetics...were seen as a threat to the continued and peaceful existence of the Roman Empire'.[127] It suggests, rather, that a Cynic with the right Stoic friends among the senatorial elite trod a tightrope between imperial favour and disfavour, because his own freedom of speech featured in the moves made by senators and emperors to define their mutual standing. There was a recognized place for the licensed maverick, but the terms of the licence were far from clear.

Dio Chrysostom describes Cynics at Alexandria who, like other beggars, accosted people in alleyways, at crossroads, and in temple gateways, and who engaged the passers-by through some form of discourse.[128] Elsewhere Lucian has self-proclaimed Cynics, former slaves and artisans, filling 'every city' and improving their lot by begging rather than working for a living.[129] Goulet-Cazé has therefore argued for bands of Cynic beggars roaming the streets of the great metropolises. She believes that Cynicism proved attractive to people in the lowest social orders, slaves, labourers, artisans, and stall-holders, for all of whom it promised escape from a hopeless plight.[130] This conviction, however, has not successfully negotiated the distorting perspective of Lucian's comic intent. If we take a Cynic whose existence is undoubted, Peregrinus, Lucian tars him with the charge of parricide, but presents the philosopher as born among the ranks of the wealthy.[131] We know more of Cynic identity as a literary type, and of how it might be viewed and used by others, than about those who understood themselves to follow the Cynic way of life.

LENTIL SOUP WITH CORIANDER – RIVAL SCHOOLS BUT A COMMON FRUGALITY

Stoics looked back to Zeno of Citium and his student Cleanthes as ascetic paragons at the head of their school. In the second century AD, Athenaeus seasoned his literary dish, *The Learned Banqueters*, with a choice selection

---

[125] For doubts as to Philostratus' reliability, cf. E. L. Bowie, 'Apollonius of Tyana: tradition and reality', *ANRW* II.16.2 (1978), 1657–9.

[126] Cassius Dio, *Roman Histories*, LXVI.13; Tacitus, *Histories*, IV.40.3; for an analysis of Demetrius' defence of Celer, cf. J. Moles, '"Honestius Quam Ambitiosius"? An exploration of the Cynic's attitude to moral corruption in his fellow men', *JHS* 103 (1983), 103–23.

[127] Francis, *Subversive Virtue*, xiii–xiv.   [128] Dio Chrysostom, *Or.*, XXXII.10.

[129] Lucian, *Runaways*, 12 and 16.   [130] Goulet-Cazé, 'Le cynicisme', 2735–6.

[131] For Lucian's artfulness, cf. D. Clay, 'Lucian of Samosata: Four Philosophical Lives (Nigrinus, Demonax, Peregrinus, Alexander Pseudomantis)', *ANRW* II., 36.5 (1992), 3406–50.

of quotations from the Stoics on the topic of that quintessential dish for the frugal Greek philosopher – lentil soup. Zeno was cited as advising that no more than 'one-twelfth of a coriander seed' be thrown into the pot.[132] Elsewhere he was held to have relied on raw rather than cooked food, or to have followed a diet of bread and water, and thought to have worn a thin cloak like the Cynics. Diogenes Laertius praised Zeno for his perfect endurance and frugality.[133] His contempt of wealth was lauded in verse by Zenodotus as making for 'self-sufficiency' (*autarkeia*).[134] Cleanthes was said to be renowned for the hardships he took upon himself.[135] But whereas Cynic asceticism centred upon the figure of the beggar, Cleanthes was known to have earned a small living from menial tasks, drawing water for a garden, digging, and grinding meal.[136] Nor were these paragons for simple imitation. Zeno's contempt for wealth was not generally understood by later Stoics as requiring them to adopt a life of voluntary poverty. Wealth in itself was morally indifferent. The Seneca who held up Demetrius for admiration warned Lucilius to avoid 'rough clothing, long hair, a rather untidy beard, too pronounced a scorn of money, and a bed upon the ground'.[137] Where Cynic asceticism functioned as the shortcut to virtue which bypassed intellectual endeavour, Stoics viewed a more limited asceticism as both conducive to a thorough training of the mind and as the practical conclusion of its insight. Musonius wrote that endurance of 'cold, heat, thirst, hunger, meagre rations, hard beds' and 'avoidance of pleasures' strengthened not only the body but the soul, which was 'trained for courage by patience under hardship and for self control by abstinence from pleasures'.[138] A moderate asceticism of this kind was part of an education in virtue for young men from the governing elites.[139] Cynic 'shamelessness' was rejected in favour of a sexual ethic which manifested self-control by restraining sexual activity within socially acceptable boundaries: heterosexual rather than homosexual relations, and for the purposes of procreation within marriage. Stoics thus adhered to the cultural tradition adumbrated by Michel Foucault: 'the more one was in the public eye, the more authority one had or wanted to have over others, and the more one sought to make one's life into a brilliant work whose reputation would spread far and last long – the more necessary it was to adopt and maintain, freely and

---

[132] Athenaeus, *Deipnosophists*, IV.158b.

[133] DL, VII.26 (Ἦν δὲ καρτερικώτατος καὶ λιτότατος), in Marcovich, *Diogenes,* vol. I, 461.

[134] DL, VII.30.   [135] Ibid., VII.168.   [136] Ibid., VII.168–9.   [137] Seneca, *Ep.* 5.2.

[138] Musonius, *Discourse 6, On Ascesis*, tr. C. Lutz, *Musonius Rufus, 'The Roman Socrates'*, Yale Classical Studies 10 (New Haven: Yale University Press, 1947), 55.

[139] Francis, *Subversive Virtue*, 18 and 24.

deliberately, rigorous standards of sexual conduct.'[140] Nonetheless, behind these differences between Cynic and Stoic asceticism lay a common respect for frugality, especially in matters of food and drink; Musonius favoured 'inexpensive food' (*tēn eutelē trophēn*).[141]

A virtue of frugality, though it might be understood variously within a wider ethics or meta-ethics, and variously related to practice, was in fact shared by the different philosophical schools. To some extent the Sceptics might be considered to have excluded themselves from this shared virtue: the wealthy sceptic philosopher Arcesilaus was remembered for his love of fine food and being 'highly extravagant' (*poluteles*).[142] Yet Sceptics tended to adopt a conformist ethic in which frugality also featured as a form of indifference to sensual pleasures. Epicureans likewise embraced a frugality which might surprise us. Epicurus had certainly refused to abstain from the pleasures of food and sex, and held pleasure the supreme good.[143] He further held that self-sufficiency (*autarkeia*) was worth striving for, not because people were always to make do with what was simple and cheap, but so that they could manage on the basics when necessary. However, he, too, therefore argued for a simple diet and 'spat' on 'extravagant pleasures' (*tais ek poluteleias hedonais*).[144] Poverty when assessed in the light of our natural make-up turns out to be true wealth.[145] Cutting down is not to be taken to excess, but a senseless fear of frugality leads people into worse anxiety.[146] Furthermore, Epicurus recognized that a simple lifestyle gave authority to a philosopher's teaching.[147]

A PYTHAGOREAN TRADITION?

Porphyry, as we have seen, appealed to the authority of the sixth-century sage Pythagoras and his followers rather than to Diogenes. To what extent, then, was there a Pythagorean ascetic tradition? Antiquity recognized a

---

[140] Foucault, *The Use of Pleasure*, 60.

[141] Musonius, *Discourse* 18A, *On Food*, tr. Lutz, *Musonius*, 113.

[142] DL, IV.40, πολυτελής τε ἄγαν ὤν, in Marcovich, *Diogenes*, vol. I, 286. It is possible that Diogenes (IX.110) likewise describes Timon as being fond of his wine (φιλοπότης), but Marcovich (*Diogenes*, vol. I, 705) emends the received text at this point to read φιλοπο<ιη>τής, 'friend to poets'.

[143] Athenaeus, *Deipnosophists*, XII.546e.

[144] Epicurus, *Letter to Menoeceus*, 130–1, ed. G. Arrighetti, *Epicuro, Opere*, 2nd edn (Turin: Giulio Einaudi, 1973) 113–15; *Epistularum fragmenta*, 58 and 124, in Arrighetti, *Epicuro*, 429 and 472.

[145] *Gnomologium Vaticanum*, 25, in Arrighetti, *Epicuro*, 145: Ἡ πενία μετρουμένη τῷ τῆς φύσεως τέλει μέγας ἐστὶ πλοῦτος.

[146] Ibid., 63, in Arrighetti, *Epicuro*, 153; fr. 235 (Arrighetti) = Porphyry, *To Marcella*, 28.

[147] Epicurus, *Epistularum Fragmenta*, 125, in Arrighetti, *Epicuro*, 473: 'what you say will appear all the more splendid for a pallet bed and ragged cloth: these things will not just be spoken of but demonstrated.'

variety of conflicting traditions concerning Pythagoras' dietary observances, and scholars have argued that Pythagoras and his immediate followers were not strict vegetarians but avoided only those meats which were not sacrificed to the gods in public cult. A strict vegetarianism, it is surmised, was characteristic only from the fourth century BC after Pythagoreanism collapsed as an influential political movement in the Greek cities of southern Italy, a development which perhaps allowed surviving Pythagoreans instead to establish an 'ascetic counterculture'.[148] Vegetarianism in this context was in part the practical consequence of belief in the transmigration of souls between animals of different species; the other elements in this counterculture prove difficult to determine. There is disputed evidence that very early Pythagorean communities held their property in common.[149] The *Golden Verses*, a pedagogical text which has been attributed to a Pythagorean movement in the period 350–300 BC, does not show common ownership, however; it merely stresses the importance of controlling one's anger and appetites for food, sleep, and sex.[150] It further exhorted readers not to sleep at night before undertaking a careful examination of their conduct during the day.[151] That a distinctive ascetic tradition continued to be practised across the Hellenistic period and into Roman imperial times may only be conjectured. The *Pythagorean Notebooks* specified how the purity (*hagneia*) required for worshipping the gods is achieved through 'purifications and baths and ablutions and keeping oneself pure from funeral rites and childbirth and all pollution, and by abstaining from meat and carcasses and red mullet and blacktail fish and eggs and egg-laying animals and from beans and from other things forbidden by those who perform ritual initiations (*teletai*) in the sanctuaries'.[152] Whether this prescription was actually observed in any Pythagorean community is unknown. Gillian Clark has rightly noted that 'there is no evidence for Pythagorean brotherhoods' after the Pythagoreans 'diaspora' in the fourth century BC.[153]

What Porphyry exploited in advancing his own Neoplatonist asceticism was the emergence of Pythagoras at a very early date as a figure in literature whose wisdom, physical asceticism, and knowledge of cult was intimately associated with the divine. Aristotle recorded Pythagorean traditions which made the sage a prophet with powers to foretell the future, who was greeted

---

[148] C. H. Kahn, *Pythagoras and the Pythagoreans: A Brief History* (Indianapolis: Hackett, 2001), 9.
[149] Iamblichus, *On the Pythagorean Life*, 6.30. On this topic, cf. P. Garnsey, 'Pythagoras, Plato and communality: a note', *Hermathena*, 179 (2005), 77–87.
[150] *Golden Verses*, lines 9–12, in J. C. Thom (ed.), *The Pythagorean Golden Verses* (Leiden: Brill, 1995), 94. For date and context, cf. 58 and 80.
[151] *Golden Verses*, lines 40–6, in Thom, *The Golden Verses*, 96.   [152] Kahn, *Pythagoras*, 83.
[153] G. Clark, in Iamblichus, *On the Pythagorean Life*, tr. G. Clark (Liverpool University Press, 1989), 1.

by the river Cosas or Nessus as he crossed over, and who could bi-locate. His thigh, so tales ran, was golden. He was not man nor god but some third kind of rational being.[154] Diogenes Laertius cited Heraclides of Pontus (still alive at the time of Aristotle's death in 322 BC), as the source for the story that Pythagoras was thought to be the son of Hermes with the power to remember a series of lives before his present incarnation.[155] Scholars trace much other material in the literary tradition back to a lost *Life* by a contemporary of Heraclides, Aristoxenus.[156] Pseudonymous treatises supposedly presented Pythagoras' ascetic teachings, including the advice to keep sexual pleasures for the winter when they were least harmful to health.[157] A certain Antiphon's *On the Life of Those Who Come First in Virtue* was Porphyry's source for Pythagoras' training in 'endurance' (*karteria*) at the hands of the Egyptian priests.[158] Much else came to him from Antonius Diogenes' *The Incredible Things Beyond Thule*, a story of fables set within fables, wondrous journeys of discovery, written at the end of the first century AD.[159]

Ewen Bowie, in examining the background to Philostratus' *Life of Apollonius*, has concluded that by AD 160 Pythagoras was the model by which the author fashioned the life of its holy man and wonderworker Apollonius. In Bowie's view, Apollonius' return from the cave of Trophonius at Lebadeia with Pythagoras' *doxai* or key teachings (at VIII. 19) is related by Philostratus 'in such a way as to suggest it was already in the tradition'. Though the lost *Life of Pythagoras* attributed to Apollonius was probably not composed by him, the attribution belongs to the same tradition, and the historical Apollonius (of whom little can be said with confidence) may have seen himself as a Pythagorean.[160] The *Life of Apollonius* thus drew on established parallels when it opened with a deft summary of how Pythagoras was envisioned by his admirers: his reincarnations, his renunciation of meat and of clothes made from animal skins, his possession of a divine knowledge which came from intimate association with the gods; all of which served to introduce Apollonius as yet more divine.[161] Philostratus

---

[154] D. Ross, *The Works of Aristotle*, vol. XII, *Select Fragments* (Oxford: Clarendon Press, 1952), 134–7.

[155] DL, VIII.4–5.

[156] Édouard des Places SJ, *Porphyre: Vie de Pythagore, Lettre à Marcella* (Paris: Les Les Belles Lettres, 1982), 15.

[157] DL, VIII.9.   [158] Porphyry, *Life of Pythagoras*, 7.

[159] Ibid., 10. For this novel-like work, cf. T. Hägg, *The Novel in Antiquity* (Berkeley and Los Angeles: University of California Press, 1991), 118–21. For a fuller account of the figure of Pythagoras in ancient literature, cf. J. Dillon and J. Hershbell, *Iamblichus: On the Pythagorean Way of Life* (Atlanta: Society of Biblical Literature, 1991), 4–13.

[160] Bowie, 'Apollonius of Tyana', 1672–3 and 1691–2.   [161] Philostratus, *Life of Apollonius*, I.1–2.

portrays his Pythagorean hero as a strict ascetic who drinks water not wine, who is stricter than Pythagoras in spurning marriage, resists seduction by powerful officials, and whose voluntary poverty is attested by a letter from Vespasian![162]

Such asceticism characterizes a life which has godlike powers. Pythagoras can turn away plague, stop violent winds, and calm the sea.[163] Extraordinary self-deprivation becomes a sign of divine identity. Iamblichus, writing at the end of the third century or beginning of the fourth century AD, related that when, on the voyage to Egypt, the young Pythagoras 'behaved with his habitual self-control and decorum', his fellow travellers 'saw something superhuman in the lad's self-discipline'.[164] They recognized that the boat cut a direct course towards its destination 'as though some god were present'. Asceticism ceases to be the restraint of appetites within the limits set by human needs to become a superhuman feat: the youth eats and drinks nothing for three days and two nights, and scarcely sleeps.[165] In the figure of Apollonius, however, asceticism of this type is now associated with the charge of being a *goēs* – either a true or fake sorcerer. Philostratus opens the *Life of Apollonius* with the admission that his protagonist was falsely accused of being a *magus*.[166] Niketas Siniossoglou has recently sought to contrast an extreme Christian asceticism with the 'moderation and self-control' he ascribes to Graeco-Roman philosophical asceticism; any such contrast must be qualified by recognition of this more extreme asceticism constructed as a literary type in Neoplatonic and other pagan texts.[167]

If the figures of Pythagoras and Apollonius share a similar asceticism in the authors on whom I have drawn, and form a second literary type of ascetic, those authors do not put these figures to the same use. The *Life of Apollonius* has the form of a novel; Tomas Hägg may even understate the case when noting deftly that the 'historical core almost disappears in the romantic pulp'.[168] The work exists primarily to entertain its readers who are to enjoy the spirited defence which Philostratus mounts of his hero. The accusations of sorcery and other nefarious crimes put by Apollonius' foe Euphrates partly exist as rhetorical artifices which justify the animated narration of events and wonders. Apollonius, for example,

---

[162] Ibid., 1.12–13; 11.35; VIII.7.   [163] Porphyry, *Life of Pythagoras*, 29.
[164] Iamblichus, *On the Pythagorean Life*, 3.15, tr. Clark, 6–7.
[165] Ibid., 3.16. This episode may be shaped by the legendary *inedia* of the apostle Peter on his boat-journey to Rome. Cf. *Actus Vercellenses*, 5, *NTA*, vol. 11, 291.
[166] Philostratus, *Life of Apollonius*, 1.2.   [167] Niketas Siniossoglou, *Plato and Theodoret*, 31–2.
[168] Bowie, 'Apollonius of Tyana', 1665; Hägg, *The Novel*, 115.

must acquit himself in an eloquent, lengthy *tour de force* before the tyrant Domitian.[169]

A very different use may be ascribed to the figure of Pythagoras in the writings of Porphyry and Iamblichus. Here, the ascetic sage stands to a varying extent as an embodiment of the authors' pagan philosophical systems, and stands in opposition to competing models of ascetic sanctity in Late Antiquity, whether to the Apollonian wonderworker, to rival figures within the philosophical schools, or (less probably) to the figure of Jesus and contemporary Christian ascetics. Gillian Clark has prudently noted that Porphyry's *Life of Pythagoras* 'as it now survives, does not suggest any special commitment to Pythagoras, his teachings and his way of life, whether as rival to Christ or as rival to Plato', but a concern for purification at once ritual and moral is shared by its author and subject.[170] Clark readily acknowledges that Pythagoras exemplifies the philosophic life for Iamblichus: the biography stands at the head of a much longer exposition of Neopythagorean philosophy. She further suggests that it begs comparison to the life of Plotinus with which Porphyry had prefaced the *Enneads*. One version of pagan philosophical asceticism is related to another.[171] Iamblichus makes no mention of celibacy on the part of Pythagoras' followers; his asceticism differs in this respect from that of Apollonius in Philostratus' *Life*.

Any intended opposition to Christianity on the part of Iamblichus is highly disputed. The placing of a miracle story about a catch of fish (the number of which Pythagoras correctly predicts to the amazed fishermen) on his arrival in Italy may be intended to outdo the encounters of Jesus with the fishermen who become his disciples at the outset of his public ministry in the Synoptic Gospels.[172] Pythagoreans at Kroton are described as not only students of the master's philosophy but 'coenobites' (*koinobioi*) sharing a common life. After the sage's death some followers become solitaries in lonely places.[173] Gillian Clark has pointed out that the word *koinobioi* is rare outside Christian literature, while the description of solitaries echoes

---

[169] Philostratus, *Life of Apollonius*, VIII.6–7. For an opposing view of Philostratus' intent as the 'rehabilitation' of his protagonist, cf. James, *Subversive Virtue*, 83–97.

[170] G. Clark, 'Philosophic Lives and the Philosophic Life: Porphyry and Iamblichus', in T. Hägg and P. Rousseau (eds.), *Greek Biography and Panegyric in Late Antiquity* (Berkeley, Los Angeles, and London: University of California Press, 2000), 33; Porphyry, *Life of Pythagoras*, 7, 12, 17, 45, 46. For a view sympathetic to an anti-Christian dimension in Porphyry's biography, cf. Dillon and Hershbell, *Iamblichus*, 14.

[171] Clark, 'Philosophic Lives', 34–5, 39–40, and 45–6.

[172] Iamblichus, *On the Pythagorean Life*, 8.36; Dillon and Hershbell, *Iamblichus*, 26.

[173] Iamblichus, *On the Pythagorean Life*, 6.29 and 35.253, tr. Clark, 11 and 105.

later Christian language for desert anchorites. If Iamblichus did not intend Pythagoras and his disciples to figure in opposition to emerging forms of Christian asceticism, that opposition certainly exists later as Christian authors echoed pagan characterization of Pythagoras to present their own saints for emulation.[174]

To see through these texts into the actual practice of asceticism among Neoplatonist philosophers or wandering figures such as Apollonius is extremely difficult. Iamblichus portrays a Pythagorean community which belongs within a literary tradition of such closed philosophical communities, but we cannot read off from this ideal the practice of his own school in Syria.[175] It is possible, though, to conclude first that there was no one established set of practices underlying the literary figures or the virtues they characterized. Porphyry's writings, for example, reveal that Castricius felt able to differ in his diet from the vegetarianism practised at Plotinus' school in Rome.[176] Castricius and Zethus both disagreed with Plotinus on the degree of proper involvement in politics.[177] Rogatianus, on the other hand, withdrew from the *cursus honorum*, gave up his house and household, and ate only on alternate days, a diet Porphyry ascribes to no one else in the circle.[178] We are told that Plotinus held him up as an example to other philosophers, which in itself suggests the exceptional nature of his asceticism. The master had no house at Rome of his own, and appears to have been celibate, but Zethus was married and owned the property in which the philosopher occasionally stayed.[179] Porphyry eventually married but professed to live as a celibate. Second, whatever form ascetic practices took, *some* physical asceticism was essential to the Neoplatonists' pursuit of wisdom and holiness.

CONCLUSIONS

This chapter has sketched versions of asceticism practised and idealized by pagans in the Graeco-Roman world which are largely unfamiliar from the perspective of Judaeo-Christian tradition. Cynics won a limited if contested license to flout the conventions governing food, sexual activity, and deference to authority, thereby asserting the wisdom of a life lived in strict accordance with nature; they could fashion for themselves a characteristic identity by their counter-cultural practices. Their asceticism centred upon

[174] Clark, 'Philosophic Lives', 45.
[175] A.-J. Festugière, 'Sur une nouvelle edition du "*De vita Pythagorica*" de Jamblique', *Revue des Études Grecques* 50 (1937), 470–94, at 476–7; Dillon and Hershbell, *Iamblichus*, 21.
[176] Porphyry, *Life of Plotinus*, 2.   [177] Ibid., 7.   [178] Ibid.   [179] Ibid., 7 and 9.

the figure of the beggar whose poverty brought disrepute and the status of an outsider to the Greek house and city, but who was nonetheless a public figure within that city. Such asceticism was not associated with ritual abstention, purity, or cult; it neither required sexual renunciation, nor emphasized the importance of sexual restraint, but devalued marriage. By the imperial period the movement had probably muted its original 'shamelessness'. It *represented*, but never in itself *constituted*, a threat to law and order. Stoics drew upon, and redrew, Cynic models in the idealization of their moderate asceticism which, however, did not centre upon the condition and stance of the beggar, but upon the restraint of appetite within conventional limits. This served to train the individual in detachment from anything that was not unqualifiedly good. Sexual restraint was therefore valued within the confines of marriage and procreation. Neoplatonists drew on the figure of Pythagoras to develop quite other versions of asceticism. Through appeal to cultic abstention and ritual purity they advocated an asceticism in food, drink, and all sexual activity, constructive of a moral and intellectual purity essential for union with the divine. They sought detachment from mundane concerns but differed on how far detachment required withdrawal from urban life and politics. Although no one set of agreed practices underlay the ascetic ideal, these forms of philosophical asceticism, like their Cynic and Stoic counterparts, were not ritualized in periodic abstinence. Nor were they penitential in aspect, the means to articulate a sinner's contrition before a judging deity; but they were integral to a life of virtue and holiness. Finally, those who adopted some form of asceticism, from whatever tradition, could be variously appraised by others who did not share their outlook. In the same way that Lucian could cast the Cynic Peregrinus as a glutton for fame, Hermippus satirized Pythagoras as faking a visit to the underworld.[180] Yet even such unfavourable appraisal presupposed that some physical asceticism was a characteristic part of the holy life.

[180] Dillon and Hershbell, *Iamblichus*, 8.

CHAPTER 2

Asceticism in Hellenistic
and Rabbinic Judaism

MOSES – THE ASCETIC PHILOSOPHER-KING

In his *Life of Moses*, the Alexandrian Jewish exegete Philo (*c.* 15 BC–AD 50) related, in the absence of any biblical account of Moses' upbringing, how the future leader of the Ancient Israelites had been educated within the Egyptian royal household. The boy rapidly outstripped his Egyptian and Greek tutors to master mathematics, geometry, music, the language of the Assyrians, and the Chaldaeans' knowledge of the heavens.[1] It was, in other words, an education to rival that of any Pythagoras. To match the knowledge of the Greek sages was not merely a feather in Moses' cap. Nor was it simply an opportunity to claim the superiority of Judaism over the dominant Hellenistic culture. Such wisdom was, as Philo conceived it, essential to Moses' inspired leadership: the Israelite was envisaged as a type of philosopher-king, one who excelled in the moral and intellectual virtues required of a just lawgiver. It was the philosopher's contemplative intimacy with God which allowed him to enshrine faithfully the divine wisdom in the timeless legislation of the Jewish Law (the Torah).

Moses, the uncrowned philosopher-king, was thus portrayed in terms drawn from the Greek philosophical tradition. The rule of others presupposed self-control; moral excellence lay in a Platonic subjection of the passions to reason, so that the 'violent affections' of his soul were reined in like a 'restive horse', an allusion to the famous description of the virtuous soul in Plato's *Phaedrus*.[2] This subordination involved asceticism in food, drink, sexual pleasures, and the various trappings of wealth, where the virtues proper to kingship included self-control, prudence, and 'disdain for pleasure'.[3] Moses had become 'masterful in needing little'.[4] Philo presented

---

[1] Philo, *Life of Moses*, 1.5.20–4.
[2] Ibid., 1.6.26, tr. C. D. Yonge, *The Works of Philo*, 2nd edn (Peabody, Mass.: Hendrickson, 1993), 461; Plato, *Phaedrus*, 246a–b.
[3] Philo, *Life of Moses*, 1.27.154.   [4] Ibid., 1.6.29 (ἀσκητὴς ὀλιγοδεείας), Ph*DVM*, 38.

such self-discipline as the rational restraint of appetite within the limits set by nature: Moses 'never lavished on his stomach anything more than the necessary tribute appointed by nature', and 'ignored the pleasures of the organs below the stomach except to father legitimate children'.[5] Unlike other rulers, the Israelite commander had not amassed silver, gold, palaces, servants, and possessions through taxation, nor 'anything else extravagant (*eis poluteleian*)'. He had, rather, despised wealth as 'blind'. He cultivated 'the frugality (*euteleia*) and plainness (*eukolia*) of a private person'.[6]

A Middle-Platonist set of ascetic virtues integral to the contemplative life likewise serves as the interpretative frame for a number of specific ascetic practices. The fast from all food and drink on the Day of Atonement (Yom Kippur) is said to be observed 'so that people can keep the feast with pure thoughts unhindered or pestered by any bodily passion'.[7] The forty-day fast from all food, drink, and sexual relations, which Moses undertook when receiving the Law at Mount Sinai (Exodus 34:28), is understood as a purification before prophesying or exercising priestly powers: 'he had first to purify his body as much as his soul, so that it was attached to no passion, but was pure from everything of mortal nature, from food and drink, and from all relations with women'.[8]

This mixture of generalities and specifics allowed Philo first to make a virtue of necessity: Moses lacks the riches attendant on power because he virtuously renounces their acquisition, and not because taxes and proper-ties presuppose a settled or productive life incompatible with the exodus journey through the wilderness. The Israelite is presented as without need for private wealth, because, like a Greek sage, he shares in all that belongs to God. Philo applies to Moses the proverb that 'the property of friends is common', which Cynics and others had drawn upon to claim the use of what belonged to God.[9] Philo likewise draws on Cynic tradition to term the good man a 'citizen of the world'.[10] Second, Philo approximated the total abstention of the Jews from forbidden foods (see below) to the restraint from excess characteristic of Graeco-Roman diatribe against lux-ury. He occluded what was odd from a Graeco-Roman perspective to focus on what was more obviously praiseworthy: dietary laws are implicitly transmuted into sumptuary laws. The distance between Jewish and Greek conceptions of the holy man was thus foreshortened.

This does not mean that Philo advocated the adoption by Jews of the ascetic *practices* which characterized some forms of Greek philosophical

---

[5] Ibid., 1.6.28.   [6] Ibid., 1.27.152–3.   [7] Ibid., II.4.24.   [8] Ibid., II.14.68–9.
[9] Ibid., 1.28.156.   [10] Ibid., 1.28.157.

tradition. He rejected the Cynic pose of the philosopher as a homeless ill-clad beggar who sleeps outdoors on the bare ground and flouts the conventions governing when to eat and bathe. The claim of such a figure to self-control is dismissed as spurious.[11] Philo's characterization of Moses shows, however, the deep influence which a Platonic understanding of asceticism exercised on him and on Jews who, like him, had received the Hellenistic philosophical and literary education which was the preserve of the governing classes. Strong acculturation served to reinterpret Judaism in what amounted to a limited assimilation or 'integrative accommodation' with the dominant culture in defence of distinctive forms and tenets.[12] A conceptual framework encapsulates and reinterprets ascetic practices which have very different religious and cultural origins where they bore quite different meanings. This raises thorny questions about asceticism in ancient Judaism. How widely was Philo's understanding of asceticism shared by fellow Jews in the diaspora and for how long? Peter Brown wisely cautioned readers to 'bear in mind the composite nature of any overall presentation of Judaism' in Late Antiquity, 'drawn as it is largely from the Palestinian and Babylonian Talmud – that is, from writings of widely differing periods and regions.'[13] There is good reason to think, as we shall see, that Second Temple Judaism was no less pluriform. With what other Jewish interpretations of asceticism did Philo's circulate and compete? And where there was more than one interpretative framework, what variety, if any, of ascetic practice underlies this diversity?

THE *THERAPEUTAE* – FACT OR FICTION?

It is still widely held that Philo's advocacy of asceticism was partly informed by his admiration for a group of Jewish men and women known as the *Therapeutae* ('Worshippers' or 'Attendants'), whom he portrayed in terms appropriate to a Greek philosophical school (*proairēsis*) in his treatise *On the Contemplative Life*.[14] Philo described these *Therapeutae* as numerous in Egypt, and as a 'race of worshippers' (*therapeutikon genos*) widely scattered across the diaspora;[15] they were to be found not in the confusion of urban life but in the greater solitude of suburban or outlying districts, and, above

---

[11] *The Worse Attacks the Better*, 7.19.

[12] Cf. J. Barclay, *Jews in the Mediterranean Diaspora: From Alexander to Trajan (323 BCE–117 CE)* (Edinburgh: T&T Clark, 1996), 92–8.

[13] P. Brown, *The Body and Society: Men, Women and Sexual Renunciation in Early Christianity* (London and Boston: Faber, 1989), 35 n.7.

[14] Philo, *The Contemplative Life*, 1.2, Ph*DVC*, 78.   [15] Ibid., 2.11 and 3.21, Ph*DVC*, 84 and 90.

all, in a religious 'colony' established outside Alexandria near Lake Mareotis. Here they devoted themselves to the contemplation of God withdrawn from public life, having left behind 'brothers, children, wives', their wider family and friends.[16] Surpassing even the Greek sages Anaxagoras and Democritus, each member of the colony entrusted their former wealth to others.[17]

Philo's description of their lifestyle centres around a repeated contrast between a spurned extravagance (*poluteleia*) and their chosen frugality (*euteleia*): their individual houses are 'basic' (*euteleis*) and spaced somewhat apart from one another so as to facilitate both 'solitude' and 'community' (the pattern of later Christian semi-anchoretic monasticism).[18] Each dwelling contained a 'shrine' or 'monastery' (*monastērion*) from which food and drink were excluded and where a worshipper remained alone for six days of the week in contemplation of God's Law and Scriptures.[19] Philo presented this as an *askesis* or philosophical exercise which engaged them so deeply, and offered such spiritual sustenance, that they not only fasted daily from food and drink until sunset but some men continued to fast for days at a time. On the sabbath, solitary fasting gave way, not to anything costly (*poluteles*), but to a common meal of plain bread (*arton eutele*) seasoned with salt and sometimes hyssop, washed down with water.[20] Philo stressed that their clothing was 'as basic as possible' (*eutelestatē*).[21] At their banquets, perhaps held every seven weeks, they sat on 'basic' (*eutelē*) papyrus matting, not expensive (*poluteleis*) cushions.[22] The community had no slaves to wait upon them.[23] Women as well as men were members of this celibate community, though they sat separately at common meals. Philo stated that there were many elderly virgins among the women in the community who had freely chosen a state of purity (*hagneia*) in their desire for contemplation.[24]

What realities should the historian detect behind Philo's portrait of the *Therapeutae* as a widespread philosophical movement and ideal contemplative community? The 'race of worshippers' scattered across the diaspora is probably none other than the Israelite nation itself, the wealthier, educated members of which might enjoy in the suburbs a more leisurely life

---

[16] Ibid., 2.18 and 2.20–3.22.   [17] Ibid., 3.13.
[18] Ibid., 3.24, Ph*DVC*, 92.   [19] Ibid., 3.25 and 30, Ph*DVC*, 94 and 98.
[20] Ibid., 4.34–7, 9.73, and 10.81–2, Ph*DVC*, 104, 134, and 140.   [21] Ibid., 4.38, Ph*DVC*, 106.
[22] Ibid., 8.65 and 9.69, Ph*DVC*, 124 and 128–30. Cf. V. Nikiprowetzky, 'Le *De vita contemplativa* revisité', in J. Leclant (ed.), *Sagesse et religion: colloque de Strasbourg (octobre 1976)* (Paris: Presses Universitaires de France, 1979), 105–25, at 117–23; and D. Winston, *Philo of Alexandria: The Contemplative Life, The Giants, and Selections* (Mahwah: Paulist Press, 1981), 320 n.38. A few scholars see an annual feast, e.g., Boyarin, *Carnal Israel*, 39.
[23] Philo, *The Contemplative Life*, 9.70.   [24] Ibid., 8.68.

enriched by a good library.[25] Philo casts the *Therapeutae* as representative of the Jewish nation, but this only sharpens the question about the nature of their movement or community. Renan argued that the *Therapeutae* had no existence outside the pages of Philo's text. A recent historian, Shaye Cohen, has by contrast largely taken Philo at his word to write of the *Therapeutae* as groups of men and women 'scattered throughout Egypt' who 'abstained from marriage' and 'practised moderation and self-mastery'.[26] Neither verdict does justice to the complexities of a text marked by more than one interpretative frame. Philo's account of the *Therapeutae's* diet, in particular, repeatedly havers between two different interpretations. A predominant ascetic interpretation centres upon the diet's 'frugality', which is contrasted at length with the excesses of Greek *symposia*. In this frame, having one's fill is thought harmful to body and soul, and hyssop is a concession for those accustomed to more sumptuous fare. A second, symbolic, interpretation relates the common meal to the similar food (the unleavened bread seasoned with salt and hyssop) which was reserved for the priests on a table in the Jerusalem Temple.[27] Both understandings of the diet explicitly approximate the *Therapeutae* to, but do not identify them with, the Temple priests in Jerusalem. Both may be termed forms of asceticism, but they are not the *same* forms of asceticism. If Philo read the diet in this twofold fashion, nothing requires us to believe that the *Therapeutae* shared his Greek philosophical version of asceticism. This possible gap, between a major plank of Philo's interpretative framework and the life he describes, throws doubt on Cohen's confident collapse of meanings into practices (moderation and self-mastery): 'what the book mainly offers is a picture of thinkers without their thoughts'.[28]

How, then, may other ascetic elements in the description of the *Therapeutae* be read? Withdrawal from the strife-torn city to form a separate philosophical community can be recognized as a Greek philosophical *topos*. Philo, however, may also have in mind the separate cities given to the Levites in the Book of Numbers (35:2): the description of the *Therapeutae* leaving their families behind closely resembles Philo's account elsewhere of the Levites – the priestly tribe.[29] Once again we find two fields of meaning

---

[25] For the Israelite nation as the θεραπευτικὸν γένος, cf. Philo, *Life of Moses*, II.35.189. For the good man's life in the suburbs as companionship with long-dead authors, cf. *On Abraham*, 4.22–3.

[26] Shaye J. D. Cohen, *From the Maccabees to the Mishnah* (Philadelphia: Westminster Press, 1987), 171.

[27] Philo, *The Contemplative Life*, 4.37, 9.73, and 10.81–2; Nikiprowetzky, 'Le *De vita contemplativa* revisité', 109.

[28] D. M. Hay, 'Things Philo said and did not say about the Therapeutae', *SBLSP* 31 (1992), 673 n.2.

[29] J. Riaud, 'Quelques réflexions sur les Thérapeutes d'Alexandrie à la lumière de *De Vita Mosis* II, 67', in E. Hilgert, D. T. Runia, D. Hay, and D. Winston (eds.), *Heirs of the Septuagint: Philo, Hellenistic*

within which to interpret practice. Identification with the Levites may explain the absence from Philo's account of any details concerning the economic life of the community at Lake Mareotis. This silence may hide a greater integration into society than desired by Philo's ideal of withdrawal into solitude, including continued ties of economic dependence with the families supposedly left behind.[30] The *Therapeutae* may have seen themselves as entitled, like the Levites, to the gifts of others. Philo, however, could not readily encode this aspect of the community within his Greek interpretative frame: the latter offered the model of the Cynic beggar, whose status was at odds with that of priestly contemplatives. All this strongly suggests that the *Therapeutae* saw themselves in priestly terms.

What, then, of the sexual abstention of the *Therapeutae*? Vincent Desprez has written that the elderly virgins reported by Philo 'no doubt... embraced this kind of life in their youth, as did the men', but this seems implausible in a Graeco-Roman and Jewish culture that favoured marriage for young women often before the age of twenty.[31] Virginity may possibly be a state of mind for Philo which can be recovered through abstinence. It has been suggested that the celibates who sing together at the close of the treatise symbolize the inner harmony of the mind. Behind Philo's symbols of the ideal contemplative life may lie a community comprising many widows and couples who have not so much 'abstained from marriage' as from the marriage-bed. Here, too, it must be considered highly probable that abstinence was understood by this community in priestly terms, a field of meaning not given by the text but, once again, to be found in the Jewish Scriptures: abstinence secured the necessary ritual purity of the priests who performed the Temple sacrifices, a purity lost by intercourse or other seminal emissions. In place of Philo's Greek interpretative frame we must locate the significance of asceticism for the *Therapeutae* in the meanings given to abstention within the Jewish Scriptures.

ABSTENTION IN THE JEWISH SCRIPTURES: SEPARATION, PETITION, AND REPENTANCE

All Jews in the Graeco-Roman world revered and accepted the authority of the Pentateuch, the Books of the Prophets, and the 'writings' or *Ketubim*, a

Judaism and Early Christianity, *Studia Philonica Annual* 3 (Atlanta: Scholars Press, *c.* 1991), 184–91, at 188.

[30] Hay, 'Things Philo said', 679 n.34; Barclay, *Jews*, 118.

[31] V. Desprez, 'Jewish Ascetical groups at the time of Christ: Qumran and the Therapeuts', *American Benedictine Review* 41.3 (1990), 291–311, at 309. For marriages among pagans, cf. Jens-Uwe Krause, *Witwen und Waisen im Römischen Reich*, 4 vols., (Stuttgart: Steiner, 1994–5), vol. 1, 22–7.

collection which came to include the other books we know from the later
Hebrew Bible, though these collections were not necessarily to be thought
of as a single Bible, and Jews did not necessarily agree on *how* the sacred
texts were to be read. Even the language in which they were read varied:
as well as Hebrew, there were also Aramaic and Greek versions (many of
which were adopted by the early Church in its Septuagint).[32] We should
therefore examine the forms of abstention from food, drink, and sexual
pleasure, which the inspired texts of this threefold canon laid down and
variously valued.

In Leviticus, chapter 11, God's Law prohibited the Jewish People from
eating certain foods: they were not to eat camel meat, rabbit, pork, or any
quadruped without cloven hooves and which did not chew the cud; seafood
that lacked the scales and fins characteristic of fish was likewise forbidden;
the People were not to eat certain species of birds, sometimes identified by
scholars as the eagle, vulture, osprey, falcon, raven, ostrich, sea gull, owl,
cormorant, ibis, and pelican. With the exception of certain types of locust,
all flying insects counted as forbidden food, as did all 'swarming' creatures,
rodents, and reptiles. No meat was to be eaten unless it had been drained
of its life-blood (Leviticus 7:26–7). It was forbidden to boil a kid in its
mother's milk or to eat flesh that had been seized by scavenging animals
(Exodus 22:31, 23:19, and 34:26). These divine prohibitions separated the
Israelite people from other nations to be holy as God is holy: 'holiness was
given a physical expression in every encounter with the animal kingdom
and at every meal'.[33] They functioned in relation to the sacrificial cult;
what could not be eaten, could not be offered. Mary Douglas has further
suggested that the author of Leviticus forbids all slaughter of domestic
livestock not intended for sacrifice. Eating meat in accordance with the
rules for its offering is seen as a way of entering into obedience to God and
respect for his ordering of the world.[34] The much later rabbinic *Mishnah*
(see below) thus dealt with dietary laws in the Order of Holy Things.

Some animals not only counted as forbidden food, their carcasses were
also sources of ritual impurity. They were among a number of such sources

[32] The authoritative status of the Pentateuch was recognized widely by the fourth century BC, that
of the Prophets by the mid-third century BC. Agreement over the books numbered among the
Prophets and Writings, and thus the closure of a canon, may well date to the second century BC,
but the length and nature of this process of closure is contested: the closure of the *Ketubim* might
date to the second century AD. Jewish sects also revered texts which formed a further group outside
the threefold canon. For different views, cf. Roger Beckwith, *The Old Testament Canon of the New
Testament Church and its Background in Early Judaism* (Grand Rapids: Eerdmans, 1985), esp. chapter
4 and 164–6; James A. Sanders, 'The canonical process', *CHJ*4, 230–43.
[33] M. Douglas, *Purity and Danger* (Harmondsworth: Penguin, 1970), 57.
[34] M. Douglas, *Leviticus as Literature* (Oxford University Press, 1999), 75 and 93.

stipulated by the Mosaic Law: human corpses, but also menstrual blood, semen, other forms of genital discharge, and leprosy. Although it was forbidden to have sexual relations with a woman during her monthly period (Leviticus 18:19), ritual impurity did not in itself imply moral failure; it was incurred in the performance of virtuous and morally required acts: begetting lawful children or the burial of the dead. The Law laid down the duration of such impurity and the means for its removal, both of which might vary with respect to the person who had contracted the impurity: a priest, or a person who had undertaken a Nazirite vow, might be required to perform acts of ritual purification different to those enjoined on other Jews.[35] As in ancient Greek and Roman religion, ritual purity was essential to Jewish religious rites: what was impure must not come into contact with the holy. Here, again, abstention serves a desired separation, consecration to God. To neglect this, to eat flesh from a sacrificial offering while in a state of ritual impurity, was to cut oneself off from Israel (Leviticus 7:20–1). The presence of God, whether on Mount Sinai, or in the Jewish camp on the exodus, or in the Jerusalem Temple, therefore necessitated various forms of abstention by those who entered His presence and offered sacrifice. At Exodus 19:15 the Israelite men were instructed to abstain from sexual relations for three days in preparation for God's gift of the commandments. It is a measure of Moses' extraordinary intimacy with God at Sinai that he abstained miraculously for forty days even from pure foods, from bread and water.

Scripture ordained (Leviticus 16:29 and 31; 23:27; Numbers 29:7), that on Yom Kippur, held on the tenth day of the seventh month, the entire nation was to 'afflict' or 'humble' itself, (LXX *tapeinōsate*), a command which appears to have been universally understood as a 'technical term for fasting in the Priestly Code'.[36] Scripture also established a distinctive pattern of abstention for someone who took a Nazirite vow of self-dedication to God. The Nazirite vowed to 'separate himself to the Lord': he or she was to drink no wine and consume nothing taken from the vine for the duration of the vow; neither was a person to cut their hair in that period. All contact with the dead was to be avoided (Numbers 6:1–12). The Septuagint made explicit that the vow brought the devotee into a state of religious purity.[37]

---

[35] H. K. Harrington, *The Purity Texts* (London and New York: T&T Clark, 2004), 11.
[36] J. Muddiman, 'Fast, fasting', in N. Freedman (ed.), *Anchor Bible Dictionary*, vol. II (New York and London: Doubleday, 1992), 773–6, at 773.
[37] Stuart Chepey, *Nazirites in Late Second Temple Judaism* (Leiden: Brill, 2005), 25–30.

Outside the strictures of the Mosaic Law the Scriptures revealed other forms of abstention acceptable to God, and commented upon cultic abstention. Jeremiah, chapter 35, showed God's favour for the 'house of the Rechabites' who on the command of Jonadab ben Rechab had refrained from drinking wine, viticulture, and settled agriculture generally, to return to their nomadic tents. While this practice is exceptional, fasting repeatedly appears within the texts as an adjunct of successfully petitioning God in prayer. A collective fast, often decreed by the king, seeks to win God's decisive support in war: the Israelite army fasts for a day at Bethel after incurring heavy losses in battle with the tribe of Benjamin and before asking whether it is God's will that they continue to fight (Judges 20:26–8). Israel fasts for a day at Mizpah when Samuel beseeches God's help in the war against the Philistines (1 Samuel 7:5–6). Saul binds his army by a curse not to eat before conquering the Philistines in battle, a curse which nearly cost Jonathan his life (1 Samuel 14:24–45). Jehoshaphat decrees a fast on learning of the threat posed by the Moabites and Ammonites (2 Chronicles 20:3). The fast-day on which Baruch reads from Jeremiah's scroll may have been precipitated by the threat of Nebuchadnezzar's armies (Jeremiah 36:6 and 9).[38] By extension such public fasting could accompany prayer for deliverance from other pressing dangers: an army of locusts (Joel 2:12), severe drought (Jeremiah 14:12), a threatened pogrom (Esther 4:16).[39] In different circumstances Ezra decrees a collective fast at the river Ahava before leading his band of exiles back to Jerusalem (LXX Ezra 8:21–3): an act of humility before God secures their safe passage. Public fasting can also express humble penitence: the pagan Ninevites demonstrate their repentance and avert divine punishment through a total fast which includes not only every person in the city, but the livestock and beasts of burden (Jonah 3:5–10).

Individuals likewise fast as a form of humble or penitent petition. David fasts 'until evening' in penitence for the murder of Uriah, hoping vainly to placate God and so save the life of the child whom he had fathered in adultery (2 Samuel 12:16–23). Ahab fasts in sackcloth when he learns of his punishment for Naboth's murder (LXX 1 Kings 20:27–8), an action which the Lord describes to Elijah as Ahab being 'cut to the quick in my

---

[38] J. A. Thompson, *The Book of Jeremiah* (Grand Rapids: Eerdmans, 1980), 623.
[39] The Book of Esther, the original version of which may have been composed as early as the fourth century BC, evolved in multiple Hebrew and Greek versions; it was known in Palestine by the early first century BC; cf. J. D. Levenson, *Esther* (London: SCM Press, 1997), 26–7; L. M. Wills, *The Jewish Novel in the Ancient World* (Ithaca and London: Cornell University Press, 1995), 93–131.

presence'.[40] Fasting also expresses mourning. The inhabitants of Jabesh-gilead fast for seven days after Saul's burial (1 Samuel 31:13 and 1 Chronicles 10:12). David and his attendants fast in mourning for the death of Saul and Jonathan (2 Samuel 1:12). These different uses of fasting are not always separable or univocal: when Ezra refuses even bread and water after the failure of the Israelites to abandon their foreign wives, this is described as an expression of mourning, but the fast accompanies his prayer and confession of sin on behalf of the nation (LXX Ezra 9:5 and 10:6). Nehemiah fasts in grief but also in petition when he learns of the plight of the Jews in Jerusalem (LXX Ezra 11:4 = Nehemiah 1:4). Hannah refuses to eat in sorrow at her failure to bear a child (1 Samuel 1: 7), but this abstinence can be seen in retrospect as a fast which precedes her successful prayer to God at Shiloh.

In the Psalms, fasting is characteristic of the humble and contrite man of prayer. The worshipper who recites the psalm in cult or private prayer ritually takes their words on his or her lips, identifies himself or herself with this figure or type of heartfelt devotion. The Prophets, on the other hand, point with anger towards a mendacious gap they perceive between the meaning of fasting and the real disposition of worshippers who merely adopt the pose of the penitent.[41] The Prophets therefore re-describe concern for God's righteousness as true fasting. The intention is not to end cultic fasts, but to shape their meaning for participants, or to clarify that meaning as a linguistic act before God that is either true or false.[42] In this context we may consider the puzzling account of fasting in the Book of Zechariah, where a question from the shrine at Bethel, about fasting in the fifth month, leads the prophet to speak of four annual fast-days in the fourth, fifth, seventh, and tenth months; in future these are to be held as 'seasons of joy and gladness, and cheerful feasts' (RSV Zechariah 8:19).[43] How is this paradoxical command to be understood given the predominant meanings associated with fasting in the above discussion? Some scholars hold that the prophet decrees the continuation of the fasts but a radical change in their meaning;[44] others think that a fast-day is to be replaced by a feast-day, though only in God's good time.[45]

---

[40] ὡς κατενύγη Αχααβ ἀπὸ προσώπου μου.

[41] LXX Pss. 34 (35):13; 68 (69):11; 108 (109):24; Is. 58:3–6.

[42] M. Fishbane, *Biblical Interpretation in Ancient Israel* (Oxford: Clarendon Press, 1985), 304–7.

[43] The fast on the fifth month was probably to mourn the destruction of the first temple, that of the seventh month the murder of Gedaliah; cf. Thompson, *The Book of Jeremiah*, 657.

[44] Muddiman, 'Fast, fasting', 774.

[45] For a brief discussion, cf. R. J. Coggins, *Haggai, Zechariah, Malachi* (Sheffield Academic Press, 1987), 50.

Finally in this section we should note the motif of fasting as a preparation for divine revelation. Daniel fasts before making his great prayer of intercession on Israel's behalf (9:3), and this is associated with penitence, 'sackcloth and ashes', but his action is rewarded by the appearance of the archangel Gabriel. Daniel fasts again in mourning at 10:2–3, and here, too, the fast results in an angelic vision.

SECOND TEMPLE JUDAISM

In this biblical frame, we can see more clearly the coherent meaning of the different ascetic practices deployed by the *Therapeutae* to identify themselves with, and make for, a priestly holiness. The suspicion must be that Philo's philosophical interpretative frame is redundant. Nowhere in the Septuagint is fasting or any other form of abstention characterized as a part of a virtuous *euteleia*. The cognate adjective appears four times in the Book of Wisdom always in a pejorative sense to mean what is worthless: the superlative form characterizes the 'utterly debased' hope of the man who fashions idols from clay (15:10).

How, though, did other groups within late Second Temple Judaism use the different forms of abstention they found in the Sacred Scriptures? Some practices may be presumed to be all but universal, such as the day of fasting on Yom Kippur, though different Jewish groups might disagree about when the tenth day in fact fell.[46] The author of *Jubilees* possibly interprets the fast as a penitential act.[47] The abstention from forbidden foods appears to have been widely, but not universally observed, subject to intense cultural pressures to assimilation, and therefore a focus for anxiety in Jewish texts both in late Second Temple Judaism and the early Rabbinic period.[48] In the rabbinic period, preparation for the religious festivals by those who observed them might involve abstaining from intercourse immediately beforehand, as well as the ritual washing of themselves and their clothing.[49] This was probably common practice earlier.

---

[46] Cf. Barclay, *Jews*, 416. More than a dozen sectarian calendars were found in Cave Four at Qumran. Cf. G. Vermes, *The Complete Dead Sea Scrolls in English* (London: Penguin, 1997), 20.

[47] *Jubilees*, 5.17–18, tr. O. S. Wintermute, *OTP*, vol. ii, 65; cf. J. Kugel, *Traditions of the Bible: A Guide to the Bible As It Was at the Start of the Common Era* (Cambridge, Mass.: Harvard University Press, 1998), 751.

[48] For resistance to assimilation, cf. 3 Maccabees 7:11, and 4 Maccabees 1:32–5; for a survey of the literary evidence, cf. Barclay, *Jews*, 434–7.

[49] H. K. Harrington, *Holiness: Rabbinic Judaism and the Graeco-Roman World* (London and New York: Routledge, 2001), 111.

During the Maccabean wars of the second century BC the Hasmoneans apparently sought to conform the army and Jewish nation to the biblical patterns we have already outlined: the army is described as fasting in sackcloth and ashes before battle (1 Maccabees 3:47) and a general fast is declared at a time of heightened military threat (2 Maccabees 13:10–12). Although we cannot exclude the possibility that these reports owe more to the biblical modelling pursued by the historians (who narrated the campaigns at the end of that century or beginning of the first century BC) than they owe to that of the Hasmoneans themselves, their historical accuracy is highly probable.[50] Josephus related that during the Jewish war a similar fast was declared at Tiberias at a time of supposed military threat. He questioned the motives which prompted the declaration, but his misgivings were outweighed by the need to participate in an action so publicly associated with piety (*eusebeia*).[51] There is also considerable evidence that individuals in the Second Temple era undertook Nazirite vows, in seeking to be cured of illness, or in petitioning some other gift from God, and commonly abstained for a thirty-day period. The destruction of the Temple, however, rendered impossible the Nazirite's offering of hair, and observance of the practice thereafter, though discussed at length in the *Mishnah*, is hard to prove.[52]

A number of texts show the value of personal fasting as a prized element in a life of holiness unassociated with the Nazirite vow. The Book of Tobit, probably originally composed in Aramaic at some point in the late third century or early second century BC, seemingly included the angelic counsel that 'Prayer with fasting, almsgiving, and righteousness is good' (12:8).[53] Although Tobit was not included in the Hebrew canon, its widespread circulation and status in some Jewish communities are measured by its inclusion in the Septuagint and the discovery of both fragmentary Aramaic and Hebrew copies at Qumran. The Book of Judith, a fictional tale about the assassination of an invading general, Holofernes, by the courageous heroine of its title, was probably composed in the early part of the first

---

[50] For the dates of composition, cf. J. A. Goldstein, *1 Maccabees* (New York: Doubleday, 1976), 62–4; R. Doran, '2 Maccabees', in J. Barton and J. Muddiman (eds.), *The Oxford Bible Commentary* (Oxford University Press, 2001), 735.

[51] Josephus, *Life*, 290–2.

[52] For evidence from Philo and Josephus for its relation to illness and prayer, cf. Chepey, *Nazirites*, 50–3, and 57–61; for the thirty-day period, ibid., 57, 78–80, 119–20 and 133–5; for an aristocratic Nazirite of probably the early first century AD, cf. N. Avigad, 'The Burial vault of a Nazirite family on Mount Scopus', *Israel Exploration Journal* 21 (1971), 185–200.

[53] J. Fitzmyer, *Tobit*, (Berlin and New York: de Gruyter, 2003), 25, 51–2, 285 (translation) and 292. The text varies in the extant Greek recensions. Fitzmyer holds that the later Short recension (which reads 'fasting' where the Long recension reads 'fidelity') is more faithful to the likely Aramaic original.

century BC.[54] It indicates the high value which its author and readers placed upon fasting as a mark of personal piety and Jewish identity. Judith fasts daily throughout the year (how is unspecified), except on Fridays and the following Sabbath, on the day of the new moon and the day preceding the new moon, and on the feast days of the Jewish calendar (8:6). These exceptions remind us that abstention can be significant through being forbidden to the devout at certain times as well as being enjoined on them. Judith also refuses offers of marriage to remain a widow until her death in extreme old age when she leaves her money to members of her husband's family (16:22 and 24). No actual practice of daily fasting by Second Temple Jews can be read off from this portrait where an ideal is taken to extremes, but the figure of a widow whose piety is expressed in fasting (as well as the eventual virtuous dispossession of wealth), at least affirms a conventional pattern of holy conduct.[55] The popularity of the book is hard to assess: it would be found in the Septuagint, but was not included among the Hebrew *Writings*. It has not been discovered among the writings copied at Qumran, nor does the story appear in Philo or Josephus, although these two latter omissions may reflect the authors' desire to present Judaism as a peaceable religion acceptable to a Graeco-Roman audience.

The Pentateuch insisted upon the purity to be observed within the Israelite cult and camp. But what counted as the camp in changed circumstances after the (re-)establishment of the Jerusalem Temple? This question was variously answered in the Second Temple Period. The archaeological remains on the Temple mount of baths for purification suggest that for many it was only this area immediately surrounding the Temple which was to count as the camp.[56] But other groups might think the camp extended to the whole city, might regard the incurrence of ritual impurity with more or less gravity, and might apply to themselves purity regulations which others regarded as obligatory only for priests. The New Testament offers evidence for the seriousness with which the Pharisees regarded the adoption by ordinary Jews of purity regulations.

---

[54] A.-J. Levine, 'Judith', in Barton and Muddiman (eds.), *The Oxford Bible Commentary*, 633. For an earlier date, cf. C. A. Moore, 'Why wasn't the Book of Judith included in the Hebrew Bible?', in J. VanderKam (ed.), *'No One Spoke Ill of Her': Essays on the Book of Judith* (Atlanta: Scholars Press, 1992), 65.

[55] A. D. Roitman, 'Achior in the Book of Judith: his role and significance', in VanderKam, *'No One Spoke Ill of Her'*, 43 n.33. For disputed evidence from non-Jewish sources that some Jews *did* fast on Saturdays cf. L. H. Feldman and M. Reinhold (eds.), *Jewish Life and Thought Among Greeks and Romans: Primary Readings* (Edinburgh: T&T Clark, 1996), 366–71; for discussion, cf. J. Tabory, 'Jewish festivals in late antiquity', *CHJ4*, 561–2.

[56] Cohen, *From the Maccabees*, 130.

THE ESSENES AND THE QUMRAN COMMUNITY

Philo contrasted the contemplative life practised by the *Therapeutae* with the active life practised by another Jewish sectarian movement, the Essenes. This movement, which probably originated in the mid-second century BC and lasted until the Jewish revolt of AD 68, was portrayed in antiquity by Philo, the Elder Pliny (AD 23/4–79), and Josephus (b. AD 37/8). In recent decades scholars have repeatedly debated the relationship of the Essenes to the movement whose collected writings have been recovered from eleven caves close to Khirbet Qumran by the Dead Sea, prompted by the similarities and dissimilarities between the communities described, presupposed, or desired in the different texts. Such differences have been commonly explained by the existence of two branches of an evolving Essene movement, the more sectarian of which came to occupy the settlement at Qumran until the Romans destroyed it after the revolt; but differences may also be explained by the idealizing nature of some Qumran texts, which legislate for how things should be rather than describing actual practice. What is clear is that the Essenes known from Latin and Greek sources and the movement behind the Dead Sea Scrolls valued very similar patterns of abstention, though these have been set in different interpretative frames.

The Elder Pliny briefly describes the Essenes as a 'solitary tribe' (*gens sola*) of men by the Dead Sea; they are world-weary fugitives from society whose sexual abstinence, like their refusal of monetary commence, is symbolic of a retreat from ordinary human exchange brought about by 'dismay at others' lives'.[57] Philo, as we expect, presents the movement in terms drawn from the Greek philosophical tradition. In *Every Good Man is Free* he relates that the Essenes withdraw to a host of villages not from lassitude but to avoid the morally corrupting influence or 'lawlessness' of the cities, though elsewhere he admits that many in fact inhabit the Judaean towns;[58] they reckon wealth to lie in 'wanting little and being easily satisfied'. Like classical lovers of wisdom, they avoid 'impulses to greed' by abstaining from commerce. Like Cynics, they 'labour upon the ethical part of philosophy', although, unlike Cynics, they are guided by ancestral laws.[59] The Scriptures which they study are supportive of the Greek ascetic virtues: 'detachment from pleasure, self-control, endurance, wanting little, plainness, being easily satisfied, freedom from pride'.[60] It is in this context that Philo details their common ownership of goods. In his *Hypothetica* lack of private property

---

[57] Pliny, *Natural History*, v.73.   [58] Philo, *Every Good Man is Free*, 12.76; *Hypothetica*, 11.1.
[59] Philo, *Every Good Man is Free*, 12.76–80.   [60] Ibid., 12.84.

serves as proof that the Essenes are 'neither washed away by the body's currents nor carried off by their passions', a concern which is to explain the absence of children and youths from the movement.[61] In terms familiar from his account of the *Therapeutae* Philo describes the Essenes as 'lovers of the need for little, who turn away from luxury as an illness of body and soul'.[62]

Josephus likewise presents the Essenes in familiar Greek terms as an ascetical philosophical school 'numerous in every town' of Palestine who 'practise holiness' (*semnotēta askein*) by spurning pleasures and excelling in self-control (*enkrateia*). Thus, most avoid marriage not because of any inherent evil in the institution, but supposedly to escape women's licentiousness; a further group marry but restrict sexual activity to procreation. Those who seek admission by following the sect's way of life for a probationary year are said to prove their self-control and 'endurance' (*karteria*).[63] In the same interpretative vein Josephus describes their refusal to use money in terms of common ownership and exchange based upon need.[64] The Essenes' diet, with its two daily meals of bread and water, is also presented in terms of a Greek philosophical frugality which restricts food to a necessary minimum: Josephus ascribes to their communities a mysterious silence which derives from their 'unbroken sobriety and the meting out of just enough food and drink to satisfy them'.[65] The Essenes' longevity is put down to the 'simplicity of their lifestyle', which included abstention from the use of oil to anoint the body.[66] Such description of the Essenes' ascetical virtues is matched by Josephus' account of their eschatological hopes which they supposedly 'share with the sons of the Greeks'.[67]

The Qumran scrolls give the same patterns of abstention a very different meaning. They are explained, above all, by a predominant concern for advancing in holiness through the strict observance of ritual purity, and, second, by a penitential understanding of fasting. Thus, the scrolls indicate a group or groups who placed great importance on forms of withdrawal from ordinary society including the formation of a separate community. The caves yielded eleven or more partial copies of a text known as the *Community Rule* or *Manual of Discipline* which was probably composed around 100 BC.[68] It prescribes the customs of a group who thought of itself as a 'unity' or *yahad* organized in units of a thousand, one hundred, fifty, and ten, just as Moses had organized the Israelite camp at Exodus

---

[61] Philo, *Hypothetica*, 11.3–4.   [62] Ibid., 11.11.
[63] Josephus, *The Jewish War*, 11.119–21, 124, 138, and 160.   [64] Ibid., 11.127.
[65] Ibid., 11.133.   [66] Ibid., 11.123 and 151.   [67] Ibid., 11.155.
[68] The oldest copy apparently dates to between 100 and 75 BC; cf. Vermes, *Dead Sea Scrolls*, 97.

18:25.[69] Where Pliny and Philo stress what members withdrew *from*, the scrolls stress what members withdraw *to*: an Israelite camp, morally and ritually pure, and so fit for the presence of God. Another treatise pieced together partly from the scrolls and partly from medieval texts, the so-called *Damascus Document* relates the history of a religious movement inspired some twenty years after its foundation by a 'Teacher of Righteousness'. Perhaps written at much the same time as the *Community Rule*, it likewise contains rules for members in 'camps' with an organization into units of a thousand, one hundred, fifty, and ten.[70]

Sexual abstinence is required to maintain the level of purity appropriate to life in the Israelite camp, though the scrolls recognize more than one such pattern of abstinence. The *Damascus Document* distinguishes between married and celibate members, and it is plausible, though not certain, that the latter belong to a distinct camp of 'perfect holiness', a sectarian branch who maintain a higher level of ritual purity within the community than that required of others.[71] This tallies with the celibacy of the sect members at Qumran, which may be inferred from the burials at the site: the bodies have been discovered of over one thousand adult males, but (lying separately from the main burials) the remains of only eleven women and five children.[72] Several texts, the *Temple Scroll* and *Damascus Document*, prescribe sexual abstinence within the holy city of Jerusalem.[73] The latter explicitly states that this is to avoid defiling the Temple city through 'uncleanness'. Hannah Harrington believes that the *Damascus Document* also forbids married Essenes to have intercourse on the Sabbath.[74] Some stipulations within the texts are obscure. The *Damascus Document* rules that 'whoever approaches to fornicate with his wife, which is not according to the regulation, shall depart and never return', but does not specify the nature of the crime.[75] On the grounds that the same treatise forbids intercourse with one's pregnant wife, Hannah Harrington has plausibly argued that the offence is 'sexual intercourse for pleasure' rather than procreation.[76]

Dietary abstinence is determined in large part by concern for ritual purity. Only those who are ritually and morally pure are admitted to the

---

[69] *Community Rule*, 1QS, col. 2, tr. *DSS*, 128.
[70] *Damascus Document*, Genizah A, cols. 12–14, tr. *DSS*, 70–1.
[71] Ibid., Genizah A, col. 7, tr. *DSS*, 57; Harrington, *The Purity Texts*, 13.
[72] Harrington, *The Purity Texts*, 14.
[73] *Temple Scroll*, 11Q19, col. 45, tr. *DSS*, 477; *Damascus Document*, col. 12, tr., *DSS*, 69.
[74] Harrington, *The Purity Texts*, 17.   [75] *Damascus Document*, 4Q270 fr. 11 col. 1, tr. *DSS*, 73.
[76] Ibid., 4Q270 fr. 9 col. 2, tr. *DSS*, 65; Harrington, *The Purity Texts*, 47.

common meal described in the *Community Rule*. It is 'pure food';[77] Harrington reads the treatise as implying that it was 'harvested, stored and eaten in a state of purity; all members had to bathe before eating it'. She thinks that the Qumran sectarians 'combined the purification rules addressed to all Israel in Leviticus 11–15 with the purity required to eat sacrificial portions in Leviticus 7:19–21'.[78] Maintaining such purity, and purifying oneself after defilement, has a strongly penitential dimension wholly absent from the Greek philosophical frame. The *Damascus Document* punishes numerous breaches of discipline with reduced rations for varying numbers of days, several months in the case of more serious infractions, and understands this discipline within a biblical frame of penitential fasting. The text cites Joel 2:12 – 'Return to God with weeping and fasting'.[79] The *Community Rule* closely associates repentance and acceptance of the discipline established by the *yahad*.[80]

How do the scrolls suggest that we should understand the movement's ideal of common property? This, too, is related to purity. The *Community Rule* asserts that the 'wealth' of members was to be controlled by the 'Sons of Aaron' – i.e. given to the priests who exemplify the holiness of the community – and not to be confused with 'that of rebellious men, who have failed to cleanse their path by separating from perversity'.[81] Commerce with the morally impure is defiling just as ritual impurity is contagious. These normally distinct categories of impurity seem to merge in the scrolls.[82] The probationary or formation period for entrants to the sect correlated the handing over of property to the group with permission to touch the ritually pure property of the community. After the first year, the entrant can touch the pure vessels of the group, and his own goods are removed, but they are not yet considered safe to be used by the full members.[83] For group members common ownership thus functioned to protect purity, while acting in sociological terms as a powerful agent of social separation and cohesion. Such an ideal could not be readily practised in the cities, however, and the *Damascus Document* instead stipulates the mutual aid which members owed one another; it requires each man to give the 'Overseer' the earnings of at least two days each month for distribution in alms by the 'Judges'; it forbids business partnerships without the approval of the Overseer, and all commerce with the corrupt.[84]

---

[77] *Community Rule*, 1QS col. 6, tr. *DSS*, 134.   [78] Harrington, *The Purity Texts*, 23 and 25.
[79] *Damascus Document* 4Q266 fr. 18 cols. 4 and 5, and 4Q270 fr. 11 col. 1, tr. *DSS*, 72–3.
[80] *Community Rule*, QS1, col. 3, tr. *DSS*, 129.   [81] Ibid., col. 9, tr. *DSS*, 139.
[82] J. Klawans, *Impurity and Sin in Ancient Judaism* (Oxford University Press, 2000), 79–85.
[83] *Community Rule*, col. 6, tr. *DSS*, 134–6.   [84] *Damascus Document*, 13–14, tr. *DSS*, 71–2.

RABBINIC JUDAISM

The destruction of the Temple at the end of the Jewish war, which ended the sacrificial cult, together with the annihilation of the Essene movement in the course of the war, brought about a cataclysmic upheaval within Judaism. Out of this there gradually emerged over four hundred years what we now refer to as Rabbinic Judaism, a movement which advanced as authoritative the decisions of the *tannaim*, the Palestinian rabbis of the first and second centuries AD, as these (often disputed) decisions were codified in the *Mishnah* around the year AD 200. This collection was glossed and supplemented by the *Tosefta* (*c.* AD 300), but also variously weighed and debated by later sages in far-distant parts of the diaspora; their judgements would in turn be edited in the *Jerusalem Talmud* (*c.* AD 375–425) and the *Babylonian Talmud* (*c.* AD 600).[85] One must recognize, however, that not all Jews in the Graeco-Roman world after AD 70 observed the decisions laid down and argued over in these different collections; indeed, a great many decisions could not be observed, because '[m]uch of the Mishnah speaks of matters not in being in the time in which the Mishnah was created'.[86] The rabbis codified what, in their view, *should be*.[87] Furthermore, it is notoriously difficult to date individual decisions or debates within the Talmud, many of which cannot be ascribed with confidence to the rabbis who voice them.[88] Nonetheless, the *Mishnah*, and to a lesser extent the *Talmud*, offer crucial insight into Jewish ascetic practices, and the values that might be ascribed them in a religion which would not develop the same tools for constructing orthodoxy or enforcing orthopraxis as Christianity.

The *Mishnah* details the fasts and abstinence which should or could accompany certain events. Thus, on the Day of Atonement it is forbidden to eat, drink, to anoint oneself with oil, or to have sexual relations, but children are dispensed from fasting, which is also moderated for the sick, the pregnant, and those who have been weakened by near-starvation.[89] The Ninth of Av was kept as a day of fasting to mourn the destruction of the

---

[85] On the *Mishnah*, cf. D. Kraemer, 'The Mishnah', *CHJ4*, 299–315; on the *Tosefta*, cf. P. Mandel, 'The Tosefta', *CHJ4*, 316–35; on the *Palestinian Talmud*, cf. A. Goldberg, 'The Palestinian Talmud', in S. Safrai (ed.), *The Literature of the Sages*, First Part (Assen and Philadelphia: Van Gorcum and Fortress Press, 1987), 303–22.

[86] J. Neusner, *The Mishnah: A New Translation* (Yale, New Haven, and London: Yale University Press, 1988), xvi.

[87] For the *Mishnah* as 'an ideal taxonomy', cf. J. Lightstone, *The Rhetoric of the Babylonian Talmud: Its Social Meaning and Context* (Waterloo, Ontario: Wilfred Laurier University Press, 1994), 254–6.

[88] Diamond, *Holy Men*, 19, claims that although sayings are often wrongly ascribed to a particular sage, they are usually ascribed to a figure from the period and place in which they originate. I do not share his confidence.

[89] *Yomah* 8.1 and 8.4–6.

Temple; the rabbis stipulated that on the preceding evening 'a person should not eat two prepared dishes, nor should one eat meat or drink wine'.[90] The Palestinian Talmud specified that fasts were permitted on the day before and after the sabbath and festival days.[91] The rabbis also referred to a first-century text, the *Megillat Ta'anit* (the *Scroll of Fasting*), which listed thirty-five days in the year when mourning and fasting were forbidden in celebration of great events in Israel's history.[92] A later gloss on the *Mishnah* required abstention from meat and wine by mourners between a person's death and the burial of the corpse, except on the Sabbath.[93] Mourners likewise abstained from sexual relations, this time including the Sabbath.[94]

If the Hebrew scriptures repeatedly gave value to fasting as a form of prayer in the face of military threat, the *Mishnah* stipulates the public fasts to be called under threat of drought. If rain has not fallen in a given town or locality by the seventeenth day of Marsheshvan, a sequence of fasts is to be undertaken by appointed individuals on a Monday, Thursday, and the following Monday; on these days food is not eaten until after dark. If there is still no rain by the new moon of Kislev, further public fasts are ordained, during which ashes are imposed on each person's head, and prayers recited. As the situation deteriorates, the fasts are repeated with more stringent conditions: abstention from sex, from work, from bathing, and anointing with oil. A citation from Jonah (3:10) makes clear that this fasting has a penitential dimension: the drought is perceived as a sign of God's displeasure at sin.[95] Public fasting was similarly the proper response to plague.[96] We should reckon such public fasts an intermittent feature of life in Palestinian Jewish settlements under Roman rule.

Several versions of the Book of Esther had promoted the celebration by Jews of the Purim festival. One version of the Hebrew text referred (at 9:31) to fasting in relation to the festival's adoption, and scholars have disputed the text's dating and significance, but the Jerusalem Talmud reveals a lively debate about which days it was permitted or forbidden to fast on in the month of Adar before Purim itself on the fourteenth and fifteenth of Adar.[97]

---

[90] *Taanit* 4.7 D, tr. Neusner, *The Mishnah*, 315.   [91] Palestinian Talmud, *Taanit* 2:12, III.A.
[92] J. Geiger, 'Sophists and Rabbis: Jews and their past in the Severan age', *Sev*, 444–5.
[93] Palestinian Talmud, *Mo 'ed Qat.* 3:5; Babylonian Talmud, *Mo 'ed Qat.* 23b.
[94] Palestinian Talmud, *Mo 'ed Qat.* 3:5.
[95] *Mishnah*, *Taanit* 1.4–2.1. The Palestinian Talmud (*Taanit* 1:4) specifies that the individuals who fast are appointed by the community and should have a reputation for holiness.
[96] *Taanit* 3:4.
[97] Levenson, *Esther*, 131; C. A. Moore, *Daniel, Esther and Jeremiah: The Additions* (New York: Doubleday, 1977), 243; R. J. Coggins and S. Paul Re'emi, *Israel Among the Nations* (Grand Rapids and Edinburgh: Eerdmans, 1985), 138; Palestinian Talmud, *Taanit* 2:12, II.A–B, tr. Neusner, *The Talmud*, 202.

One form of communal fasting described in the *Mishnah* almost certainly belongs to the realm of an ideal order without actual practice: rules lay down the fasting to be undertaken by the *maamad*, delegations of Jews who had fasted when a given group of priests was responsible for the Temple cult.[98] But this ideal may have further promoted other forms of regular fasting. Luke's Gospel portrayed one of the Pharisees as fasting twice a week (18:12). It is not clear with what confidence, if any, this portrait may be used to determine the fasts of Pharisees generally before AD 70, but evidence does suggest regular, twice weekly, fasting by Jews in the rabbinic period. The *Didache*, in part an early 'church-order' which describes ideal Christian practice, ordains fasting on Wednesday and Friday unlike the 'hypocrites' who fast on a Monday and Thursday.[99] It seems likely that the latter are non-Christian Jews. If so, a pattern of fasting ordained for appointed individuals or for the whole community *on specific occasions* may have been increasingly adopted by private individuals on a regular basis. The passage seemingly suggests the desire within some Christian communities to differentiate themselves from a practice which marks out, in their eyes, an opposing religious community, but which is also attractive to their own members, for whom it may be a tradition received from Jewish Christians. The *Babylonian Talmud* favours fasting by individuals as a penitential act through numerous stories of sages who fasted severely in response to seemingly minor sins.[100] It also praises those who endure deprivation and hardship, including lack of food, for the sake of Torah study.[101]

The impact of the *Mishnah* and Talmudic literature on actual fasting in the Roman period is impossible to assess. A text which may date as early as 100 BC, or as late as AD 175, the *Apocalypse of Zephaniah*, presents the seer confronted by a scroll in which, among his other sins, are noted the days on which he failed to fast.[102] It is a useful reminder of both how actual life may not have squared with texts, but also how texts sought to comment upon and influence the conduct of (potential) backsliders.

The *Talmud* also contains echoes of debates within the emerging Rabbinic Judaism over the value of sexual abstinence within marriage outside the fast days on which it was required, in particular when occasioned by absence from home for the purposes of Torah study. The *Mishnah* recognizes that a person may vow all kinds of periodic abstention, especially from particular foodstuffs, but restricts sexual abstinence of this kind to

---

[98] *Taanit* 4:3; Diamond, *Holy Men*, 103.
[99] *Didache* 8.1; Diamond, *Holy Men*, 104; S. D. Fraade, 'Ascetical aspects', 275–6.
[100] Diamond, *Holy Men*, 72–3; Fraade, 'Ascetical aspects', 275–6.   [101] Diamond, *Holy Men*, 31–2.
[102] *Apocalypse of Zephaniah*, 7:6, tr. O. S. Wintermute, *OTP*, vol. I, 513. For the date, ibid., 500–1.

not longer than one or two weeks. A man, however, may leave his wife for a longer period, a month, for the purposes of *Torah* study.[103] In the Palestinian Talmud one opinion holds that this period may be extended with the wife's consent.[104] This can be seen as a 'kind of ascetic sexual practice', alongside the other forms of deprivation endured for this purpose.[105] Some held that sexual relations were to be motivated only by the desire to conceive children.[106]

Long-term sexual abstinence is associated in the *Babylonian Talmud* with R. Hiyya b. Ashi (a Babylonian sage of the third century AD). Some scholars see this as the reflection of a debate in diaspora communities of a practice made attractive by Syrian Christians.[107] The *Babylonian Talmud* opposes such abstinence, but its final verdict may presuppose an earlier pluriformity of opinion and practice which later rabbis were concerned to suppress.[108] Daniel Boyarin has argued that Talmudic debates should be seen as attempts to propose 'utopian solutions to cultural tensions'.[109] These may have turned on whether men should defer marriage for the sake of Torah study, and whether a wife could be left for extended periods of study. The difficulty for the historian of the Graeco-Roman world lies in knowing when to date and where to place these tensions, but Naomi Koltun-Fromm has identified them in texts from the third century which explore Moses' supposed sexual renunciation during the Exodus.[110]

Related to this issue are the disputed origin, date, redaction history, and readership of various works, including *Joseph and Aseneth*, the *Testaments of the Twelve Patriarchs*, and the *History of the Rechabites*. These all attribute to their heroes forms of prolonged voluntary sexual abstinence. In the *Twelve Patriarchs* and the romance *Joseph and Aseneth* this is abstinence *before* marriage, together with the refusal to marry a pagan. Aseneth, like the other women at the Egyptian court, is struck by Joseph's beauty, but he will only meet her when he thinks that she is determined to remain a virgin. When he realizes her desire, he refuses to kiss a pagan woman. Only when Aseneth repents of her idolatry, and fasts in sackloth and ashes,

---

[103] *Mishnah, Nedarim* 6:1–7:2, and *Ketubot* 5:6, tr. Neusner, *The Mishnah*, 417–19 and 388–9.
[104] Palestinian Talmud, *Ketubot* 5:7, II.B, tr. Neusner, *Talmud*, vol. XXII (1985), 189.
[105] Boyarin, *Carnal Israel*, 47.
[106] Palestinian Talmud, *Taanit* 1:6, VIII.N, tr. Neusner, *Talmud*, vol. XVIII, 170.
[107] Shlomoh Naeh, 'Freedom and celibacy: a Talmudic variation on tales of temptation and fall in Genesis and its Syrian background', in J. Frishman and L. Van Rompay (eds.), *The Book of Genesis in Jewish and Oriental Christian Interpretation* (Louvain: Peeters, 1997), 73–89.
[108] Boyarin, *Carnal Israel*, 35.   [109] Ibid., 15.
[110] Naomi Koltun-Fromm, 'Zipporah's Complaint: Moses is not conscientious in the deed! Exegetical traditions of Moses' celibacy', in Reed and Becker, *The Ways that Never Parted*, 283–306.

will Joseph consent to kiss her. He will sleep with her only when they are married.[111] The text, which plays on the conventions of the Hellenistic novel (the *topoi* of preserving virginity and the delayed consummation of sexual desire), sets up a strong analogy between fornication and marriage outside the religious community. Likewise, the implied readers of the *Testament of Reuben* are urged to '[p]ay no heed . . . to the beauty of women and do not set your mind on their affairs . . . until the Lord will give you a wife'.[112] In the *Testament of Issachar*, its eponymous hero does not marry until the age of thirty, too preoccupied before that point even to think of 'pleasure with a woman'.[113] The *History of the Rechabites*, on the other hand, presents a utopian island community, the purported descendants of Jonadab ben Rechab, where married women live separately from their ascetic husbands and likewise dedicate themselves to fasting and prayer.[114] Husbands sleep only once with their wives; the women bear two children, one of whom in turn marries, while the other remains a virgin.[115]

These texts have been given both early Jewish and later Christian origins. Contrary to much earlier scholarship, some now hold that we cannot determine whether Jewish originals lie behind each of the extant *Testaments*; nor, where they do, can we reconstruct their contents. We have only Christian texts which presuppose various debates with Jews.[116] Modern scholars are divided over the Jewish or Christian origin and date of *Joseph and Aseneth*.[117] The *History of the Rechabites* is recognized by many scholars as a Jewish text, which, though later redacted and interpolated by Christians, may predate the second century AD. Eliezer Diamond has opined that the work 'may reflect to some degree the sexual practices, or at least the ideals, of a group of Jews living in the late Second Temple or early rabbinic period'.[118] We should limit ourselves to saying that by the third century these novelistic texts, which circulated in a milieu where Jews and Christians were not hermetically sealed in separate spheres, entertained

---

[111] *Joseph and Aseneth* 6:1, 8:5, 10:17, 21:1 and 9.

[112] *Testament of Reuben*, 4.1, tr. H.W. Hollander and M. de Jonge (eds.), *The Testaments of the Twelve Patriarchs: A Commentary* (Leiden: Brill, 1985), 96–7.

[113] *Testament of Issachar*, 3.5, tr. Hollander and de Jonge (eds.), *The Testaments*, 239.

[114] *History of the Rechabites*, 10:7.   [115] Ibid., 11:6–8.

[116] Hollander and de Jonge (eds.), *The Testaments*, 67 and 85. For an alternative view, cf. Boyarin, *Carnal Israel*, 68.

[117] For a Jewish origin between 100 BC and AD 117, cf. R. D. Chesnutt, *From Death to Life: Conversion in Joseph and Aseneth* (Sheffield Academic Press, 1995) 80–1; for Christian authorship unlikely to be earlier than the third century AD, cf. R. Kraemer, *When Aseneth Met Joseph* (Oxford University Press, 1998), ix.

[118] Diamond, *Holy Men*, 35.

their readers with a model of holiness in which sexual abstinence figured as a form of religious devotion.

Finally, we can observe the motif of fasting to receive a vision in Jewish apocalyptic literature of the period: two texts dated to around AD 100, 4 Ezra and 2 Baruch, both relate how these recipients of angelic visions had first to fast for periods of seven days.[119] These texts cannot be shown to bear directly upon Jewish practice in the rabbinic period, but they would prove influential in later, Christian, monastic circles.

CONCLUSIONS

Jews in the Graeco-Roman world practised various forms of abstention. Of these, observance of the food laws and the purity laws were, generally speaking, central to their religious self-understanding as the Chosen People. The food laws were widely observed, but variously understood. The purity laws were revered but applied very differently by different groups. They did not prevent Jews who wished from taking an active part in the civic life of the Graeco-Roman cities: a gravestone of AD 243/244 at Acmonia in Asia Minor honours Titus Flavius Alexandros as a Jew who served as *agoranomos* or market overseer, *sitones*, or public corn-buyer, and who was also a council member, *strategos* and *eirenarch*.[120] Here, then, was a man of some importance in the local community and responsible for keeping the peace. When one Rufina, the head of the synagogue at Smyrna in the third century AD, provided a tomb for the members of her household, she made the fines for any violation of the tomb payable to the Jewish association or *ethnos*, but also placed a copy of the inscription in the civic archives.[121] It was for such Hellenistic Jews that Philo's attempt to make sense of Jewish patterns of abstention in terms derived from the Greek philosophical tradition will have been attractive, but Philo is not to be relied upon for the meaning of the rules concerning food, sex, and property among the *Therapeutae* or *Essenes*. For tightly structured sectarian groups such as these in the Second Temple period the food and purity laws were a major element in their dissociation from what they perceived to be impure societies as they recreated the holiness proper to the Israelite camp. The laws combined with permanent sexual renunciation to symbolize social separation, where 'the body, always modified by the social categories through which it is known,

---

[119] 4 Ezra 5:20, 6:31, and 35; 2 Baruch 9:1, 12:5, 20:50, and 21:1.
[120] P. Trebilco, *Jewish Communities in Asia Minor* (Cambridge University Press, 1991), 62–3.
[121] P. Harland, *Associations, Synagogues, and Congregations: Claiming a Place in Ancient Mediterranean Society* (Minneapolis: Fortress Press, 2003), 86.

sustains a particular view of society' and 'strong social control demands strong bodily control'.[122] After the Temple's destruction and with the slow rise of rabbinic Judaism, permanent sexual renunciation largely disappeared when sectarian groups were no longer tolerated. Temporary abstinence for the purposes of Torah study was acceptable only within disputed limits. More widely, fasting had a strongly penitential role as a form of humble prayer, a meaning which was absent from Graeco-Roman ascetic tradition.

[122] M. Douglas, *Natural Symbols* (Harmondsworth: Penguin, 1973), 93 and 100.

CHAPTER 3

Christian asceticism before Origen

Study of pagan and Jewish asceticism has taught us that asceticism can be variously practised and understood. The asceticism portrayed in literary texts is not a simple window on what actually happened, nor a sure guide to how practitioners understood their ascetic acts. Furthermore, we have seen the influence of Greek Neoplatonist asceticism on Jewish Hellenistic thought. What influence, then, would Graeco-Roman and Jewish beliefs have on nascent Christianity? How would Christians use abstention from food and sexual relations? By approaching these questions from the perspective of common fasting, we shall see how indebted early Christianity was to Judaism in this respect, though we shall also see its wish to deny that debt. Fasting became a powerful means of distinguishing Christians from Jews and of defining different Christian groups. On turning to sexual restraint we shall see a distinctive practice of permanent renunciation which was widely advocated by appeal to a cluster of New Testament texts, but which was variously related to baptism and accompanied by differing accounts of marriage. In text and life the sexually abstinent, widows and virgins, made for groups within the Church which together displayed the life of heaven. Finally, we shall see the degree to which a highly educated Christian, Clement of Alexandria, was drawn (like Philo and to some extent by Philo) to re-cast popular ascetic practices within a Greek philosophical frame.

MOURNING SET IN STONE

At Rome, early in the third century AD, two calendars were carved prominently on the sides of a stone statue of a seated figure, while the monument was inscribed elsewhere with the titles of various theological treatises.[1] The calendars tabulated the date each year from AD 222 until 333 of the Jewish

---

[1] M. Guarducci, *Epigrafia Greca*, vol. IV (Rome: Instituto Poligrafico dello Stato, 1978), 535–45.

Passover (14 Nisan), and of the following Sunday in the Roman calendar when certain Christians now kept their separate feast of Passover or Easter, while one of the listed treatises was itself *An Exposition of the Dates of Passover and What is in the Table.* An inscription above the Passover calendar stipulated that no one was to fast when the Passover fell on a Sunday.[2] Whatever the identity and symbolism of the statue's seated figure (probably a woman), these texts and tables drew on epigraphic traditions which honoured authors by displaying their works, and which published civic and other edicts in this way for common observance; they thus presented an authoritative ritual set in stone for contemporary and future readers who were cast as members of an enduring polity or worshipping community.

How many Christian readers accepted the authority thus articulated, and for how long, we cannot know, but the inscription points first to the importance such third-century readers attached to a communal fast in the period before Easter. Such a fast may have been already ancient: Justin (*c.* AD 100–*c.* 167), the head of a Christian school or house-church at Rome in the mid second century, describes a fast undertaken by catechumens before baptism while other members of the church fasted and prayed for them.[3] Justin does not say when their baptism occurred, but it was probably at Easter: a later church order, the *Apostolic Tradition*, placed the catechumens' fast on the day before their Easter baptism.[4] An Easter fast was certainly not limited to Rome. Tertullian (*c.* AD 170–*c.* 220) reveals that it was universally observed by Christians at Carthage in the early third century, many of whom regarded it as the only absolute fast required of all believers. This was the fast of which Jesus spoke in the Synoptic Gospels 'when the bridegroom is taken away', understood as the period of mourning between his death and resurrection.[5] The Gospels of Matthew, Mark, Luke, and John, which were increasingly regarded as authoritative in many Christian communities, were silent as to the apostles' observance of this fast on the first Easter Saturday, but the Easter fast seemingly influenced the mid-second-century *Gospel of Peter* in which Peter relates how he and the other disciples 'were fasting and sat mourning and weeping night

---

[2] ἀπονηστίζεσθαι δὲ δεῖ οὗ ἂν ἐνπέσῃ κυριακή.

[3] Justin, *First Apology*, 61.2. This pre-baptismal fast may have been influenced by that of St Paul before his baptism at Damascus in Acts 9:9–19.

[4] *Apostolic Tradition*, 20. The *Didache* (7.2) legislates for baptism at other times: it prescribes a one- or two-day fast by the baptismal candidate, a fast by the minister, and by others if possible, stipulations which would be senseless during the communal Easter fast.

[5] Mark 2:19–20; Matthew 9:15; Luke 5:34–5; Tertullian, *On Fasting*, 2.2.

and day until the sabbath'.[6] Likewise, in the *Gospel of the Hebrews* the apostle James 'had sworn that he would not eat bread from that hour in which he had drunk the cup of the Lord until he should see him risen from among them that sleep'.[7] This work probably originated within a Greek-speaking Jewish-Christian community of the early second century, and was certainly read in the Alexandria of the late second or early third century.[8] It, too, presumed and reinforced observance of the Easter fast as mournful prelude to the celebration of Christ's resurrection.

The inscriptions also point to a serious and long-running dispute among Christians at Rome about when or how to keep this widespread fast: the stipulation concerning what to do when Passover fell on a Sunday would have no point unless it settled, for some, a contentious issue.[9] Some such dispute had proved divisive in the city during the closing decades of the second century. Eusebius of Caesarea (*c.* 260–*c.* 340) inserted into his *Church History* a letter sent by Irenaeus (*c.* AD 100–*c.* 170), a church leader in Gaul with close links to the Roman church, to Victor, the bishop who presided over one of the many Christian house-churches in the metropolis from AD 189 to 199.[10] The letter agreed with Victor that Easter was properly celebrated on the Sunday, but censured him for his breach of communion with those who followed an older tradition of celebrating Easter on 14 Nisan (the so-called 'Quartodeciman' practice). Irenaeus described how some Christians fasted for one day at Easter, but others for two or more, some for a day comprising forty hours, a variety of practice which in his view was of long-standing. Earlier Christians had held to their custom through 'simple and popular devotion' and disagreement about the fast only confirmed their 'common mind concerning the faith'.[11] Such diversity had not previously led to a breach of communion between churches.

---

[6] *Gospel of Peter*, 7.27, tr. *NTA*, vol. I, 224. The work predates the end of the second century. The privileged status of the Four Gospels is seen in (i) their being copied together; (ii) their place in the harmonized account of Jesus' life by Tatian (*c.* AD 120–80/90); (iii) Irenaeus' advocacy of them as authoritative versions (*Against the Heresies*, III.11.8).

[7] *Gospel of the Hebrews*, fr. 7, tr. *NTA*, vol. I, 178.

[8] *Gospel of the Hebrews*, ed. Vielhauer and Strecker, *NTA*, vol. I, 176.

[9] Allen Brent, *Hippolytus and the Roman Church in the Third Century: Communities in Tension before the Emergence of a Monarch-Bishop* (Leiden and New York: Brill, 1995), 67.

[10] For Victor's contested presidency, cf. P. Lampe, *From Paul to Valentinus: Christians at Rome in the First Two Centuries*, tr. M. Steinhauser (London: T&T Clark, 2003), 395–7; Brent, *Hippolytus*, 446.

[11] Eusebius, *Church History*, v.24.12–13, SC 41, 70. My 'simple and popular devotion' translates καθ' ἁπλότητα καὶ ἰδιωτισμόν. Deferrari's translation of ἰδιωτισμόν as 'permits personal preference' assumes that the observance of the Easter fast was a matter of individual decision. At issue here is probably divergence of practice between different house-churches in Rome. Cf. Eusebius, *Ecclesiastical History*, Books I–V, tr. R. Deferrari, FC 19 (New York, 1953), 337.

Jonathan Smith has argued that Christians at the end of the second century formed 'a heterogeneous collection of relatively small groups, marked off from their neighbours by a rite of initiation (chiefly, adult baptism), with their most conspicuous cultic act a common meal', but these disputes over the Easter fast indicate the importance of communal fasting for the group-identity of some churches and, as Irenaeus suggests, for a common Christian identity which transcended local communities.[12] It is one of the means whereby Christians, who were not generally marked out by observance of the Mosaic food laws, asserted their 'alien citizenship' and refused 'assimilation into the imperial city or state'.[13] Fasting transcended divisions of gender and social rank. In a culture where the very poor were inured to periodic hunger, it was a devotion from which they were not easily excluded.[14] Minucius Felix, author of a Christian apologetic dialogue before the mid third century, had his pagan interlocutor describe Christians as an unholy conspiracy bound together by 'solemn fasts' amongst other things.[15] It has been argued that Early Christian asceticism reveals 'an intense orientation toward the development and articulation of an individual subjectivity';[16] such a view, however, with the definition of asceticism on which it depends, occludes the importance of fasting as a communal activity among many Christians of the second and third centuries, and reveals the lingering influence exerted on the history of asceticism by the figure of the fourth-century ascetic monk or virgin.

The disputes outlined above further suggest the bearing of communal fasting on the changing understanding of unity in Early Christianity. Irenaeus' paradoxical argument for unity of faith from diversity of practice makes sense rhetorically in a context where the opposite was also argued. Victor's attempt to persuade other Roman churches to adopt the practice of his own or face excommunication makes sense in a context where the unity of these house-churches now appeared compromised by their diverse calendars, and that appearance may have given Victor an opportunity to

---

[12] J. Z. Smith, *Drudgery Divine: On the Comparison of Early Christianities and the Religions of Late Antiquity* (University of London, 1990), 129–30.

[13] R. Williams, *Why Study the Past? The Quest for the Historical Church* (London: Darton, Longman and Todd, 2005), 47.

[14] Sexual renunciation, by contrast, was not necessarily a '*carrière ouverte aux talents*', contra Peter Brown, *The Body and Society*, 61. To remain widowed or to live without the support of offspring in old age was not always an option open to the poor, even within churches where some elderly women could hope for regular alms.

[15] Minucius Felix, *Octavius*, 8.4. For a second-century date, cf. S. Price, 'Latin Christian Apologetics: Minucius Felix, Tertullian, and Cyprian', in M. Edwards, M. Goodman, and S. Price (eds.), *Apologetics in the Roman Empire: Pagans, Jews, and Christians* (Oxford University Press, 1999), 112.

[16] R. Valantasis, *The Gospel of Thomas* (London: Routledge, 1997), 24.

assert his authority over these groups; this was one move in the direction of a single bishop presiding over the entire Roman church.

Victor's disapproval of holding Easter on 14 Nisan may have been motivated in part by the belief that it did not mark a sufficient breach between Jews and Christians. Origen (*c.* 185–254) preached some forty years later against the observance by Christians of Jewish fasts.[17] The stone calendars certainly witness to the value which some Christians saw in determining the date of Passover independently of local Jewish custom.[18] Such concerns may have resulted in part from, or built upon, the outcome of yet another contested fast. We saw in the previous chapter how the *Didache* stipulated that Christians were to fast on Wednesdays and Fridays rather than on the Tuesdays and Thursdays, because the latter were days on which the 'hypocrites' fasted (a likely echo of Christ's words at Matthew 6:16). It is probable that the 'hypocrites' were either non-Christian Jews or (less probably) Jewish Christians, and that the author of the stipulation, like Victor, was acting to strengthen symbolic boundaries between groups whose practices did not cleanly demarcate wholly separate religions. As with the inscription on the chair, we may suppose a diversity of practice behind the text which the author sought to resolve.[19] The dating of the *Didache* is disputed, but most consider it to be earlier than the late second century and to have enjoyed a wide readership in that century. We do not know how successful the *Didache* was in fixing the timing of these twice-weekly, and probably voluntary, fasts, nor what proportion of the Christian population observed them; but some such 'stations' were customary at Rome by the mid second century at the latest.[20] A half century later, many North Africans observed them without regarding them as obligatory, and without complete agreement on how the station was to be kept, whether those who fasted should exchange a kiss of peace with those who did not fast, and whether they should stay away from the Eucharist to preserve their fast.[21] These stational fasts did not simply strengthen unity among existing Christians; they made for their unity as Christians over and against Jews and Jewish-Christians.

---

[17] Origen, *Homilies on Jeremiah*, 12.13.
[18] T. Thornton, 'Problematical Passovers: difficulties for Diaspora Jews and early Christians in determining Passover dates during the first three centuries AD', *SP* 20 (1989), 402–8, 407.
[19] *Didache*, 8.1. Cf., S. G. Wilson, *Related Strangers: Jews and Christians 70–170 CE* (Minneapolis: Fortress Press, 1995), 224–5. For arguments against seeing the target as Jewish Christians, cf. K. Niederwimmer, *Die Didache* (Göttingen: Vandenhoeck and Ruprecht, 1989), 165–7.
[20] *Shepherd of Hermas*, Similitude 5.1.1. See n.30 below.
[21] Tertullian, *On Fasting*, 2.2–3, and 10.1; *On Prayer*, 18 and 19.

'IN FASTING AND SELF-ABASEMENT'

Stational fasts thus figure among the very early 'technologies for the production of self and other' which contributed to the formation of Christianity over and against Judaism.[22] Nonetheless, they should not obscure how far the practice and meaning of early Christian fasting derived from Judaism. As Judith Lieu has observed, there is a 'tension between continuity, and the creation of difference within it'.[23] Early Christians took from Judaism the role which fasting played as an expression of mourning (as already seen in mourning the death of Christ), its function in expressing penitence and humility, together with its consequent role in accompanying prayer for divine aid, whether for forgiveness or revelation. This understanding was mediated through the Septuagint as this was read in Christian liturgies and reprised in writings such 1 Clement and the *Epistle of Barnabas* (though neither text contains direct exhortation to fasting). 1 Clement is a letter sent in the late first or early second century from the Roman church to the church at Corinth. It recalls both how Moses (Exodus 34:28) had remained on Mount Sinai for forty days 'in fasting and self-abasement' and how Esther's prayers had found favour with God 'on account of her fasting and self-abasement'.[24] The *Epistle of Barnabas*, a Greek text probably composed in the first half of the second century, but which was also circulating in Latin by the end of that century, twice recalls Moses' fast at Sinai, and relates that the prophet fasted 'in order to receive the covenant'.[25] The *Protevangelium of James*, which dates to the second half of the second century, shows how a Christian author could then make Moses the dramatic pattern for successful prayer: Joachim miraculously fasts in prayer for forty days and nights in the wilderness, like Moses on Mount Sinai, refusing to eat or drink 'until the Lord my God visits me'.[26]

Joachim was not the only Jew whose piety was characterized by an early Christian author in terms of prayer and fasting. Luke's Gospel presented the prophetess Anna as fasting and praying in the Temple precincts (Luke 2:37). Its sequel, the Acts of the Apostles, echoed her piety in its portrayal of the house-church at Antioch, the members of which were fasting when instructed by the Spirit to chose Barnabas and Saul as missionary preachers

---

[22] D. Boyarin, *Dying for God* (Stanford University Press, 1999), 18.
[23] J. Lieu, *Christian Identity in the Jewish and Graeco-Roman World* (Oxford University Press, 2004), 161.
[24] 1 Clement 53.2 and 55.6.
[25] *Epistle of Barnabas* 14. Cf. P. Prigent and R. Kraft (eds.), *Épître de Barnabé*, SC 172 (1971), 25–7.
[26] *Protevangelium of James*, 1.2, tr. *NTA*, vol. 1, 426.

(Acts 13:2–3). It is not simply that Luke-Acts shares the Jewish understanding of fasting as a proper disposition for prayer and the reception of divine revelation. This continuity is one element in the assertion of a rather more complex continuity, the transmission to the Pauline house-churches and Gentile mission of God's promises to Israel, and the grant of apostolic authority: at Acts 14:23 prayerful fasting forms the setting in which Paul in turn ordains presbyters 'in every church'. It is unlikely that Acts 13 and 14 offer a reliable guide to the history of the Pauline mission; we cannot deduce from these verses a role for fasting in the appointment of elders; but they indicate roles which fasting might play in Christian literature of the second century, whether to characterize holy protagonists or to act as an authenticating sign of holiness (roles to which I return below). Polycarp exhorted the Philippians to be 'sober in prayer and persistent in fasting'.[27] How such fasting was practised, however, by the bishop, or in the community to which he wrote, remains unclear. Yet some continuity with Jewish practice is further evident in the way that Christians in Roman North Africa, for example, observed communal fasts as acts of prayer in response to drought on the instruction of their bishops.[28] Such fasting was recognized as manifesting a proper 'humility of mind'.[29]

The relationship between humble prayer and fasting was explored with polemical intent in the *Shepherd of Hermas*, a work widely regarded in Rome and central Italy, Gaul, North Africa, and Egypt by the late second century, and which was revered as inspired scripture in many churches before the fourth century.[30] The personified figure of the Church explains to Hermas that his prayer to understand her changing appearance would fail unless made in the proper spirit through humble fasting: 'Every request requires humility. So fast, and you will receive what you ask from the Lord.'[31] This teaching, however, is seemingly contradicted later in the work. The angelic Shepherd warns Hermas, and through him the Christians of Rome, that their stational fasts of bread and water were useless as prayers unless the money which they had not spent on food were given in alms to the poor who would then pray on behalf of their benefactors. Only fasting of this kind amounted to a virtuous humility.[32] The two teachings feature in parts of the work which in some places circulated separately, at least in the mid

---

[27] Polycarp, *Letter to the Philippians*, 7.2.
[28] Tertullian, *Apology*, 40.14–15; *Ad Scapulam*, 4.6.   [29] *On Fasting*, 12.2 and 13.4.
[30] C. Osiek, *Shepherd of Hermas, A Commentary* (Minneapolis: Fortress Press, 1999), 4–8, and 20; Metzger, *The Canon*, 65. The work may date in part to the closing years of the first century, but a mid-second-century date has also been proposed.
[31] *Shepherd of Hermas*, Vision 3.10.6, tr. Osiek, *Shepherd*, 83.
[32] *Shepherd of Hermas*, Similitude 5.1.1–4 and 5.3.7.

third century, and which may reflect two stages in the work's composition.[33] The teaching presented by the figure of the Church is found in what is perhaps the earlier stage of composition, and presupposes an ancient link at Rome between fasting and humble prayer, while the *Shepherd*'s criticism of this teaching is found in what is sometimes held to be a later addition; it may be a polemical development, part of a wider concern by the author or redactor to promote greater almsgiving within the Roman churches; but a developmental account of fasting in the *Shepherd* does not depend on any redaction; it also fits to a wider pattern in which the narrator, and through him the reader, is led to a deeper religious understanding.

NEW FASTS

The *Shepherd of Hermas* concerned itself with the meaning of fasting as an established set of practices, where that meaning was confirmed by relation to the distinct practice of almsgiving; it did not seek to alter the fasting practices themselves. The late second and early third century, however, also saw a growing conviction among some Christians that more frequent and rigorous fasts were required. Tertullian's *On Fasting* reveals a movement, to which its author belonged, that viewed the Carthaginian practices we have already met as dangerously lax. Its members welcomed the prophetic ministries and teaching on fasting made popular by Montanus and his followers during the final decades of the second century, though Montanists would soon be denounced as 'radish-eating' heretics by the Roman author of the *Elenchos*, and Tertullian would later be represented as belonging to a schismatic group outside the Catholic Church.[34] Tertullian, and those like him, regarded their stations as obligatory; they continued them further into the evening, and outside these occasions practised 'xerophagy': for two weeks in the year they adopted a diet from Monday to Friday which avoided wine, succulent meats and fruits, the moisture of which was held to fuel the body's sexual appetite.[35] Such discipline had been commanded by the Holy Spirit whose prophesies were thought to arm the Church in face of threatened persecution.[36] Xerophagy habituated the Christian to hardship, anticipated a prison regime to strengthen the Christian for actual

---

[33] Osiek, *Shepherd*, 3–4, and 8–10. For the work's literary unity, cf. S. Young, 'Being a man: the pursuit of manliness in *The Shepherd of Hermas*', *JECS* 2 (1994), 238.

[34] *Elenchos*, VIII.19.2. For the third-century date and authorship of the *Elenchos*, cf. M. Simonetti (ed.), *Ippolito: Contro Noeto* (Bologna: EDB, 2000), 63–7; on the Montanist movement in North Africa, cf. D. Rankin, *Tertullian and the Church* (Cambridge University Press, 1995), 27–51.

[35] Tertullian, *On Fasting*, 1.4, 13.3, and 15.2.   [36] Ibid., 13.5.

imprisonment and martyrdom.[37] Fasting thus addressed the anxiety that one might lose through physical frailty the eternal life promised to the faithful. Tertullian complained that opponents of the movement condemned the 'unity' or unified action of their fasts, dry foods, and stations; he revealed that they further accused the movement's members either of Judaizing or of lapsing into the kind of ritual abstention practised by the followers of Isis.[38] Such polemic indicates the extent to which patterns of fasting could be identified with particular religions for rhetorical purposes but also confirms my earlier stress on the degree to which communal fasting was held to identify or delimit the Christian body-politic.

It is in this context that we may compare the *Acts of Peter* and *Acts of Paul*, two popular apocryphal works probably from Asia Minor and written towards the end of the second century.[39] These tales, which drew upon the Greek picaresque novel, differed from the romances not least in the prominence given to fasting, though this featured differently in each work. The earliest Greek *Acts of Peter* have been largely lost, but the *Actus Vercellenses*, a fourth-century Latin translation of a later redaction, presents St Paul as fasting for three days at Rome before the vision which sends him to Spain.[40] When Simon Magus seduces most Roman Christians into apostasy, the handful who remain faithful are said to have 'mourned and fasted'.[41] St Peter fasts on the ship ferrying him to Rome and refuses all offer of food from the crew.[42] He relates at Rome how, in Judaea, after fasting for three days, he had been granted a vision that revealed what Simon Magus had stolen from a wealthy matron.[43] He now urges them to fast and pray so that Simon may be thwarted at Rome. Peter duly fasts before his victorious contest with him.[44] Fasting is thus the principal action which distinguishes the heroic apostles from the villains, and which unites the saints with the enfeebled community whose cause they champion; it manifests unwavering faith in God, evokes visions, and secures God's miraculous power to triumph over a heretical opponent.

The *Acts of Paul* have to be reconstructed in part from papyri fragments and in part from an early derivative text, the *Acts of Paul and Thecla*. They apparently presented the Christian community at Damascus as fasting

---

[37] Ibid., 12. [38] Ibid., 13.4, 14.1, and 16.7.

[39] For the provenance and dating of these *Acts*, cf. C. M. Thomas, *The Acts of Peter, Gospel Literature, and the Ancient Novel: Rewriting the Past* (Oxford University Press, 2003), 27–8.

[40] *Actus Vercellenses* 1, ed. Schneemelcher, *NTA*, vol. II, 287. Thomas argues that chapters 1 to 3 belong to a redaction effected in the late second century. On the *Actus Vercellenses* and evolving nature of the Greek *Acts*, cf. Thomas, *The Acts of Peter*, 10, 15, 17, 21–39.

[41] *Actus Vercellenses*, 5, *NTA*, vol. II, 290. [42] Ibid., 5.

[43] Ibid., 17. [44] Ibid., 18 and 22.

before the apostle's arrival there.[45] Anchares fasts after the death of his son before Paul raises the boy back to life.[46] Paul fasts in prayer for six days with Onesiphorus, his wife and children, in an open tomb on the road from Iconium to Daphne so that Thecla is miraculously rescued from the pyre on which she is due to be executed.[47] Paul fasts in prayer for three days at Sidon.[48] At Philippi he fasts for two days with the prisoners in the knowledge of the violent death they are to undergo, and later raises Frontina from death.[49] Two disciples, Artemilla and Eubula, fast in grief at Paul's sufferings.[50] At his departure from Corinth for Rome, Paul probably says (the text has to be restored), 'Brethren, be zealous about <fasting?> and love. For behold, I go away to a furnace of fire < . . . > and I am not strong except the Lord <grant> me power.' The distressed Christians duly fast while one of their number, Cleobius, is inspired to announce that Paul must complete his mission.[51] Finally, exhausted by his fasts and vigils, Paul falls asleep on the boat for Rome.[52] Fasting, while remaining something which unites the community with its apostolic champion, is here vital to securing deliverance from persecution or winning the grace to persevere under threat of persecution; it is the non-violent counter to the violence of pagan authorities, rather than a badge distinguishing the orthodox from the heretical. These apocryphal acts draw upon the narrative models and heroes of the Old Testament to create 'non-violent figures of the apostles' whose divine power enables them to 'set aside and supersede the pagan world'.[53] Fasting, however, plays a key role as the defence shared by the apostle, the beleaguered community or its individual members within the narrative, and the communities in which these texts were read.

Fasting as a practice shared by the text and its readers raises the question of how these works fed into the Montanist movement. They seemingly originated in the region where Montanism first became popular. In addition, the *Acts of Paul* present the Holy Spirit coming upon a woman, Myrta, who then prophesies to the brethren assembled for the celebration of the Eucharist, a role for women which echoes that of the Montanists, Prisca and Maximilla.[54] Tertullian apparently knew of women who appealed to the *Acts of Paul* (or the *Acts of Paul and Thecla*) to justify the right of

---

[45] *Acts of Paul*, fr. Ry, *NTA*, vol. II, 237. This portion of the reconstructed *Acts* is conjectural.
[46] Ibid., fr. PHeid, *NTA*, vol. II, 238.   [47] Ibid., *Acts of Paul and Thecla*, 23–4, *NTA*, vol. II, 243.
[48] Ibid., fr. PHeid, 35–9, *NTA*, vol. II, 249.
[49] Ibid., fr. PHeid 41–2, *NTA*, vol. II, 256.   [50] Ibid., *NTA*, vol. II, 253.
[51] Ibid., PH 6, tr. *NTA*, vol. II, 257–8.   [52] Ibid., PH 7, *NTA*, vol. II, 258.
[53] I. Karasszon, 'Heroism in the Acts of Paul and in the Bible', in J. Bremmer (ed.), *The Apocryphal Acts of Paul and Thecla* (Kampen: Pharos, 1996), 188.
[54] *Acts of Paul*, PH 7, *NTA*, vol. II, 258.

women to teach and baptize. At the time of writing *On Baptism*, Tertullian disapproved of the work for this reason, ascribing the *Acts* to a presbyter writing in Roman Asia in around AD 170.[55] Were the *Acts*, therefore, meant to encourage the more frequent fasts which Tertullian came to advocate, and to legitimate controversial roles for women? The *Acts of Paul* would surely have been well received by Montanist sympathizers; the work fitted neatly with Tertullian's view of fasting as a discipline preparatory to persecution, and presumably gave solace to readers who felt threatened by the authorities.[56]

Readers also found support for fasting in a third apocryphal text, the *Acts of Peter and the Twelve Apostles*. This composite work, though known only through a later Coptic version, may well date to the second century.[57] It tells how Peter and his fellow apostles sail to an island-city which is home to those who practise the central Christian virtue of 'endurance'.[58] Christ, disguised as a pearl merchant, invites them to his own city by means of a dangerous journey that demands daily fasts between each night-stop, travelling without bread, water, meat, or vegetables. On arrival there they speak 'humbly' with Jesus before he sends them back with instructions about the food and healing they are to provide for the poor as well as a warning for the church's ministers against partiality towards the rich.[59] Although the provenance and circulation of this work is unknown before its translation into Coptic at the beginning of the fifth century, the text contains nothing that suggests a Gnostic origin. Its emphases on frequent fasting until evening, with what appears to be a concern for xerophagy and a resultant humility, together with its veiled criticism of church leaders, would have recommended it to Montanist sympathizers.[60] While Yves Tissot is correct to say that the apostles of the apocryphal Acts rarely give their readers 'préceptes alimentaires', his conclusion that their 'frugalité est plutôt un trait arétologique' needs qualification.[61] The Greek Acts do not characterize fasting, nor abstinence from meat and wine, in terms of the classical virtues

---

[55] Tertullian, *De Baptismo*, 17.

[56] Cf., W. Rordorf, 'Terra incognita: recent research on Christian apocryphal literature, especially on some Acts of Apostles', *SP* 25 (1993), 154–5.

[57] Cf. H.-M. Schenke, *Acts of Peter and the Twelve Apostles*, *NTA*, vol. II, 414; D. Parrott, 'The Acts of Peter and the Twelve Apostles', *NHL*, 289.

[58] For 'endurance' (ὑπομονή) as a name for the Church, cf. Clement of Alexandria, *Paedagogus*, 1.5.22.2, *CA*, vol. I, 103.

[59] *Acts of Peter and the Twelve Apostles*, tr. Schenke, *NTA*, vol. II, 420–4.

[60] R. Valantasis, 'Nag Hammadi and asceticism: theory and practice', *SP* 35.4 (2001), 181, argues implausibly that the account of fasting indicates 'some sort of graded system of advancement'.

[61] Y. Tissot, 'L'encratisme des *Actes de Thomas*', *ANRW* 25.6 (1988), 4417.

of frugality (*euteleia* and *litotes*) examined in Chapter 1, though the *Acts of Thomas* associate fasting and plain food with the apostle's 'simplicity'.[62]

While some early Christians fasted more severely than others as a matter of principle, there were others who did not observe the weekly stations on principle, or who rejected the meanings so far elucidated.

The *Gospel of Thomas*, composition of which has been variously placed in the second century, contains a number of sayings attributed to Jesus on fasting.[63] In Logion 6 the disciples ask Jesus how to fast, to pray, and to give alms, and what dietary regimen to observe. Jesus responds by urging them not to lie, nor to perform hateful deeds, which, as Joseph Fitzmyer pointed out in restoring the Greek version, does 'not answer the questions . . . but insists on other things'.[64] The saying *might* mean that unexceptionable but overvalued practices are subordinated to the more important business of honesty and avoiding wrong-doing. If, however, fasting and almsgiving are understood as forms of penitential prayer, ways of seeking forgiveness, then the saying should be interpreted as a rejection of these practices, because the disciples were to avoid those sins which necessitated them. It is notable that the Coptic version of Logion 6 differs precisely in that the disciples ask not *how* but *whether* to fast.[65] Jesus' answer then reads as a more explicit rejection of fasting and almsgiving.

Internal evidence suggests this change reveals how the *Gospel of Thomas* was generally understood by its readers. In Logion 14 of the *Coptic Gospel of Thomas* Jesus warns his disciples that 'If you fast, you will give rise to

---

[62] τὸ ἁπλουν αὐτοῦ. *Acts of Thomas* 20.10, tr. A. F. J. Klijn (Leiden: Brill, 2003), 65 (with note on Greek).

[63] Origen regarded the *Gospel of Thomas* as heretical; a Greek fragment from Oxyrhynchus may date to as early as AD 200 and is no later than 225. As an ordered collection of sayings, the *Gospel of Thomas* post-dates Matthew because Logion 14 shows use of this Gospel: cf. R. Uro, 'Thomas and oral gospel tradition', in R. Uro (ed.), *'Thomas' at the Crossroads: Essays on the 'Gospel of Thomas'* (Edinburgh: T&T Clark, 1998), 32. For a date no earlier than the mid second century, cf. P. Jenkins, *Hidden Gospels: How the Search for Jesus Lost its Way* (Oxford University Press, 2001), 70–2. For arguments in favour of an earlier date, cf. H. Koester, *Ancient Christian Gospels: Their History and Development* (London: SCM, 1990), 84–128; Valantasis, *The Gospel of Thomas*, 13–21.

[64] πῶς νηστεύ[σομεν, καὶ πῶς προς]
[ευξό]μεθα καὶ πῶς [ἐλεημοσύνην ποιή]
[σομεν, κ]αὶ τί παρατηρήσ[ομεν ὅταν δειπ]
[νῶμε]ν; λέγει Ἰη(σοῦ)ς· [μὴ ψεύδεσθε καὶ ὅ]
[τι μισ]εῖται μὴ ποιεῖ[τε· . . . . J. Fitzmyer, 'The Oxyrhynchus *logoi* of Jesus and the Coptic Gospel according to Thomas', *Theological Studies* 20.4 (1959), 528–9.

[65] *Coptic Gospel of Thomas*, 6.

sin for yourselves; and if you pray, you will be condemned; and if you give alms, you will do harm to your spirits.'[66] This saying is so far unparalleled among the Greek papyri fragments, but scholars have pointed out that its thematic relationship to Logion 6 strongly suggests that it may once have stood as Jesus' direct answer to the disciples' question, whether in a postulated sayings collection which served as a source for the *Gospel of Thomas*, or because its present position in the Nag Hammadi codex arises from a copyist's error.[67] It is implausible to see it as a late addition to the work. The saying works by paradox or irony: the very fasting and almsgiving which are wrongly thought by many to be redemptive, purgative of sin, in fact constitute sins. Jesus states in Logion 27, which does survive in Greek, that 'if you do not fast to the world, you will not find the kingdom of God'.[68] Fitzmyer has taken this to mean 'withdrawal from a worldly or secular outlook'; Tjitze Baarda, on the other hand, sees a rejection of the creation and of its creator, understood as the demiurge.[69] Clement of Alexandria glosses an almost identical phrase, 'fasting from the world', as the avoidance of sin.[70] The saying is sufficiently opaque that different readers may well have taken the saying in one or other of these ways depending on their own interpretative prejudices. Nonetheless, the practice of penitential fasting has been replaced with a metaphorical substitute.

Only Logion 104 in the *Coptic Gospel* indicates anything other than a complete rejection of fasting. When the disciples suggest to Jesus that they pray and fast, Jesus asks 'What is the sin that I have committed, or wherein have I been defeated? But when the bridegroom leaves the bridal chamber, then let them fast and pray.'[71] This re-working of the Synoptic saying concerning the bridegroom (Mark 2:19–20, etc.), may imply that the *Gospel of Thomas* rejected all voluntary fasting but recognized the communal fast immediately before Easter. This depends, however, on what is understood by leaving the bridal chamber. In Logion 75 we are told that only the solitary will enter the chamber.[72] It is not the world into which Christ comes to call the disciples, and from which he is absent at his death, but the realm into which the disciples are called from this life. The

---

[66] Ibid., 14, tr. *NHL*, 128.
[67] Uro, '*Thomas* and oral gospel tradition', 30.   [68] Fitzmyer, 'The Oxyrhynchus *logoi*', 532.
[69] For further discussion, cf. Wilson, *Related Strangers*, 90–1; Lieu, *Christian Identity*, 133; and T. Baarda, '*If you do not sabbatize the Sabbath . . .* The Sabbath as god or world in Gnostic understanding (Ev. Thom., Log. 27)', in R. Van Den Broek, T. Baarda, and J. Mansfeld (eds.), *Knowledge of God in the Graeco-Roman World* (Leiden: Brill, 1988), 178–201.
[70] Clement of Alexandria, *Stromata*, III.15.99.
[71] *Coptic Gospel of Thomas* 104, tr. *NHL*, 137.   [72] Ibid., 75.

compiler of the *Gospel of Thomas* probably rejected all fasting, though its message will have been variously understood and appropriated by a diverse readership.

The freedom with which readers might appropriate the teachings on fasting in the *Gospel of Thomas* is evident in a letter by a biblical exegete and speculative theologian Ptolemaeus. This pupil of Valentinus was active at Rome in the mid second century and possibly executed there for his Christian faith. He was later labelled a heretic for what we now term Gnostic beliefs about the emergence of a spiritual realm through a series of emanations, the creation of the world by a demiurge, and the non-material nature of Jesus Christ.[73] Ptolemaeus explained to a Roman noblewoman Flora (and through her, to other Christians) that the offerings, fasts, the Passover, and circumcision ordained by the Jewish Law, were signs of spiritual realities and that what Christ enjoined under the name of fasting was only the spiritual reality which it signified – 'abstaining from all that is worthless'. Physical fasting 'among us' might serve as a helpful reminder of the spiritual reality and was not observed merely because a day had been set for the purpose.[74] Ptolemy's school allowed followers to retain customary practices while reinterpreting their significance; it is probable that a good number therefore avoided the voluntary stations while remaining within Christian communities that kept the communal fast. Some may nevertheless have chosen to form separate Christian groups.[75]

MEAT, DRINK, AND SEX

The *Coptic Gospel of Thomas* has Jesus say, 'Wretched is the body that is dependent upon a body, and wretched is the soul that is dependent on these two.'[76] This may be understood either as a rejection of eating meat, or as condemnation of sexual desire and intercourse.[77] Indeed one saying may serve two related morals. We are directed away from abstention in the form of periodic fasts to abstention from particular foods and drink, and

---

[73] On Ptolemaeus, cf. Lampe, *From Paul to Valentinus*, 239–40, 296–7, 317, and 388–9. On the 'Gnostic' label and its limited value, cf. M. Williams, *Rethinking Gnosticism: An Argument for Dismantling a Dubious Category* (Princeton University Press, 1996).

[74] Ptolemaeus, *Letter to Flora*, 5.13.

[75] Some Gnostics formed intellectual circles within larger churches, cf. C. Markschies, *Gnosis: An Introduction*, tr. J. Bowden (London and New York: T&T Clark, 2003), 111 and 114. For 'Sethian' Gnostic texts read within an 'audience cult', cf. Williams, *Rethinking Gnosticism*, 113.

[76] *Coptic Gospel of Thomas*, 87, tr. *NHL*, 135.

[77] Cf. S. Davies, *The Gospel of Thomas Annotated and Explained* (London: Darton, Longman and Todd, 2002), 108; J.-É. Ménard, *L'Évangile selon Thomas* (Leiden: Brill, 1975), 188–9.

to abstention from sexual intercourse, as alternative ascetic and symbolic practices.

Scholars who have noted the rejection of fasting in the *Gospel of Thomas* to deny the presence therein of an asceticism based upon abstention may be misled by thinking that early Christian asceticism or 'encratism' has a single abstemious form.[78] This mistake reflects the polemical endeavour of Irenaeus and the author of the *Elenchos* who condemned an 'Encratite' sect marked by a triple abstention from meat, wine, and sexual relations.[79] Historians have since recognized that this 'sect' is the creation of its detractors who sought to marginalize and denigrate ascetic practices of which they disapproved, but which were common in churches of the Eastern, Graeco-Roman world. The assumption has remained, however, that 'encratism' is normally a threefold rejection of meat, wine, and sex.[80] We shall see that some Christians indeed advocated and practised this interlocking asceticism. Furthermore, abstention from meat was frequently paired with abstention from wine, and these dietary restraints might be perceived as enabling sexual restraint as we saw in Tertullian's defence of xerophagy. However, we should not presume that where one form of abstention is found, all three are extolled. We must also distinguish between those who advocated a given pattern of asceticism as virtuous, but did not require it of every Christian, and those who required it of all the baptized. There were those who argued for sexual restraint within marriage and those who rejected marriage. Nor may we assume that the meaning of abstention in any instance is given independently of its place in a wider nexus of beliefs and practices. Finally, in this list of caveats, we must be wary when deriving the practices of groups from the advocacy of individual writers. Irenaeus, for example, related that Saturninus condemned marriage and procreation, while many of his followers abstained from meat to practise what Irenaeus regarded as a feigned self-control (*enkrateia*).[81] Nothing is said here about abstention from wine; a teaching on sexual restraint is mirrored amongst Saturninus' devotees by abstention from meat, but the latter practice is not a universal discipline. I shall examine dietary abstention first.[82]

---

[78] Cf., Valantasis, 'Is the Gospel of Thomas ascetical?' 59 n.7 and 64.   [79] *Elenchos*, VIII.20.1.

[80] G. Quispel, 'The study of encratism: a historical survey', in U. Bianchi (ed.), *La tradizione dell'enkrateia* (Rome: Edizioni dell'Ateneo, 1982), 49. For encratism as 'une praxis ascétique susceptible d'être diversement théorisée', cf. Tissot, 'L'encratisme des *Actes de Thomas*', 4417.

[81] Irenaeus, *Against the Heresies*, I.24.2, SC 264 (1979), 325.

[82] I acknowledge my extensive debt to Andrew McGowan's *Ascetic Eucharists: Food and Drink in Early Christian Ritual Meals* (Oxford: Clarendon Press, 1999) in this section, though I frequently differ from his reading of the evidence. Where he relies on 'the implications of all the parts for the whole'

Much meat available in the Graeco-Roman cities had first been sacrificed in pagan temples, and this generated disputes among first-century Christians about the morality of its consumption. St Paul distinguished between what was merely obtained, on the one hand, in the market and could be consumed without qualm at home or at a banquet to which one had been invited, and, on the other hand, what was specifically offered by a pagan as 'a sacrificial offering' (1 Cor. 10:25 and 28). To refuse this meat made clear the Christian's non-participation in worship of demons. He warned against eating *eidōlothuta*, meat sacrificed to idols and consumed in the temple precincts or as part of a religious festival, even if the believer personally rejected the religious significance of the meal. Others in the church might compromise their beliefs through participation in these meals (1 Cor. 8:1–13). The apostle intervened to adjudicate between differing views. A few years before AD 60, he likewise attempted to settle a dispute among Christians at Rome between the 'weak' who confined themselves to a vegetable diet and those who ate meat; while not forbidding its consumption, the apostle again advised that it was right not to eat meat nor drink wine if this caused fellow Christians to fall into sin (Romans 14:21).

Little suggests that St Paul's judgement settled the matter for early Christians. Another letter attributed to Paul in the early Church, but which may well date to the early second century, drew on the apostle's authority to condemn those who insisted on abstention from *brōmata*, a Greek word for food which frequently means meat (1 Timothy 4:3).[83] Letters which were probably incorporated into the Book of Revelation during the reign of Trajan (AD 98–117) condemn Christians at Pergamon and Thyatira who still ate what the author considered to be *eidōlothuta* (Rev. 2:14 and 20). It has even been suggested that these Christians were in some sense 'heirs' to Paul's permitting the consumption of sacrificial meats.[84] In the mid second century Justin could not deny the charge put by Trypho that many Christians ate *eidōlothuta*, though the apologist replied that all who did so were heretics.[85] That some Christians wished to do so indicates

---

(idem, 17), I am less confident as to how pieces of evidence fit together, and doubt the value for the second century of fourth-century writers whose use of sources is not open to critique.

[83] Scholars generally consider 1 Timothy pseudepigraphal and date it to the early second century. For a dissenter open to Pauline authorship, cf. Luke Timothy Johnson, *The First and Second Letters to Timothy* (New York and London: Doubleday, 2001). For the view that the letter was written to oppose Marcionites, cf. R. J. Hoffmann, 'Women in Marcionite churches of the second century', *SP* 18.3 (1989), 166.

[84] Cf. D. Aune, *Revelation 1–5*, Word Biblical Commentary, vol. LII (Dallas: Word Books, 1997), cxxxii and 193; P. Prigent, *Commentary on the Apocalypse of St John*, tr. W. Pradels (Tübingen: Mohr Siebeck 2004), 20–1, and 175.

[85] Justin, *Dialogue*, 35.

how far participation in civic cult and social standing interlocked.[86] If the communal Easter fast readily contributed to a shared Christian identity at little social cost, refusal of *eidōlothuta* was a sign of religious allegiance that cost more by way of social separation.

Hegesippus, a second-century author of *Memoirs* concerning the early Church, portrayed James the Just, leader of the Jerusalem church, not only as a Nazirite who avoided wine, but also as not eating meat.[87] The title of Hegesippus' work suggests comparison with Xenophon's *Memoirs* of Socrates, an attempt to relate Christianity to the Greek philosophical tradition, so Hegesippus and his educated readers may have conflated Jewish patterns of heroic asceticism with a Pythagorean or Neo-Platonic pattern in which vegetarianism was highly respected. Nothing can be proven about James' actual conduct or its significance.[88] But if this reported abstention reflects an early tradition about James, it need not be seen through the lens of Greek philosophy. The previous chapter showed that fasting from *both* meat and wine was stipulated as a form of mourning in rabbinic Judaism. The *Gospel of the Ebionites*, composed for a Jewish Christian group, portrayed the Baptist as surviving, not on a diet of locusts and wild honey, but honey only, and had Jesus question his disciples whether he desired to 'eat flesh' with them at the Passover; these variants suggest some form of abstention from meat within the Jewish Christian movement which used this Gospel.[89] Nothing suggests that we add sexual renunciation to the discernible pattern of abstention.

Marcion (*c.* 120–*c.* 160) and Tatian (*c.* 120–post 180?), both of whom accepted Paul's Letter to the Romans, were accused by Tertullian of requiring permanent abstention from meat.[90] Marcion broke from the Roman churches in AD 144 and established alternative communities in which the Old Testament was rejected as enjoining worship of a baleful creator rather than the God and Father of Jesus Christ. He edited the existing collection of Pauline letters and rejected 1 Timothy as well as the other 'Pastoral

---

[86] A prohibition against consumption of εἰδωλόθυτα is also found at *Didache* 6:3; abstention from sacrificial meat is vaunted as a mark of Christian superiority at Aristides, *Apology*, 15.5.

[87] Eusebius, *Church History*, 11.23.5.

[88] For James' abstention from meat as part of an anti-cultic and anti-sacrificial portrayal, cf. McGowan, *Ascetic Eucharists*, 149–50; cf. also, Chepey, *Nazirites*, 174–7.

[89] *Gospel of the Ebionites*, frs. 2 and 7, ed. P. Vielhauer and G. Strecker, *NTA*, vol. I, 169 and 170. I hesitate to label this abstention vegetarianism on the limited evidence available.

[90] Tertullian, *On Fasting* 15.1. For Tatian's use of Romans, cf. E. J. Hunt, *Christianity in the Second Century: The Case of Tatian* (London and New York: Routledge, 2003), 36–8; Marcion did not accept the whole of Romans, but is not known to have rejected 14:21. Cf. E. Evans (ed.), *Tertullian, Adversus Marcionem*, 2 vols. (Oxford: Clarendon Press, 1972), vol. II, 645.

Epistles'.[91] The scriptural impediment to a ban on meat was thus removed. Tertullian's claim that Marcion taught abstention from meat is supported by the author of the *Elenchos* who (implausibly) saw in the heretic's teaching ideas taken from Empedocles.[92] Whether and how Marcionite churches also practised fasting is unclear, but I presume that they kept the Easter fast.[93] The meaning of their abstention from meat is impossible to reconstruct with confidence. Andrew McGowan has interpreted it in terms of a wider rejection of the 'cuisine of sacrifice' and opposition to the demonic powers of this world, though his reading depends in part on the belief that Marcionites also abstained from wine (on which more below) and on extrapolation from the meaning of such abstention among other Christians.[94] In the case of Tatian, while little in his *Oration* confirms his supposed teaching, its attack on gladiatorial shows suggests that the slaughter of men in the arena satisfies a lust for blood in the same way that the sacrifice of animals satisfies the pagans' desire for meat.[95] The *Diatessaron*, Tatian's harmonization of the Gospel story based principally (not solely) on the Four Gospels, omitted locusts from the Baptist's diet in the wilderness, but in this he may simply have followed the reading known to him.[96]

Much harder to assess is the evidence concerning wine in early Christianity. Origen ascribed to Montanism an oracle in which the speaker claimed 'I am a Nazirite of God: like them, I do not drink wine'.[97] Should this be understood in terms of the xerophagy already discussed above, or did Montanism outside Roman North Africa practise a different pattern of abstention to that outlined by Tertullian? No definite answer can be given. A number of Gnostic texts encouraged readers to refrain from wine, disparaged for inducing the drinker to sexual intercourse. A text from Nag Hammadi, the previous history of which is uncertain, condemns wine as 'the debaucher'.[98] Another relates that the grapevine sprouted up together with Eros from the first blood shed over the earth, with the result that 'those who drink of it conceive the desire of sexual union'.[99] These texts are a useful corrective when assessing the claims of their opponents that

---

[91] Tertullian, *Adversus Marcionem*, V.21. [92] *Elenchos*, VII.30.3.

[93] For the assumption that Marcionites fasted, cf. H. Drijvers, 'Christ as warrior and merchant – aspects of Marcion's Christology', *SP* 21 (1989), 83 and 84.

[94] A. McGowan, 'Marcion's love of creation', *JECS* 9.3 (2001), 304–7. [95] Tatian, *Oration*, 23.2.

[96] M.-É. Boismard, *Le Diatessaron: De Tatien à Justin* (Paris: Librarie Lecoffre, 1992), 75; W. Petersen, *Tatian's Diatessaron: Its Creation, Dissemination, Significance, and History in Scholarship* (Leiden: Brill, 1994), 20.

[97] *Oracle* 19, in Origen, *Letter to Titus*, PG 14.1306, tr. R Heine (ed.), *The Montanist Oracles and Testimonia* (Belgium and Macon, Ga.: Peeters and Mercer University Press, 1989), 9.

[98] *Authoritative Teaching*, 24, tr. G. MacRae, *NHL*, 306.

[99] *On the Origin of the World*, 109, tr. H.-G. Bethge and B. Layton, *NHL*, 178.

Gnostics were guilty of licentiousness, but circumspection is required in determining how these texts shaped the drinking habits of their readers.

Andrew McGowan has argued for the widespread celebration within the Eastern empire of a Eucharist without wine which features prominently in the apocryphal acts.[100] There is no doubt that some groups celebrated such a Eucharist, given Clement of Alexandria's explicit condemnation of the practice.[101] The difficulty lies in identifying the Christians concerned, and in estimating the custom's prevalence. Irenaeus, for example, attacked the docetism of a group whom he termed Ebionites (a group not necessarily to be identified with that which used the *Gospel of the Ebionites*) as a refusal to mix the wine of heaven with the water of this world.[102] This is plausibly explained by the statement of the fourth-century bishop Epiphanius that the Ebionites celebrated the Eucharist with water rather than wine, though, if so, these Jewish Christians may not have understood the symbolism of this act in the way Irenaeus uses it. Furthermore, Epiphanius 'was used to reading documents with great attention to see what he could infer from them', so that the bishop may have reached his conclusion from this very passage of Irenaeus.[103] There is no certainty that Epiphanius got it right.

Other candidates for churches or movements which held bread-and-water Eucharists in this period are equally elusive. The Valentinian Gnostic Theodotus, in a text preserved by Clement of Alexandria, wrote about the sanctification of bread and oil, but does not mention wine in this context.[104] McGowan thinks it 'possible or likely that Theodotus used water rather than wine in a eucharistic cup, and even clearer that wine did not come into the picture in any event'.[105] What relationship, however, should we postulate between Theodotus' 'picture', his theological interests and commentary, and the rites of Valentinian communities, if and where these existed apart from other churches?[106] In the case of Marcion, who did establish separate churches, McGowan argues from the silence of Tertullian and the late accusation of Epiphanius.[107] This builds too much

---

[100] McGowan, *Ascetic Eucharists*, passim.   [101] Clement of Alexandria, *Stromata*, 1.19.96.1.

[102] 'They set aside the mingling of the heavenly wine and wish to be only the water of this world, not accepting the God who would mingle with them'. Irenaeus, *Against the Heresies*, v.1.3.

[103] Epiphanius, *Panarion* 30.16; F. Williams, *The Panarion of Epiphanius of Salamis, Book I (Sects 1–46)* (Leiden and New York: Brill, 1987), xix. McGowan occludes a key interpretative step to assert, 'Irenaeus says that the Ebionites used only water in the cup of their Eucharist' (*Ascetic Eucharists*, 144–5).

[104] Clement of Alexandria, *Excerpta ex Theodoto*, 82.   [105] McGowan, *Ascetic Eucharists*, 163.

[106] For Valentinian ecclesiology of the church as comprising two concentric bodies, the inner 'pneumatics' and outer, 'physics', cf. Lampe, *From Paul to Valentinus*, 387.

[107] McGowan, *Ascetic Eucharists*, 164, with reference to Epiphanius, *Panarion*, 42.3.3 and Tertullian, *Adversus Marcionem* 1.14.3. McGowan reasserts Marcionite rejection of wine in 'Marcion's love of creation', 303.

on too little. McGowan follows Harnack to argue that all references to wine at the Eucharist in the commonly received text of Justin's *Apology* (especially at 65.3) may well be interpolations, but Harnack's view has not won general acceptance, and the most recent editors of the text do not adopt it.[108] McGowan thinks it 'probable' that Tatian shared a 'bread-and-water tradition of eucharistic meals' and that this may 'help tip the scales of probability in the more radical direction' when determining Justin's practice.[109] However, what we do not know about Tatian should not figure largely in what we surmise about Justin.

The evidence concerning Tatian is hard to evaluate. The *Diatessaron* (widely used throughout Syria in both Greek and Syriac versions until the early fifth century) probably did not contain all the references to Jesus and the disciples drinking wine which we know from the canonical Gospels. Jesus may not have figured as the drunkard of Matthew 11:19. His assertion at the Last Supper that he would not drink wine again until the arrival of the kingdom, may not have been contradicted by the offer of wine and gall at Calvary (Matthew 27:34).[110] There was probably no indication that Jesus would drink wine in the kingdom.[111] It is possible that Tatian transferred the exhortation 'do this in remembrance of me' (which at Luke 22:19 comes after the division of the bread and immediately before the second instruction concerning the cup) to a 'later position, after the vow of renunciation, thus apparently making the ascetic lifestyle, rather than the liturgical ritual alone, the authentic *anamnesis* of the saviour'.[112] Some such changes saved Jesus from the charge of excess, and removed inconsistencies in the Gospel story, a matter of concern to early Christians when such a charge and any inconsistency might be exploited by Celsus and other pagan critics. Yet the *Diatessaron* did not suppress the miraculous multiplication of wine at Cana, though it suppressed the genealogies.[113] The claim that 'Jesus' self-identification as the "true vine" (John 15:1) became "I am the tree of the fruit of truth"' is not supported by Robert Murray, who ascribes to the *Diatessaron* the Syriac term *karma* meaning both 'vine' and 'vineyard of truth'. The *Diatessaron* alone cannot support Tatian's advocacy of a bread-and-water Eucharist.[114]

---

[108] McGowan, *Ascetic Eucharists*, 151–5. I am grateful to Denis Minns OP and Paul Parvis for allowing me to consult their forthcoming edition of the *Apology*. They remove a reference to wine at 54.6 as a gloss upon the original, but emend the text of 65.3 to read ποτήριον ὕδατι κεκραμένον, which they translate as 'a cup of wine mixed with water'.

[109] McGowan, *Ascetic Eucharists*, 155 and 158–9.   [110] Petersen, *Tatian's Diatessaron*, 378–9.

[111] On these changes, cf. Hunt, *Christianity*, 148–9; Petersen, *Tatian's Diatessaron*, 370–1.

[112] McGowan, *Ascetic Eucharists*, 157.

[113] Petersen, *Tatian's Diatessaron*, 42 and 75; Ephrem, *Commentary on the Diatessaron*, 5 and 12.

[114] McGowan, *Ascetic Eucharists*, 157; Murray, *Symbols*, 95–6.

On the other hand, Jerome's *Commentary on Amos* ascribes to Tatian an unspecified prohibition on drinking wine grounded in his reading of Amos 2:13.[115] Authors had by then branded Tatian the heretical founder of an 'encratite' sect, and Clement of Alexandria certainly ascribed to 'encratites' a rejection of wine more thoroughgoing than his own strictures on its avoidance by youths and its moderate use among adults.[116] There was clearly *some* abstention from wine championed by Tatian and broadly shared by a wider Christian movement with which he was identified, though this need not make Tatian's opinion a universal rule within given communities.[117] To what practices, though, does the prohibition noted by Jerome and the rejection asserted by Clement refer? It is Epiphanius who explicitly accuses Tatian of using water in the Eucharist.[118] Without knowing the reasons for his accusation, it is injudicious to rely upon his testimony. The balance of probabilities tips the scale in the other direction: Justin's practice seems to have included a Eucharist with wine, and that practice may well have been followed by his pupil Tatian. In Tatian's case we should probably imagine some other abstention from wine, as from meat, and which probably did not substitute for fasting but existed alongside it.

The strongest evidence for Eucharists celebrated without wine comes from a number of apocryphal acts. While the *Acts of John* contain three accounts of Eucharists celebrated by the apostle, 'the most striking thing is that there is no mention of wine or any kind of cup'. Furthermore, two Eucharistic prayers at chapters 85 and 109–10 include 'nothing to connect the rite with the death of Jesus or communion in his body and blood'.[119] The docetism of the work (its denial of the humanity of Jesus) has been used to date its composition to the second quarter of the second century, though the work was subsequently redacted by a Gnostic author in the late second or third century.[120] There is no doubt that the *Acts of John* present a Eucharist celebrated without wine or water, and this omission may be related in part to its docetism: the absence of wine, associated with the shedding of Jesus' blood in Synoptic narratives of the Last Supper, here distances the heavenly

---

[115] Tatian, Fr. 9, in Whittaker, *Tatian,* 82. I do not agree with McGowan that Tertullian (*On Fasting,* 15.1) is 'an early witness to Tatian's prohibition of meat *and wine*' (my italics), *Ascetic Eucharists,* 155 and 155 n.38. A footnote reveals the interpretation implicit in the main text.

[116] Clement of Alexandria, *Paedagogus,* 11.2.33.1.

[117] On Tatian's relationship to encratism and to Syriac Christianity, cf. Hunt, *Christianity,* 144–75.

[118] Epiphanius, *Panarion* 46.2. Theodoret repeats the charge at further remove from events.

[119] R. H. Miller, 'Liturgical materials in the *Acts of John*', *SP* 13 (Leipzig 1975), 376 and 378.

[120] P. Lalleman, *The Acts of John: A Two-Stage Initiation into Johannine Gnosticism* (Leuven: Peeters, 1998), 60 and 270; P. G. Schneider, *The Mystery of the Acts of John: An Interpretation of the Hymn and the Dance in the Light of the Acts' Theology* (San Francisco: Mellen Research University Press, 1991), 4.

Christ from earthly suffering. The motif may be contrasted with Clement of Alexandria's description of the Word as a cluster of grapes to be crushed for our salvation; at the Eucharist, the 'blood of the grape' is mixed with water as a rich symbol of how God's grace has commingled with our flesh.[121] The second-century *Acts of Andrew* probably offered a similar account of a Eucharist celebrated without mention of wine.[122] The *Acts of Thomas* include four descriptions of the Eucharist celebrated with bread alone, one with bread and water, and one in which the contents of the cup are not identified.[123] In the *Acts of Paul*, a meal described as an *agape* comprises five loaves, some vegetables, and water, while, after Artemilla's conversion at Ephesus, the apostle 'broke bread and brought water, and gave her to drink of the word'.[124] McGowan rightly sees this as referring to 'water as the drink of the eucharistic meal'.[125] Equally striking is the account in the *Actus Vercellenses*, the Latin version of the *Acts of Peter*, in which St Paul is brought 'bread and water ... for the sacrifice'.[126]

How, though, should we interpret this literary motif in texts which circulated widely in Christian communities over several centuries? They obviously do not reflect the ritual practice familiar to all their eventual readers in the early Church, nor need they reflect the customary practice of all their intended readers.[127] Do they reflect the ritual practice of the communities in which they were first produced? An answer to this question requires consideration both of the motif's function within the texts, but also what other texts were read in those communities, and whether texts were read in the liturgy or at home, and how they were regarded. Did these communities, or members within them, also value texts that could be thought to sanction a bread-and-wine Eucharist, such as a collection of Pauline letters, or the *Didache*?[128] These apocryphal Acts reveal a high level of literary artifice and intertextuality which presuppose authors and readers who engaged with a wide range of pagan and Christian literature which

---

[121] Clement of Alexandria, *Paedagogus*, 11.2.19.3.

[122] We are dependent on Gregory of Tour's *Liber de miraculis*, 20.

[123] *Acts of Thomas* 27, 29, 49–51, 121 (bread and water), 133, and 158 (unspecified cup).

[124] *Acts of Paul* 7, PH 4, *NTA*, vol. 11, 253.

[125] McGowan, *Ascetic Eucharists*, 185.   [126] *Actus Vercellenses* 2, *NTA*, vol. 11, 288.

[127] Gamble has argued that 'the careful literary crafting' of each canonical Gospel and the small size of first-century congregations make it 'unlikely that any of the Gospels was composed for the strictly local . . . use of a single community. Broader dissemination . . . must have been intended from the outset.' A similar argument holds good for the apocryphal acts. Cf., H. Y. Gamble, *Books and Readers in the Early Church: A History of Early Christian Texts* (New Haven and London: Yale University Press, 1995), 102.

[128] It is uncertain whether the *Didache* refers to a Eucharist or Agape, and whether that distinction is valid for its earliest readers, but there is no doubt that bread and wine were used. Cf., *Didache* 9–10.

circulated over a wide area.[129] The *Acts of Andrew* have been thought by one scholar to have originated in the world of Alexandria, while the *Acts of Thomas* have been traced to Eastern Syria.[130] The setting of the former, at least, implies the wide circulation of very different texts. It is implausible that a cosmopolitan community, some of whose members will have been well educated, valued only those texts which mirrored its ritual practice. Scholars who have worked closely on the *Acts of John* differ on whether they think it describes a form of Christianity corresponding to its place of origin.[131] If the non-use of wine in these texts gains significance from the use of wine in pagan sacrificial discourse, or from the association of wine with sexual intercourse, this significance would not necessarily be lost or altered by divergence from Eucharistic practice within the author's own church. On the other hand, since the literate, theologically trained authors of the *Acts* may have practised as teachers within Christian philosophical schools, or as leaders of house-churches where they presided over the Eucharistic liturgy, the texts may well reflect *some* ritual practice. Whether those who attended such meals *also* attended Eucharists celebrated with wine, and how widespread these practices were in the second and third centuries, is impossible to ascertain.

EXCISING LUST

Justin's *Apology* related with pride how a young Christian had recently petitioned the Roman governor in Alexandria for permission to be castrated. The governor had turned down this unusual request, but Justin was pleased to note that the youth had nonetheless remained single and enjoyed the approval of those who shared his attitude to sexual desire.[132] The story may have been apocryphal, and Justin's readiness to repeat it served a rhetorical purpose: to squash definitively the slurs of sexual immorality that pagans had repeatedly made against Christianity; but to vaunt this episode in defence of Christian morals shows the degree to which some early Christians valued sexual renunciation, including permanent abstention from sex and marriage. As we shall see, however, early Christians who shared a concern for the virtues associated with sexual restraint were far from united in

---

[129] For the *Acts of Andrew*, cf. D. MacDonald, *Christianizing Homer* (New York and Oxford: Oxford University Press, 1994); for the 'learned milieu' of the *Acts of Thomas*, cf. Drijvers, in *NTA*, vol. II, 327.

[130] D. MacDonald, *The Acts of Andrew and The Acts of Andrew and Matthias in the City of the Cannibals* (Atlanta: Scholars Press, 1990), 59; Drijvers, *NTA*, vol. II, 323.

[131] Cf. Rordorf, 'Terra incognita', 150–1.   [132] Justin, *First Apology*, 29.2.

their understanding of what this meant for sexual conduct. The apocryphal *Acts of John* could appear more extreme than Justin by making sexual abstinence the mark of the baptized, but has the apostle upbraid a youth who had castrated himself to preserve his purity.[133]

Justin presented various forms of Christian sexual abstinence as expressive of chastity or continence, commonplace virtues recognized by his implied pagan readers. He insisted that Christians married (and had intercourse) only for the purpose of procreation, while those who remained single, or who did not remarry on the death of their spouse, abstained from sex.[134] His polemic finds corroboration from the pagan medical theorist Galen (*c.* 129–200), who noted that Christians showed 'restraint in cohabitation'. They included 'not only men but also women who refrain from cohabiting all through their lives' with 'individuals who in self-discipline and self-control (in matters of food and drink) and in their keen pursuit of justice have attained a pitch not inferior to that of genuine philosophers'.[135] Both texts beg questions about the practices they discuss. How widespread were the different forms of sexual abstention? Were all equally acceptable everywhere? How did permanent sexual renunciation feature within the identity of the individual who embraced it? To what extent was the meaning and value of these practices given by their relationship to the virtues identified by Justin? I shall review first the texts which advocate the different Christian stances, before assessing what account of practice we should give.

LESSONS FROM THE SCRIPTURES

A number of New Testament texts envisage sexual relations within marriage as a limited good or lesser evil. 1 Timothy condemns those who altogether forbid marriage and eating meat (4:3), evidence that this twofold abstention (associated above with Saturninus) dates back to at least the early second century; but the letter's description of the qualities desirable in a bishop or deacon also insists upon the avoidance by the candidate of a second marriage (3:2 and 12). Elsewhere, St Paul permits marriage, and remarriage for widows, but advised young men not to marry if they possessed self-control, while those already with wives should live 'as though they had none' (1 Cor. 7:37, 27, and 29). Widows would be happier if they did not remarry

---

[133] *Acts of John* 53–4, *NTA*, vol. II, 191.   [134] Justin, *First Apology*, 14.2, 15, and 29.
[135] Galen, preserved in Arabic from a summary of Plato's *Republic*, tr. R. Walzer, *Galen on Jews and Christians* (London: Oxford University Press, 1949), 15.

(1 Cor. 7:40).[136] The impact of such counsel should not be underestimated: the high status accorded to Paul's letters by many churches from a very early date may be inferred from changes made in the first century which, by omitting specifics, gave them the 'appearance of general letters'.[137] A collection of Pauline letters circulating in codex-form probably predated Marcion's edition of the mid second century.[138]

Luke's Gospel contrasted the 'sons of this age' who marry and 'those who are accounted worthy to attain to that age and to the resurrection from the dead' who 'neither marry nor are given in marriage, for they cannot die any more, because they are equal to angels and are sons of God, being sons of the resurrection' (Luke 20:34–6). It was easy to argue from such a contrast that to remain single, or to refrain from intercourse if married, was the truly Christian stance, an entry into the sexless life of heaven.[139] The questions were then whether baptism effected this entry or merely made it possible, whether the Christian's incorporation into the Risen Christ meant that one already lived the heavenly life, and what the significance was of failing to live that life. Matthew's Gospel depicted Jesus as commending those who were able to make themselves 'eunuchs for the sake of the kingdom of heaven' (19:12). If Jesus had attended the marriage of Cana (John 2), he himself had not married.[140] These texts clearly promoted sexual abstention, although they could be variously interpreted and interrelated to sanction different forms of abstention; they could be adduced in support of various judgements on those many Christians who married. Tertullian, a married man who considered sexual intercourse within marriage tantamount to fornication, allowed that Christians might enter upon a first marriage but argued forcefully against remarriage, which he equated with adultery.[141] Athenagoras, who shared Justin's belief that sex within marriage was for the purpose of procreation, likewise approximated remarriage to adultery.[142]

Some Christians were swayed by texts eventually excluded from the canon of the New Testament. In Eastern churches where the *Diatessaron* was read until the fifth century, abstinence within marriage was probably promoted through the description of Anna (the prophetess of Luke 2:36) remaining 'seven years a virgin with her husband'.[143] The *Gospel*

---

[136] For the different ascetic stances within the Corinthian church, cf., V. Wimbush, 'The ascetic impulse in early Christianity: some methodological challenges', *SP* 25 (1993), 468–76.

[137] Gamble, *Books*, 60.   [138] Ibid., 58–61.

[139] For its use in the rejection of marriage by groups opposed by Clement of Alexandria, cf., idem, *Stromata*, III.12.87.

[140] A point not lost on some groups opposed by Clement of Alexandria. Cf., *Stromata*, III.6.49.

[141] Tertullian, *Exhortation to Chastity*, 9.3; *On Single Marriage*, 10.5–6.

[142] Athengoras, *Embassy*, 33.   [143] Cf. Petersen, *Tatian's Diatessaron*, 80–2.

of Thomas contained several sayings which promoted sexual abstention.[144] Jesus promised to reveal himself when the disciples could undress without shame. This may allude to stripping for baptism; but equally and more probably it teaches sexual renunciation as the reversal of the Fall, when Adam and Eve first became ashamed of their nakedness. The saying plays upon the ancient image of the body as clothing which the individual casts aside on entering the divine realm.[145] The *Coptic Gospel of Thomas* taught that the disciples would enter the kingdom when 'you make the two one, and when you make the inside as the outside, and the outside as the inside, and the upper as the lower, and when you make the male and the female into a single one, so that the male is not male and the female not female'.[146] Entry into heaven here requires transcendence of sexual differentiation. That a popular Greek version contained a similar saying is highly probable: a version of the saying appears in *2 Clement*.[147] The *Gospel of the Egyptians*, which perhaps dates from the mid-second century, included similar versions of both sayings already noted in the *Gospel of Thomas*. It re-cast them within a dialogue between Jesus and Salome together with other passages supportive of sexual abstention. When Salome asked how long the power of death would last, Jesus replied that death would have power 'as long as women bear children'. Salome announced that she herself had done well in not having children.[148] This latter work enjoyed respect among some Egyptian Christians of Clement's day: although he was quick

---

[144] I discuss the most obviously encratite sayings likely to be found in the Greek original. For other sayings, cf., R. Uro, 'Is *Thomas* an encratite gospel?' in idem, '*Thomas' at the Crossroads*, 140–62.

[145] ΛΕΓΟΥΣΙΝ ΑΥ
ΤΩ ΟΙ ΜΑΘΗΤΑΙ ΑΥΤΟΥ
ΠΟΤΕ ΗΜΕΙΝ ΕΜΦΑ
ΝΗΣ ΕΣΕΙ ΚΑΙ ΠΟΤΕ
ΣΕ ΟΨΟΜΕΘΑ ΛΕΓΕΙ
ΟΤΑΝ ΕΚΔΥΣΗΣΘΕ ΚΑΙ
ΜΗ ΑΙΣΧΥΝΘΗΤΕ

    Fitzmyer, 'The Oxyrhynchus *logoi*', 546 (= *Coptic Gospel of Thomas*, Logion 37). For its interpretation, cf. A. De Conick and J. Fossum, 'Stripped before God: a new interpretation of Logion 37 in the Gospel of Thomas', *VC* 45 (1991), 123–50.

[146] *Coptic Gospel of Thomas* 22, tr. *NTA*, vol. I, 120.

[147] *2 Clement* 12:11–30. This work, which opposes the stance on fasting and almsgiving in the *Gospel of Thomas*, glosses the saying to teach that men and women should regard each other as brother and sister without thought of sexual difference. It is a more reliable guide to second- and third-century readings than Clement of Alexandria's interpretation in terms of anger and desire at *Stromata*, III.13.93. For the improbable view that *2 Clement* does *not* promote sexual abstinence, cf. T. Baarda, '2 Clem 12 and the sayings of Jesus', in J. Delobel (ed.), *Logia, Les Paroles de Jésus – The Sayings of Jesus* (Leuven University Press, 1982), 536–7 and 555–6.

[148] *Gospel of the Egyptians*, frs. a and d, tr. *NTA*, vol. I, 209 and 210. For composition of the *Gospel of the Egyptians* before 150, cf. Schneemelcher, *NTA*, vol. I, 215; for a date after AD 150, cf. Metzger, *Canon*, 171.

to distinguish it from the Four Gospels, he laboured to press his own interpretations of several passages. Clement condemned those who supposedly
misread them in their hatred of the created order and even of humanity,
but this is his caricature of an anthropology in which the physical body, and
its sexual differentiation, belong to the postlapsarian world.[149] Clement is
not a reliable guide to the ascetic meanings these texts held for readers
impressed by them.

The *Gospel of Thomas* probably contained sayings similar to those in the
Coptic version (Logia 16, 49, and 75) in which Jesus blesses the faithful
'solitary' whose reward is to enter the bridal chamber. Scholars dispute
whether the earlier Greek version used the term μοναχός, what term was
used in any Syriac original, and whether the Coptic has been influenced
by later ascetic development. They question the relationship between these
solitaries and the later Syriac *iḥidaya* (on which more below); and they
debate whether the sayings teach that celibacy is a requirement for baptism.
Uro rightly warns both against reliance on evidence from later periods
and against 'a clear-cut encratite interpretation' which neglects the 'multi-
dimensional imagery of the gospel'.[150] While this caution is apt, there can
be little doubt that the sayings encouraged *some* form of sexual abstention,
and probably more than one form, by its various readers.

THE GOOD OF MARRIAGE

Some early Christians championed marriage, and a few defended marital
sexual relations. Ignatius defended marriage while conceding the value of
'remaining in purity' in a letter circulated during the second century.[151] At
Edessa Bardaisan (AD 154–c. 222) seems to have argued that sexual intercourse contributed to the purity, not the impurity, of the spouses.[152] Some
Christians enjoyed the texts briefly mentioned at the close of the previous
chapter which may have originated in Jewish circles: the *Testaments of the
Twelve Patriarchs,* and *Joseph and Aseneth.* A praiseworthy virtue of sexual abstinence is limited in scope by these works to the years preceding
marriage and the raising of a family. Basilides' son, Isidore, held that intercourse was 'natural' though not necessary and defended postponement

---

[149] Clement of Alexandria, *Stromata* III.9.63, 67, and 10.70. For the anthropology of the Primordial
Man, cf. Uro, 'Is *Thomas*', 150; W. A. Meeks, 'The image of the androgyne: some uses of a symbol
in earliest Christianity', *History of Religions* 13 (1974), 165–208.

[150] Uro, 'Is *Thomas*', 156–9.

[151] Ignatius, *Letter to Polycarp*, 5.1. On circulation, cf. Gamble, *Books*, 111.

[152] Drijvers, *Bardaisan of Edessa*, 190, 192, and 205.

of marriage for the sake of prayer as well as for financial reasons or on grounds of youth.[153] Letters exchanged by three bishops towards the end of the second century, Dionysius of Corinth, Palmas of Amestris (a city in Pontus), and Pinytus of Knossus in Crete, reveal a lively debate about what sexual discipline to enforce in the churches which they led, and about the scope or proper form of 'purity' (*hagneia*). Dionysius defended the good of marriage and procreation, whereas Pinytus probably sought to impose permanent abstinence on the baptized members of his flock as the only acceptable form that purity or chastity could take for Christians.[154] The letters later featured in a collection of Dionysius's correspondence which may have circulated widely, so that this bishop's arguments were deployed in a larger attempt to stop some bishops from declaring permanent sexual renunciation obligatory for the baptized.

Clement of Alexandria repeatedly limited the scope of texts which could be used to reject the good of marital relations. He taught that St Paul's concession of marriage to those who would otherwise 'burn' was directed at second marriages and did not imply that every marriage was a response to lust.[155] Matthew 19:12 was concerned only with the case of those who were drawn to remarriage after their wife had been divorced for adultery.[156] All sexual intercourse outside marriage was forbidden, as was intercourse between husband and wife during the latter's menstrual period. Nature and propriety further dictated an appropriate time: not at the very start of the day, nor after attending church or visiting the market, but at the end of the day, and then not repeatedly.[157] Clement's strictures forestalled ascetic critics who might attack his justification of marital sex. His *Paedagogus* sanctioned procreation in marriage with appeal to God's blessing over the first couple, the call to 'be fruitful and multiply' (Genesis 1:28); he drew on St Paul's call to the Corinthians to be 'co-workers' with God (2 Cor. 6:1).[158] Elsewhere he appealed to 1 Timothy 3:2 in defence of clerical marriage.[159] Clement argued that the seed of those who were holy was itself holy, and accused those who shirked marriage of being 'unmanly'.[160] Such rhetoric, however, betrays the defensive nature of Clement's task;

---

[153] Clement of Alexandria, *Stromata*, III.1.3. [154] Eusebius, *Church History*, IV.23.6–7, SC 31, 204.

[155] Clement, *Stromata*, III.1.4 [156] Ibid., III.6.50.

[157] *Paedagogus*, II.10.88.3, 92.1, and 96.2. On these restrictions as conformity to the natural order, cf. J. F. Procopé, 'Morality and manners in Clement's *Paidagogos*', *SP* 26 (1993), 313–17.

[158] Clement, *Paedagogus*, II.10.83.2. This use of Paul is an example of what Elizabeth Clark terms 'textual implosion', taking a text which has one apparent meaning to see it as collapsing into other 'core issues', though Clement's purpose runs contrary to that examined by Clark; cf. her *Reading Renunciation: Asceticism and Scripture in Early Christianity* (Princeton University Press, 1999), 133.

[159] Clement, *Stromata*, III.12.90. [160] Clement, *Stromata*, III.6.46 and II.23.142.

it measures powerful currents pulling early Christians in the direction of sexual renunciation.[161]

HERMAS AND HOLY VIRGINITY

The *Shepherd of Hermas* offers another indicator of the currents encouraging sexual renunciation within marriage, as well as abstention from marriage, and was a major text in the promotion of asceticism. Its central character and narrator, Hermas, is a married freedman, a Christian profoundly troubled by a vision in which he is confronted by his former owner, Rhoda. This wealthy fellow Christian censures him for an episode when he had looked at her longingly by the Tiber. Though Hermas had not acted on his desire, he is made painfully aware of the sinful nature of that desire.[162] The freedman is no rake: a second visionary figure, an elderly woman who embodies the Church, calls him 'the man of self-control who abstains from all evil desire and is filled with all simplicity and great innocence'.[163] The unfolding narrative will not allow us, however, to accept this description at face value; the Church addresses Hermas in terms that he perhaps used to think about himself, and terms which readers of the work no doubt used to characterize themselves. In this way it reveals competing definitions of its central virtues, self-control and simplicity. Hermas comes to see through a second vision that he must live with his wife as though she were his sister, that is, must abstain from intercourse with her.[164] The Church itself must be rejuvenated as Hermas and others like him grow in repentant simplicity.[165] A second visionary figure, the Shepherd, requires that the husband of an adulterous wife should separate from her if she refuses to abandon her affair, but he must not remarry: he is obliged to receive her back if she later comes to her right mind.[166] As Carolyn Osiek has pointed out this command ran contrary to Roman law (however fitfully applied).[167] The Shepherd allowed remarriage but taught that to remain a widow or widower was worthy of much greater honour.[168]

---

[161] The same embattled stance is detectable in the attack on Montanism found in Epiphanius' *Panarion*, 48.8–9, which Lipsius, Voigt, and Heine attribute to an unknown source of the late second or early third century. Remarriage is permitted for widowers, except priests, as a concession to weakness that shows a lack of virtuous self-control. The defence draws heavily on 1 Timothy.

[162] *Shepherd of Hermas*, Vision 1.1.1–8. For a view which denies any sexual sin on Hermas' part, cf. Young, 'Being a man', 241 and 251.

[163] *Shepherd of Hermas*, Vision 1.2.4.   [164] Ibid., Vision 2.2.3.

[165] For a fuller account of simplicity and almsgiving in the *Shepherd*, cf. my 'Almsgiving for the pure of heart: continuity and change in early Christian teaching', in *Sev*, 419–29.

[166] *Shepherd*, Mandate 4.1.4–8.

[167] Osiek, *Shepherd*, 111.   [168] *Shepherd of Hermas*, Mandate 4.4.

At one point the Shepherd asks Hermas to review his visions, so as to enter more deeply into their meaning. He tells Hermas that he has seen everything in a noble and holy fashion 'as though through (the eyes of) a virgin'.[169] Virginity (whether that of a rejuvenated Church or Hermas after his spiritual renewal) has become a symbol of spiritual purity; sexual abstinence becomes an element in receptivity to divine revelation. In his third vision Hermas had observed seven women who symbolised seven virtues. Now Hermas sees these women again and recognizes them as virgins.[170] They instruct him to his discomfort that he is to sleep with them 'as a brother and not as a husband'. The virgins kiss Hermas and like children they play together before praying and going to sleep.[171] It is reasonable to conjecture that the scene alludes to the practice (more familiar to us in the third century) of *syneisaktism*, whereby a woman (also known in Latin as a *virgo subintroducta*) or several such women lived in permanent sexual renunciation with a celibate man, often a cleric.[172] Hermas' initial disquiet and subsequent experience might then indicate a practice both novel and controversial at Rome when the text was written, and which it then served to sanction. Some of Irenaeus' Gnostic opponents practised this form of celibacy, because he alleged that it resulted in pregnancy, though he did not condemn the practice as such.[173]

The virgins of Hermas' vision reveal his spiritual purity. Sexual abstinence, and the freedom from desire which it implies, express a deep holiness. This is reinforced by the message that the virgins represent not simply human virtues, but 'holy spirits', 'powers of the Son of God' which every Christian must acquire to be saved.[174] In a final vision Hermas is promised that the shepherd and the virgins will return to his house in future.[175] While it is noticeable that the *Shepherd* makes no reference to any order of virgins, nor requires sexual renunciation by all who are married, the work gave much impetus both to consecrated virginity and the practice of sexual abstinence within marriage.

The *Shepherd*'s symbolic nexus which related virginity to purity and visionary insight is found elsewhere in the Early Church. According to an oracle by the Montanist prophetess Prisca, 'purification produces harmony, and they see visions, and when they turn their faces downward they also hear salutary voices, as clear as they are secret'.[176] The prophetess was

---

[169] Ibid., Similitude 9.1.2, ed. Joly, *Le Pasteur*, SC 53, 288 (ὡς ὑπὸ παρθένου).

[170] Ibid., Vision 3.8.2 and Similitude 9.2.3.   [171] Ibid., Similitude 9.11.3–7.

[172] R. Joly, *Le Pasteur*, SC 53, 48; Osiek, *Shepherd*, 228.   [173] Irenaeus *Against the Heresies*, 1.6.3.

[174] *Shepherd of Hermas*, Similitude 9.13.2.   [175] Ibid., Similitude 10.4.5.

[176] *Oracle* 10, in Tertullian, *De exhortatione castitatis* 10.5, tr. Heine, *The Montanist Oracles and Testimonia*, 5.

condemned by detractors for having separated from her husband, and Montanus himself was attacked as teaching the dissolution of marriage. The latter charge perhaps conflates such separation with the condemnation of second marriages contracted by Christians, but the separation itself appears motivated by the same beliefs that found wide acceptance in the *Shepherd*.[177]

ABSOLUTE CONTINENCE

Others argued that all sexual intercourse was harmful. The 'Gnostic' *Testimony of Truth* condemned the Old Testament for its sanction of procreation in marriage. The waters of the Jordan which turned back at the approach of Jesus represent the desire for sexual intercourse.[178] Tatian apparently glossed 1 Corinthians 7:5 to teach that marital intercourse inhibited prayer and was a form of spiritual fornication; it revealed weakness of will (*akrasia*) and a heart the loyalty of which was divided between God and devil. Clement of Alexandria was keen to convict Tatian of the even more extreme position in which marriage was a diabolical invention, but it is notable that he could not find that position in Tatian's *On Correction According to the Saviour*.[179] Julius Cassianus, author of a treatise *On Self-control and Castration*, appealed to Matthew 19:12 in rejecting the argument that the reproductive organs and sexual differentiation testify to God's blessing on sexual intercourse, but also appealed to the passage from the *Gospel of the Egyptians* in which Jesus promised Salome a revelation that would take place 'when you have trampled on the garment of shame and when the two become one and the male with the female (is) neither male nor female'.[180]

Total abstention from intercourse by the baptized is a prominent theme in several of the apocryphal Acts which we have already studied. In the *Acts of Paul*, the apostle enounces a series of beatitudes which echo and re-cast the words of Jesus and Paul in the canonical Gospels and Epistles. They elaborate the beatitude which heads the series: 'Blessed are the pure

---

[177] Eusebius, *Church History*, v.18.2–3. For Montanist rejection of remarriage, cf. Tertullian, *On Monogamy*, 2.1 and 3.11; *On Modesty*, 1. For the unlikely view that Montanus uniquely annulled the marriages of Prisca and Maximilla, cf. C. Trevett, *Montanism: Gender, Authority and the New Prophecy* (Cambridge University Press, 1996), 110. For the view (with which I agree) that Tertullian's rejection of second marriages reflects the earliest strand of Montanism in Asia Minor, cf. ibid., 113–14.

[178] *Testimony of Truth*, Codex IX, 30 and 31, tr. S. Giversen and B. Pearson, *NHL*, 450. Cf. R. McL. Wilson, 'Alimentary and sexual encratism in the Nag Hammadi tractates', in U. Bianchi (ed.), *La tradizione dell'enkrateia: motivazioni ontologiche e protologiche* (Rome: Edizioni dell'Ateneo, 1985), 317–39.

[179] Clement of Alexandria, *Stromata*, III.12.80–1.

[180] Ibid., III.13.91–2; *Gospel of the Egyptians*, fr. j, tr. *NTA*, vol. I, 211.

in heart for they shall see God.' What is required for purity of heart is expounded in particular in the four beatitudes which follow:

> Blessed are they who have kept the flesh pure, for they shall become a temple of God.
> Blessed are the continent, for to them God will speak.
> Blessed are they who have renounced this world, for they shall be well pleasing unto God.
> Blessed are they who have wives as if they had them not, for they shall be heirs to God.[181]

The first macarism recalls 2 Cor. 6:14–16, where St Paul urges Christians not 'to become yoked in a mismatched team with the faithless', an exhortation that recalls the Levitical prohibition against the interbreeding of cattle (LXX Lev. 19:1). As used in the epistle, this exhortation is a general call to avoid conformity with pagan beliefs.[182] In the *Acts*, however, the promise has been attached specifically to sexual continence. To the extent that it interacted with its Pauline source, the allusion now encouraged the reader to interpret the epistle as condemning sexual relations within a 'mixed' marriage of pagan and Christian. The second macarism would be read by many in the context of beliefs already set out above concerning the place of sexual and dietary abstinence in receptivity to prophetic visions. Between this and the fourth, which radically recasts 1 Corinthians 7:29 and Romans 8:17 to make God the reward of sexual renunciation, the third macarism recalls Luke 14:33. Where Luke speaks of renouncing possessions, the *Acts* offers a more thoroughgoing renunciation of the world, but which in its immediate context is symbolized by, or summed up in, sexual abstention. Seven macarisms follow which have no explicit relationship to sexual abstention, and which concern the Christian's disposition before God, but the final blessing returns to the theme; it also serves as an interpretative frame, whereby these inner dispositions find outward expression in abstinence: 'Blessed are the bodies of the virgins for they shall be well pleasing to God and shall not lose the reward of their purity (*hagneia*)'.[183]

This call to holiness is then lived out, and its rewards manifested, in the career of Thecla, the virgin converted by St Paul's sermon 'on self-control and the resurrection', who on hearing Paul preach immediately abandons

---

[181] *Acts of Paul and Thecla*, 5, tr. *NTA*, vol. II, 239–40.
[182] J. Murphy O'Connor, 'Philo and 2 Cor 6:14–7:1', *Revue Biblique* 95 (1988), 55–69.
[183] *Acts of Paul and Thecla* 6, tr. *NTA*, vol. II, 240.

her planned marriage to Thamyris.[184] Her miracles witness to the power of
Christ active in the life of the baptized and continent Christian.[185] Rordorf
argues that the lion who seeks baptism from St Paul later in the *Acts of
Paul* represents the sexual temptation which Paul, and every Christian to
be baptized, must overcome; certainly the lion on its baptism spurns the
advances of a lioness. Rordorf, however, differs from Drijvers in thinking
that the *Acts* do not so much *require* as *recommend* absolute continence by
the baptized.[186]

THE VAGARIES OF PRACTICE

It is likely that this difference in what two modern readers make of the *Acts*
replicates a similar divergence among early Christian readers. Just as the
macarisms of the *Acts* could be used to re-interpret sayings in the canonical
Gospels and epistles, so the implications of the text for personal or communal practice might be differently perceived depending on what other texts
were read alongside. The historian thus faces considerable difficulty (often
unacknowledged or understated) in determining how the arguments and
literary texts reviewed above shaped the sexual mores of early Christians.
What theologians and polemicists thought should happen is a poor guide
in assessing what did. To judge that behind 'even the most extreme statements . . . we can usually sense the mute assent of whole churches, even of
whole Christian regions' is to go beyond the available evidence.[187] Even
Galen's account of Christian sexual restraint may have derived largely or
simply from what he had read.

Tertullian's writings offer insight in this respect. Despite his view that
remarriage was a moral failing which should bar a candidate from the
exercise of church leadership, some congregations at least were presided
over by men who had entered on a second marriage.[188] The force with
which Tertullian argued against remarriage amongst the laity measures the
degree to which remarriage was commonplace. He condemned marriage
with a pagan husband, but admits such marriages occurred.[189] Tertullian
claimed as public knowledge the large number of ordinary Christians who

---

[184] W. Rordorf, 'Quelques jalons pour une interprétation symbolique des *Actes de Paul*', in D. Warren,
A. Brock, and D. Pao (eds.), *Early Christian Voices In Texts, Traditions, and Symbols* (Boston and
Leiden: Brill, 2003), 252.

[185] For a similar connection between renunciation and the power of the resurrection in the *Acts of
Andrew*, the *Acts of John*, and the *Acts of Thomas*, cf. D. Konstan, 'Acts of love: a narrative pattern
in the apocryphal acts', *JECS* 6.1 (1998), 15–36.

[186] Ibid., 258 and 263; *Acts of Paul* 9, tr. *NTA*, vol. II, 265.   [187] Brown, *The Body and Society*, 86.

[188] Tertullian, *On Single Marriage*, 12.3.   [189] Tertullian, *To His Wife*, II.2.1.

refrained from intercourse after baptism: 'For how many are there, who set a seal on their flesh as soon as they rise from the font? How many who by mutual agreement set aside their conjugal rights, choosing to be eunuchs for the kingdom of heaven?'[190] Tertullian's rhetorical questions had the advantage of not having to number the continent, for bare numbers risk sceptical re-interpretation and denial of the significance claimed for them. The passage occurs in a treatise which advocates marriage as the context in which a man displays a virtuous self-control through not sleeping with his wife.[191] Of course such a device could only work if enough readers recognized the continent as a significant number of the faithful. Yet, a few decades later Origen reveals that some might think lifelong celibacy a matter for just pride, while others would think likewise about a ten-year period of sexual abstinence.[192] Such asceticism was thus not so common as to be unexceptional.

ORDERS OF WIDOWS AND VIRGINS

Demography of course meant that the churches contained many involuntary widows, and for these women beliefs about the virtue of abstention from sex contributed to their distinct role within the churches whereby they repaid the alms they received by their prayers and other good works on behalf of the community. An 'order' of widows emerged aided by 1 Timothy 5:3–10 which counselled the churches to support elderly widows of good character aged sixty or above who were to be 'enrolled' for this purpose. According to the *Apostolic Tradition* such women did not receive any form of ordination through the laying on of hands, but were publicly named to the order.[193] Tertullian advocated a version of *syneisaktism* whereby a widower retained one or several impoverished elderly widows who could run his household as 'spiritual wives' rather than embark upon a second marriage.[194]

A significant but small minority of Christians of both sexes chose to be consecrated virgins, who took personal vows but do not appear to have formed an institutional order within the church.[195] Their dress seems to have varied, lacking the uniformity which marks out a formal order. In North Africa Tertullian argued vociferously that virgins should go veiled

[190] *To His Wife*, 1.6.2. Cf. also, *On The Adornment of Women*, II.9.
[191] Cf. C. Conybeare, 'Tertullian on flesh, spirit, and wives', *Sev*, 430–9.
[192] Origen, *Homilies on Jeremiah*, 12.8. Nautin (SC 232, 20) dates the sermons to AD 241–4.
[193] *Apostolic Tradition*, 10.
[194] *Tertullian, On Monogamy*, 16; *Exhortation to Chastity*, 12. [195] Ibid., 12.

like married women, rather than unveiled like children, as had previously been acceptable and perhaps the prevalent custom; in this he appealed to the practice of the Greek churches. Nor were they to be accorded other marks of public honour.[196] Confirmation that there was no distinct institution before the mid third century to regulate the virgins in each local church is found in the attempt by one African church to enrol a teenage virgin in the order of widows, much to Tertullian's disgust.[197] On the other hand, by the mid third century virgins might to be perceived as a distinct group. Cyprian addressed them in a treatise as 'the more distinguished part of Christ's flock'.[198] He urged them to encourage one another in the life they had chosen.[199] The bishop enhanced his authority in the business of shaping a common life or identity for them: he argued against their presence at marriage celebrations and public baths.[200]

There was no set way of life for female virgins. We have already noted the possibility that *syneisaktism* was practised in the early Roman churches. Yet, in the mid third century Cyprian condemned the presbyter Rogatianus and fellow confessors at Carthage for what he termed sharing their beds with women, and which is probably a form of *syneisaktism*. In a letter to another bishop, Pomponius, Cyprian conceded that the custom was practised by many, but he and his fellow bishops judged that virgins living with men were to separate from them. Those who refused were to be excommunicated.[201] The exact details, however, of these virgins' living arrangements have been variously reconstructed, and it is not obvious that the men with whom they had lived, one of whom was a deacon, were also professed celibates.[202] What the story reveals is the difficulty female virgins experienced in finding affordable accommodation outside the family home to match the respectability of their ecclesial status. Where possible, widows and virgins no doubt remained in the family home.

Before the third century some churches had adopted the stance that sexual renunciation was required, *at least in theory*, of all *baptized* Christians, where it is important to note that the ages at which Christians sought baptism in the second and early third century may well have differed widely.[203] Some Syriac churches employed a baptismal rite in which the

---

[196] Tertullian, *On the Veiling of Virgins*, 1–3, and 9.   [197] Ibid., 9.
[198] Cyprian, *On the Dress of Virgins*, 3.   [199] Ibid., 24.
[200] Ibid., 18 and 19.   [201] Cyprian, *Epp.* 13.5, 14.3, and 4.
[202] Cf. G. Dunn, 'Infected sheep and diseased cattle, or the pure and holy flock: Cyprian's pastoral care of virgins', *JECS* 11.1 (2003), 11–18.
[203] Cf. D. F. Wright, 'At what ages were people baptized in the early centuries?', in *SP* 30 (1997), 389–94.

sacrament was linked to acceptance of sexual renunciation. To be baptized into Christ was to be single in purpose, and single in separation from family ties, because Christ was single in these respects. In the mid fourth century, when a traditional liturgical formula can be reconstructed from the writings of Aphrahat (fl. 340s) and Ephrem (*c.* 306–73), the rite no longer reflected a requirement of celibacy for all the baptized, but it remained as the means by which certain individuals committed themselves to the single life as 'Sons and Daughters of the Covenant'.[204] We cannot tell when the traditional rite took shape, nor when its significance was modified, but it is plausible that in the late second century these churches saw in baptism a public commitment to permanent continence.[205] Many Christians may have postponed baptism. The Pseudo-Clementine *Letters to Virgins*, which may well originate in third-century Syria, reveal celibate missionaries whose asceticism is further characterized by prayer and fasting, but who may find the only Christians with whom they can lodge are married.[206]

In Syria views on sexual renunciation must have been deeply affected by the strength of Marcionite Christianity: the sect remained strong there into the fourth century.[207] Tertullian's *Against Marcion* claims that Marcionites, who had spread quickly, restricted baptism to the unmarried virgin or widow, or to the person who 'purchased baptism by divorce', because marriage was held an 'evil thing and as a traffic in unchastity'.[208] These candidates are not necessarily converts (the unmarried virgin seeking baptism more plausibly comes from a Christian family). Marcionite rejection of marriage reflected a negative view of the physical world. Clement of Alexandria lumped Marcion with Julius Cassianus and Valentinus to claim that all three saw birth as the soul's entry into evil.[209] Avoidance of intercourse was one part of the ascetic purification by which the soul,

---

[204] Murray, *Symbols*, 14–16. For the (unlikely) view that 'baptising only those who pledged themselves to continence' continued in Aphrahat's day, cf., Giulia Sfameni Gasparro, 'Asceticism and anthropology: *Enkrateia* and "double creation" in Early Christianity', in Wimbush and Valantasis, *Asceticism*, 139.

[205] For a cautious assessment, cf. S. H. Griffith, 'Asceticism in the Church of Syria: the hermeneutics of early Syrian monasticism', in Wimbush and Valantasis, *Asceticism*, 236–7.

[206] Pseudo-Clementine Letters, *Ep.* 2, 1–3.

[207] Justin (*First Apology*, 26.5) claimed that Marcion's ideas were known by people of every nation. Marcion's rapid success is measured by (i) Bardaisan's attack at Edessa in the late second or early third century; cf. H. J. W. Drijvers, *Bardaisan of Edessa* (Assen: Van Gorcum, 1966), 217–18, and 225; (ii) Tertullian's *Against Marcion*; (iii) Celsus' knowledge of Marcionite Christianity (Origen, *Contra Celsum*, v.62, vi.53 and 74). Eusebius reveals Marcionite martyrs in early fourth-century Palestine (*Martyrs of Palestine*, 10.3).

[208] Tertullian, *Against Marcion*, 1.29, ed. and tr. Evans, Tertullian, *Adversus Marcionem*, vol. 1, 80–3.

[209] Clement of Alexandria, *Stromata*, III.17.102.

bought by Christ, ascended with him to his heavenly realm.[210] No doubt Marcionites did not always live by the high standard they themselves set: the Armenian Esnik of Colb claimed in the fifth century that they did penance for their sexual sins after baptism; but the rule did not alter.[211] Interaction between Marcionism and other Christian churches probably contributed to the high value placed upon renunciation, but may also have strengthened an opposing defence of marriage seen, for example, in the third-century church order, the *Didascalia*. Outside the Syriac and Marcionite churches, the requirement of total abstinence seems restricted to certain Gnostic groups: according to the *Elenchos*, the Naassenes, for example, reckoned heterosexual intercourse morally reprehensible.[212]

CLEMENT'S ASCETIC THEOLOGY

The great variety of early Christian asceticism is now clear. Much has been traced back to Judaism, little to Greek ascetic traditions. Yet, educated Christians, like their Hellenistic Jewish counterparts, might wish to subsume and reinterpret ascetic practices within a moral theology that owed much to Greek moral philosophy. In the final part of this chapter I turn to one such thinker, Clement of Alexandria.

Clement presents Christ as the one who teaches virtue, but we cannot possess virtue until cured of our wayward passions by this man who is free from passion (*apathēs tēn psuchēn*), where passion is understood as irrational and excessive desire.[213] We must grow in likeness to this model of virtue whose precepts Clement describes in Cynic terms as a 'short cut to eternity' guiding the soul towards purity of heart.[214] Christ is the Logos, the Divine reason, who speaks through Scripture as a whole. The biblical texts fan the 'soul's spark' and 'direct its inner eye to contemplation' by communicating the truth to which our lives must be conformed.[215] Purity enables contemplation of God's self-revelation.[216] Our proximity to divine reason should mean that we want little by way of earthly goods, but contemplation of the divine does not on its own make for virtue. Clement recognizes the need for people to habituate themselves to doing good. There is a necessary 'training' for body and soul.[217] Avoidance of

---

[210] H. Drijvers, 'Christ as warrior and merchant', 82.

[211] Blackman, *Marcion*, 8.   [212] *Elenchos*, v.7.14–15 and 9.10–11.

[213] Clement, *Paedagogus*, 1.2.4.1, *CA*, vol. I, 91. Cf. also, *Stromata*, II.13.59.6.

[214] *Paedagogus*, 1.3.9.4.   [215] *Stromata*, I.10.4.   [216] *Paedagogus*, 1.1.3.3.

[217] *Stromata*, I.1.12.2 (συγγυμνασία), and II.18.81.2–4, *CA*, vol. II, 9 and 155.

sin requires exercise (*askēsis*).[218] Moral theology is not a calculus which arrives at rules of right and wrong, but envisages life as a transformative journey towards God that requires certain ascetic virtues along the way: God 'teaches us to provide for ourselves from our own resources; he fits us for the road to eternal bliss, ensuring both that we have limbered up and have been properly kitted out, so that we are self-sufficient and simple in how we live'.[219] The Word specifically teaches us 'frugality' (*to euteles*).[220] Frugality is our food for the journey, the 'viaticum'.[221]

Clement's virtue of frugality is expressed first in a diet of plain but wholesome food which meets physical need rather than affording pleasure to the palate; in the *Paedagogus* he wins over his reader by the graphic description of an opposing cuisine, the gourmet dishes preferred by the gluttonous and the bread which they have 'feminized'.[222] He employs a traditional contrast between the 'extravagant' (*poluteles*) and the 'frugal' (*euteles*).[223] The Christian meal is 'simple' (*liton*) and 'unseasoned'.[224] The ingredients, however (vegetables, fruit, and dairy products, but also meat), matter less than how they are prepared: those which require no cooking or accompanying sauce are preferable to those which must be cooked or garnished.[225] Frequent appeal to traditional ascetic vocabulary, together with this concern for the making of the meal as opposed to its content, accompanies a reluctance to pin down exactly what counts as simple fare, and allows Clement to permit much. His readers may attend banquets and eat there more extravagant dishes which others set before them.[226] He cites St Paul on the merit in not eating meat or drinking wine, but no sooner has he done so than he insists there is no sin in their consumption.[227] Grown men may take wine in moderation during the evening.[228]

It is also noticeable that Clement's discussion of virtuous asceticism with respect to food fails to include fasting. Fasting appears in the *Paedagogus* only in the context of those biblical texts in which the prophet spiritualizes the practice and reinterprets justice and almsgiving as the one fast acceptable to God (Isaiah 58:4–6).[229] Likewise Clement will gloss fasting as 'indicating abstinence from all evils without exception'.[230] His 'Gnostic' or 'Knowing Christian' recognizes that Christians may fast on Wednesdays and Fridays, but also understands the 'riddle of the fast' on these days, the true meaning

---

[218] Ibid., II.10.47.1–2 and 13.58.3, *CA*, vol. II, 138 and 144.
[219] *Paedagogus*, I.12.98.4.   [220] Ibid., I.12.99.1, *CA*, vol. I, 149.
[221] Ibid., III.6.37.1 (chapter title). *CA*, vol. I, 258.   [222] Ibid., II.1.3.1–4.1, *CA*, vol. I, 155–6.
[223] Ibid., II.1.5.2, II.1.15.1–2, and II.1.17.1, *CA*, vol. I, 157, 164–5, and 166.
[224] Ibid., II.1.7.3, *CA*, vol. I, 158.   [225] Ibid., II.1.15.1–3.
[226] Ibid., II.1.10.2.   [227] Ibid., II.1.11.1.   [228] Ibid., II.2.22.1.
[229] Ibid., III.12.90.   [230] *Stromata* VI.12.102.3. Cf. also, *Eclogues of the Prophets*, 14.1–2.

of the practice, with the result that he or she 'fasts in their life from both love of money and love of pleasure'.[231] It is unclear whether Clement's Knowing Christian actually abstains from food on these days; if they do, the value of that abstention is not located in frugality. Where Clement offers a positive description of fasting in his sermon *What Rich Man May be Saved?* (*Quis dives salvetur?*), it is the 'continual fasting' of the grief-stricken penitent.[232]

A similar defensive pattern whereby ascetic virtue is trumpeted, vice decried, and yet much is permitted, has already been detected in Clement's account of marital sex, but it runs more widely through Clement's asceticism. Household utensils and furniture should be 'frugal' (*eutelestera*), a far cry from the ludicrous ostentation of alabaster chamber-pots.[233] 'Bedding' should be 'simple and plain'; there is no call for silver legs on the bed.[234] Yet this confident deployment of the ascetic terms allows the author to decry the harsher asceticism of those who sleep rough upon the ground as so much 'Cynic vanity'.[235] A contrast between extravagance and frugality is maintained, but cannot be mapped simply onto distinct practices or lifestyles. What matters is how things are used rather than what is possessed: 'it remains for us, however, to resolve the following objection: for whom are the more extravagant things (*ta polutelestera*) if everybody chooses the more frugal (*ta eutelestera*)? For human beings, I should say, if we make use of them without passionate attachment and partiality.'[236]

How is this to be understood? Is it sleight of hand, claiming asceticism for a life which behind the rhetorical scenery is no different from that of others in the same social milieu? John Behr's sympathetic study of Clement's asceticism has argued that 'Christ's incarnation is . . . understood by Clement as enabling the exercise of the morality taught by the Greeks.'[237] Clement certainly works to narrow any gap between familiar Middle Platonist or Stoic concepts of the ascetic virtues in Graeco-Roman culture and his own account of Christian asceticism. His broad strategy thus resembles that of Philo which we examined in the previous chapter. He cites frequently from biblical and pagan sources (Plato, Homer, Eratosthenes, and Heraclitus, etc.), so that they support each other and offer common witness to his ethic. On the other hand, the refusal to specify what counts as acceptable and unacceptable may be thought essential to the transformative, progressive nature of Clement's ascetic project: to move forward in

---

[231] *Stromata*, VII.12.75.2–76.1, *CA*, vol. III, 54.   [232] *Quis dives salvetur*, 42.15.
[233] *Paedagogus*, II.3.38.4, *CA*, vol. I, 180; and II.3.39.2.   [234] Ibid., II.9.77.3 and 78.3, *CA*, vol. I, 205.
[235] Ibid., II.9.78.1, *CA*, vol. I, 205.   [236] Ibid., II.12.121.1, *CA*, vol. I, 229.
[237] J. Behr, *Asceticism and Anthropology in Irenaeus and Clement* (Oxford University Press, 2000), 166.

the spiritual life is to find that the standards of extravagance and frugality have themselves altered. What is acceptable for the beginner may be a retrograde failing in the more advanced. What is permitted is not necessarily virtuous.

Any rapprochement of Christian and pagan ethics turns out to be limited: Clement, like Philo, is vocal in the condemnation of homosexual relations, pederasty, and infanticide.[238] Above all, he repeatedly promotes almsgiving as integral to the life of virtue: he defends the Old Testament prohibition on usury and the laws about gleaning in terms of the virtue of almsgiving to the poor;[239] a Christian banquet or *agape* is to be judged not by the food on the table but by the provision made for the poor.[240] From this perspective frugality is not a steady state, but something in which the Christian progresses through almsgiving, and which promotes almsgiving.[241] The temptation to fall short of virtue is presented as a constant assault by demonic forces against which a constant ascetic vigilance is the only defence.[242] Clement's moral theology is a form of Christian asceticism, though it is diametrically opposed to an asceticism based upon permanent renunciation of particular goods, and essentially unconcerned with the periodic asceticism of fasting.

CONCLUSIONS

Christian writers fiercely debated the degree and form of restraint they were to show with respect to food, drink, and sexual pleasure. Asceticism of some kind was integral to their faith in the first two centuries, but there was no agreement as to what form it should take. Most churches rejected the Jewish food laws which sometimes led to surprising exegesis: the *Epistle of Barnabas* (10:8) apparently explained the Mosaic prohibition on eating the weasel as a ban on oral sex. Christian abstention commonly took the form of ritual fasting, both communal and individual, but there was no universal agreement either on the form of these fasts, nor on their merit. Though some cited the Old Testament censure of fasting divorced from social justice and compassion towards the poor,

---

[238] *Paedagogus*, II.89–90; *Stromata*, II.18.93.1. Clement rarely acknowledges his extensive debts to Philo, but explicitly draws on the latter's *Life of Moses* at *Stromata*, II.19.100.3. For his use of Philo, cf. C. Mondésert, *Clément d'Alexandre: Introduction à l'étude de sa pensée religieuse à partir de l'Écriture* (Paris: Aubier, 1944), 163–83; D. Runia, *Philo in Early Christian Literature: A Survey* (Assen and Minneapolis: Van Gorcum and Fortress Press, 1993), 132–56.

[239] *Stromata*, II.18.84.4 and 18.85.3.   [240] *Paedagogus*, III.7.38.3.

[241] Ibid., III.6.35–7.39.   [242] *Stromata*, II.20.110.2 and 20.126.1.

Christian fasting drew heavily on Jewish tradition for its form and meanings, while also being used paradoxically as a means to distinguish Christians from Jews. Most Christians saw the virtue in some abstention from meat and wine, while some thought Christians should abstain from these permanently.

Although most Christians who were free to do so may be presumed to have married and raised a family, a great many writers thought that abstention from sexual activity was a virtuous participation in the heavenly life unlocked by Christ in baptism. In *c.* 208 Tertullian could write polemically of 'how many men, how many women, are numbered in the church's ranks on account of their self-control (*de continentia*), who prefer to take God as their spouse'. These men and women 'killed within themselves lustful desire and all that could not gain admittance into paradise'.[243] Athenagoras made a similar boast about the 'many' celibate men and women within the Church and presumed that 'to remain a virgin and a eunuch brings one closer to God'.[244] This attitude towards sex, virginity, and widowhood was marked by readings of Genesis that either identified intercourse with the first sin or understood sexual differentiation and desire to be a result of the Fall. Though not required of every baptised individual, permanent sexual renunciation was honoured in widows and virgins, while temporary abstinence at least was generally held up as an ideal for married couples, whose sexual activity was to be limited to procreation. The number of consecrated virgins was probably much lower than the number of widows. In Marcionite churches and some Syriac churches, however, sexual abstention was a requirement of baptism. This ideal was widely promoted in the apocryphal acts, but increasingly rejected as unorthodox by churches which shared the emerging canon of Scripture.

All these different forms of asceticism owed little to the philosophical asceticism of Greek philosophy which I sketched in the Introduction. Yet, a philosophical asceticism centred upon frugality was adapted by Clement of Alexandria and advocated for adoption by well-educated Christians. In Egypt at least such Christians already read with interest Philo's moral treatises.[245] They welcomed writings which enabled them to reconcile their Christian ascetic practices and beliefs with an overarching virtue-ethics shared with fellow members of Graeco-Roman elites. Clement and Philo

---

[243] Tertullian, *Exhortation to Chastity*, 13.4, CCSL 2, 1035. For the date, cf. T. D. Barnes, *Tertullian* (Oxford: Clarendon Press, 1985), 138.
[244] Athenagoras, *Embassy*, 33.
[245] For the third-century papyrus evidence, cf. Runia, *Philo in Early Christian Literature*, 22–3.

enabled these wealthier Christians to harmonize and hold together their different social identities. This literature thus facilitated the spread of Christianity within provincial elites. More significant still for the future, Clement's vision of a progressive asceticism would be taken forward and popularized by his fellow Alexandrian, Origen.

CHAPTER 4

Origen and his ascetic legacy

We have seen that by the early third century the periodic fasting of the many and the sexual abstention of a smaller number were significant features of many Christian churches. Fasting was commonly seen as integral to prayer. The involuntary celibacy of many widows, by being taken together with the permanent abstinence vowed by some consecrated virgins, was given by writers a symbolic role in manifesting the holiness of the Church. Absent was any widespread belief that fasting and sexual abstinence entered into a personal struggle for holiness. Christian asceticism had not yet been adapted into a popular narrative that related the difficult making of a saint in conflict with his or her own failings. We now turn to this development, and to the single most important author of this narrative: Origen. This learned exegete is notorious for supposedly castrating himself as a youth inspired by Matthew 19:12. The story may be a later slur given undue credence by Eusebius.[1] What matters here is Origen's influence on the changing understanding and growth of Christian asceticism.

THE MIDDAY SUN AT MAMRE – ORIGEN'S ASCETIC VISION

At Mamre, Origen observed in a homily, God had appeared to Abraham in the full glare of the midday sun, and had sat down with his two angels to share the banquet offered them by the patriarch. But God had not accompanied his two angels to Sodom, where in the failing light of dusk Lot gave them a simpler meal of bread. God revealed himself to the one and not to the other, because only Abraham was capable of the sight; his greater receptivity was evident in the alacrity with which he attended to his

---

[1] Eusebiuis, *Church History*, VI.8.1–3. Origen condemned this response to Matthew 19 in his later *Commentary on Matthew* (XV.3, PG 13.1257). For the castration as later invention, see Jon F. Dechow, *Dogma and Mysticism in Early Christianity: Epiphanius of Cyprus and the Legacy of Origen* (Macon, Ga.: Mercer University Press, 1988), 128–9. For the opposite view, see D. Caner, 'The practice and prohibition of self-castration in Early Christianity', *VC* 51 (1997), 401.

guests. This theophany fittingly occurred at Mamre, for the name meant 'sharp sight' or 'vision'. 'Do you see', Origen quizzed his congregation at Caesarea, 'what kind of place it is, in which the Lord can hold a feast? Abraham's keen sight and gaze delighted him. For he was pure of heart, with the result that he could see God. So it is in such a place, such a heart, that the Lord can hold a banquet in the company of his angels.' In his *Commentary on the Song of Songs* Origen explained that Abraham was sitting outside his tent, not indoors, because his mind was 'far from bodily thoughts, far from carnal desires'. The vision of God promised in the beatitudes (Matthew 5:8) was thus not something attainable only by the saints in heaven, but was a gift that God bestowed on the holy man or woman whose heart had been purged of sin.[2]

Origen taught how the heart, together with the words, thoughts, and actions which sprang from the heart, had to be purified through Christian asceticism. The starting-point, familiar from the Greek philosophical tradition, was self-knowledge. This comprised first the recognition of the soul's creation in the image and likeness of God, but also awareness of its actual disposition, intentions, evil passions, and other failings.[3] Origen's audience were to ask themselves in the silence of their hearts whether it was God whom they loved most, or some lesser thing which they had idolised: wealth, sensual pleasure, or social standing.[4] The soul was like a well which demonic powers had choked with the rubbish of earthly thoughts and carnal passions.[5] Anger and the other passions were the veil preventing our perception of God's glory.[6] The Divine Word must therefore be taken to heart as the source of all purification, and His commands practised.[7] Origen envisages the Word as shepherding into good order our otherwise irrational desires by His presence within the soul. This does not, however, absolve us of hard labour. If the soul is a piece of land rendered unproductive by the weeds of wealth, of earthly pleasures and attendant cares, then reason must be the plough to uproot them drawn by oxen taken from the Scriptures. The words of Christ, His prophets, and apostles, are seedlings

---

[2] Origen, *Homilies on Genesis*, 4.1–3; *Commentary on the Song of Songs*, II.4.27–30. Cf. also *Homilies on Exodus*, 9.3.

[3] *Commentary on the Song of Songs*, II.5.7–15. For the appropriation of this teaching by one of Origen's pupils, cf. Gregory Thaumaturgus, *Address of Thanksgiving*, 9. The traditional ascription to Gregory is defended by Timothy Barnes, *Constantine and Eusebius* (Cambridge, Mass. and London: Harvard University Press, 1981), 329 n.39.

[4] Origen, *Homilies on Judges*, 2.3.   [5] *Homilies on Genesis*, 13.3; *Homilies on Exodus*, 1.5 and 3.3.

[6] *Homilies on Jeremiah*, 5.9; *Homilies on Exodus*, 2.1.

[7] *Homilies on Jeremiah*, 2.3. Cf. also, John Clark Smith, *The Ancient Wisdom of Origen* (London and Toronto: Associated University Presses, 1992), 79–83.

to be brought on through 'memory and exercise'.[8] Otherwise, we find ourselves back in the grip of worldly pursuits.[9] Such intellectual engagement
is inseparable from the disciplining of bodily desires through abstention.
The faithful person builds a tabernacle within the heart where, in prayer
to God, the intellect sacrifices with the 'knife of self-control' the vices of
pride, anger, extravagance, and lust.[10] One of Origen's pupils wrote (with
allusion to Genesis 3:18) of how the thorns and brambles produced in the
sinful heart are cut back with both arguments and 'checks'.[11]

Christ's victory over the devil's temptations through fasting in the desert
enabled us to realise how certain demons were likewise subdued by 'prayer
and fasting' (an allusion to a variant text of Mark 9:29).[12] Penitential fasting
was only a beginning; it was to be followed by a second circumcision, the
wider cutting away of our many carnal passions.[13] Just as the Israelites
had left Egypt by way of Rameses (Exodus 12:37), so the Christian had
to part from the wealth attacked by the moths or worm indicated by this
place-name.[14] Fasting and prayer, together with 'all the pain of abstinence',
cut the hamstrings of the horses which symbolized our sensual pride or
physical desires.[15] The same spiritual combat and mortification of the flesh
was symbolized in Jael's killing of Sisara.[16] To the extent that the spiritual
life was a series of sequential processes, mortification followed upon faith
and the gift of the Spirit in preparing the Christian for God's perfection.[17]

The virtuous disciplining of appetite by reason, familiar to us from Greek
and Jewish philosophical asceticism, has been set within the narrative
of salvation history as the battleground between the opposing powers
of Christ and Satan. The philosopher's *dicta* which were rehearsed to
strengthen the mind have been replaced by Holy Writ in new spiritual
exercises. This fusion of a Christian story about sin and redemption with
the Greek philosophical project of restraint in the service of apprehending
the divine is evident in the *Address of Thanks* by one of Origen's pupils to
which I have already referred. The soul's weeds are described in terms
taken from Genesis, but the teacher's procedure is 'Socratic' in controlling
students whose behaviour closely echoes that of the wicked horse in Plato's
Phaedrus (254a and d–e). The older significance of fasting within Judaism
and Christianity as a form of mourning and humble prayer has been
subsumed.

---

[8] *Homilies on Jeremiah*, 5.6 and 13.   [9] *Commentary on the Song of Songs*, 11.5.40.
[10] *Homilies on Exodus*, 9.4.   [11] Gregory Thaumaturgus, *Address of Thanksgiving*, 7.
[12] Origen, *Homilies on Exodus*, 2.3.   [13] *Homilies on Joshua*, 1.7.   [14] *Homilies on Exodus*, 5.2.
[15] *Homilies on Joshua*, 15.3.   [16] *Homilies on Judges*, 5.5.   [17] *Homilies on Numbers*, 12.3.3.

Clement of Alexandria had rejected a literal reading of Christ's call to the rich man to sell his possessions and give the proceeds to the destitute.[18] While Origen knew this, his commentary on Matthew 19:21 offered two interpretations. An allegorical reading elaborated Clement's exposition in accordance with their common spiritual anthropology: to be perfect is to rid oneself of the irrational passions that obstruct virtue; such passions must be returned as impure spirits to the demons from which they originate. But, although Origen stands accused of disregarding the literal sense of Scripture,[19] he also defended a literal reading of the verse – perfection in the disposal of wealth – to integrate Christ's command, so understood, with his ascetic anthropology. To explain how dispossession of wealth made for virtue when it exposed the individual to temptation, he drew on Clement's theological underpinning of almsgiving: the prayers offered by the recipients of alms for their donors win a progressive acquisition of virtue.[20] Clement had cited the case of Crates to show that Jesus cannot have commanded the literal dispossession practised by pagans; Origen cited him for the opposite reason: if the pagan Crates can give up his wealth, Christians should not claim this is too difficult for them. And it was a literal reading of Matthew 19:21 which Origen presumed elsewhere in his homilies, just as he adopted a literal reading of Luke 14:33, though he confessed that he had not yet achieved in full what Christ commanded.[21]

Christians' salvation did not depend, for Origen, upon their renunciation of sexual pleasure in marriage, but such renunciation made for a purity which exalted those who embraced it above others. Thus, the perpetual virginity of Mary and Jesus could be understood as the 'first-fruits of purity in the form of chastity', a choice offering to God indicative of their pre-eminent sanctity.[22] Indeed those who wrongly believed that total sexual renunciation was required for salvation nonetheless derived great benefit from this mistake.[23] Abstention from sex within or after marriage was second in value to unbroken virginity. Marital intercourse, though not sinful, was not graced by the Spirit's presence, and made the bedroom

---

[18] Clement of Alexandria, *Quis dives salvetur*, 11.2.

[19] 'Quelque peine qu'il prenne pour illustrer le sens littéral, Origène n'a pour ce sens qu'un dédain qu'il ne cache pas.' E. de Faye, *Origène, sa vie, son oeuvre, sa pensée*, 3 vols. (Paris: E. Leroux, 1927–8), vol. I$_g$ 75.

[20] Origen, *Commentary on Matthew*, xv.17.

[21] *Homilies on Joshua*, 9.9; *Homilies on Genesis*, 16.5. For further discussion, see J. José Alviar, *Klesis: The Theology of the Christian Vocation According to Origen* (Blackrock: Four Courts Press, 1993), 181–5.

[22] *Commentary on Matthew*, x.17 (καθαρότητος τῆς ἐν ἁγνείᾳ ἀπαρχὴν), SC162, 216.

[23] *Homilies on Jeremiah*, 20.4.

an unsuitable place to pray.[24] These teachings, while defending marriage, enhanced the spiritual authority of celibate Christians, and should be seen as a key element in the later rise to prominence of celibate, ascetic bishops in the fourth century.[25]

Origen's understanding of asceticism as integral to progress in any Christian life, but as having greater purchase and more perfect form in a life of voluntary poverty and sexual renunciation, is of profound consequence for the history of Christian asceticism in the late third to fifth centuries.[26] Promoted in sermons which Origen preached to the congregation at Caesarea, and which were widely disseminated, this ascetic theology provided the seedbed or matrix from which a distinct 'ascetic' or 'monastic' life could emerge supported by the wider Christian body. The previous chapter demonstrated that permanent sexual abstinence had long been adopted by individuals, while some practised more than others the common pieties of prayer and fasting. Origen popularized a vision which united these practices, together with radical poverty and Scriptural meditation, to locate them within a single interpretative frame and in a single lifestyle.

IN THE SHADE OF THE *AGNUS CASTUS* – METHODIUS OF OLYMPUS AND CONSECRATED VIRGINS

A number of Origen's teachings were attacked after his death in the mid third century. His account of the resurrected body in particular was fiercely condemned by a learned churchman, Methodius (*c.* 260–*c.* 312/13), from Olympus in Lycia. Methodius, however, was also the author of the *Symposium*, a dialogue modelled upon Plato's work of that title, but in which the male symposiasts were replaced by a chorus of female virgins who praised virginity and *hagneia*, the virtue of sexual purity or chastity, instead of *eros*. Probably composed in the last years of the third century, the work drew partly on Irenaeus, but also on the ascetic anthropology of Clement and Origen.[27] Indeed, it is Origen's opponent who here offers us an early measure of how broadly the exegete's ascetic vision was accepted.

---

[24] *Homilies on Numbers*, 11.3.5 and 6.3.7; *On Prayer*, 31.4. Cf also, *Homilies on Exodus*, 11.7.
[25] *Homilies on Joshua*, 17.2.
[26] For Origen's delayed impact in the Syrian East through Evagrius and the late-fifth-century bishop of Mabbug, Philoxenus, see A. Vööbus, *History of Asceticism in the Syrian Orient*, vol. III (Louvain: CSCO, 1988), 123–50.
[27] L. G. Patterson, *Methodius of Olympus: Divine Sovereignty, Human Freedom, and Life in Christ* (Washington: Catholic University of America, 1997), 7–8, 83–4, 86, 88–9, 92–3, 112, and 123. For Methodius' dates and career, cf. T. D. Barnes, 'Methodius, Maximus, and Valentinus', *JThS* 30 (1979), 47–55. For an excellent close reading of the *Symposium*, cf. Jason König, 'Sympotic dialogue in the first to fifth centuries CE', in S. Goldhill (ed.), *The End of Dialogue in Antiquity* (Cambridge University Press, 2009), 102–6.

In common with Origen and the Greek philosophical tradition, Methodius understood the spiritual life as centred upon that contemplation of God which drew the rational soul into ever closer resemblance to the divine.[28] That contemplation was endangered by unruly, irrational passions: the male infants drowned by Pharaoh in the Nile were an allegory of the thoughts submerged by the devil in destructive passions, while the female infants whom he allowed to multiply were carnal, sensual promptings.[29] Like Origen, Methodius recognized the central place of disciplined meditation on the Scriptures in preventing and undoing such damage to the life of virtue.[30] Indeed, the discourses which make up the *Symposium* are largely extended meditations on Scriptural passages. Asceticism, as taught by Scripture, was an essential element in this contemplative endeavour.[31] Methodius followed Origen in holding that chastity was part of the moral excellence of those called to teach less advanced Christians.[32]

What distinguished Methodius' writings on the ascetic life from Origen was the pre-eminent role accorded to chastity, and especially virginity, in perfecting the soul.[33] Chastity, taught to humanity by the celibate Christ, was supremely capable of governing the soul, as the virgin Domnina explained.[34] The virtue anchored a moral life which would otherwise be swept away on a flood of passions; and it was therefore symbolized by the willows on which the exiled Israelites had hung their harps beside the waters of Babylon.[35] Such chastity was essential for salvation and required at least some form of sexual abstention even within a faithful marriage.[36] The married might have intercourse to beget children, but chastity forbade making procreation the mere excuse for sexual pleasure.[37] Furthermore, the virgin Thallousa argued with respect to Numbers 6:1–4 that sexual purity was a form of self-offering to God, a sacrifice and 'great prayer'.[38] We have already noted Origen's interiorization of the tabernacle where the 'knife of self-control' made an offering at the altar in excising vice. Elsewhere Origen presented the Church's faithful as an altar on which prayers rose to God, and which therefore had to be purified for this purpose.[39] Others had traditionally seen widows as an altar to God on which the rich could make an offering to God by giving alms.[40] Methodius now merged these

---

[28] Methodius, *Symposium*, VI.1.133. Cf also VII.2.153, and VIII.1.171.   [29] Ibid., IV.2.97.
[30] Ibid., I.1.14.   [31] Ibid., IX.4.247–8 and XI.1.279.   [32] Ibid., III.8.73–4.
[33] Ibid., VIII.1.171 and IX.4.251.   [34] Ibid., X.1.258 and X.4.269.   [35] Ibid., IV.3.98.
[36] Ibid., IX.4.252.   [37] Ibid., III.10.78.
[38] Ibid., V.4.116.   [39] Origen, *Homilies on Joshua*, 9.1–2.
[40] E.g., Polycarp, *Letter to the Philippians*, 4.3. On the history of this image, cf. Carolyn Osiek, 'The Widow as altar: the rise and fall of a symbol', *The Second Century* 3 (1983), 159–69.

concepts and extended the image to virgins who formed a golden altar within the holy of holies in comparison with the widows' bronze altar.[41]

By playing on its Platonic antecedents, in its literary form and in allusion to the *Phaedrus*, Methodius' *Symposium* claimed that Christianity was the true philosophy, heir to what was best in the classical tradition. Virginity actualizes a 'sublimated Erotic ideal' to take the place of Platonic Eros in the ascent to the Good.[42] Like Socrates and Phaedrus in the *Phaedrus*, the virgins converse in the shade of the highly scented *agnus castus*, but only they explicitly defend the chastity which the tree symbolizes.[43] Where the *Phaedrus* ends with a short prayer to Pan, Methodius concludes with an extended prayer to Christ.[44] If virgins already served as symbolic markers of holiness within the churches (as suggested by *Hermas*), so, in this Platonic frame, they now marked the superiority of Christianity over paganism and Judaism.

Methodius' *Symposium* inspired a new genre of sermons and treatises in praise of consecrated virginity, typified by the female virgin. The extant corpus includes a Greek homily *On Virginity*, by an unknown author from the first half of the fourth century, which shares with Methodius the image of the virgin as a 'pure altar';[45] and a sermon *On Virgins* by Eusebius of Emesa (also before 350) which follows the *Symposium* in presenting Christ as the teacher of celibacy whose advent enables our escape from demonic immorality.[46] Basil of Ancyra penned a lengthy treatise, *On the True Purity of Virginity* (before 358), which, like Methodius, draws on Plato's *Phaedrus*: the virgin's winged soul gazes on the beauty and incorruptibility of God and thus comes to share that immortality.[47] There are two letters in this genre by Athanasius, the second perhaps written between 350 and 370, while his early treatise *On the Incarnation* shares with Methodius the belief that Christ is

---

[41] Methodius, *Symposium*, v.8.130.

[42] J. Rist, 'Basil's "Neoplatonism": its background and nature', in P. Fedwick (ed.), *Basil of Caesarea: Christian, Humanist, Ascetic,* 2 vols. (Toronto: Pontifical Institute of Medieval Studies, 1981), vol 1, 178.

[43] Plato, *Phaedrus*, 230b; Methodius, *Symposium*, Prologue 8 and IX.4.250.

[44] Plato, *Phaedrus*, 279b–c; Methodius, *Symposium*, XI.1.284.

[45] Anon., *On Virginity*, II.41, ed. D. Armand and M.-C. Moons, 'Une curieuse homélie grecque inédite sur la virginité adressée aux pères de famille', *RB* 63 (1953), 42.

[46] Eusebius of Emesa, *On Virgins*, 6–8. For a summary of the sermon, which survives only in a Latin translation of the late fourth or fifth century, cf. É. M. Buytaert, *Eusèbe d'Emèse: Discours conservés en latin, textes en partie inédits*, 2 vols. (Louvain: Spicilegium Sacrum Lovaniense, 1953 and 1957), vol. I, l-lii. For the probable date of composition, cf. David Amand de Mendieta, 'La virginité chez Eusèbe d'Emèse et l'ascéticisme familial dans la première moitié du IVe siécle', *Revue d'Histoire Ecclésiastique* 50 (1955), 777–820.

[47] Basil of Ancyra, *On True Purity of Virginity*, PG 30, 672b–c; Methodius, *Symposium*, VIII.1.171 and 2.173–4.

the teacher of virginity.[48] There is also a *Treatise On Virginity* dubiously ascribed to Athanasius, and a further such work wrongly attributed to him.[49] Gregory of Nyssa drew heavily on Basil of Ancyra's earlier work, and likewise presented virginity giving wings for the ascent to God, when he wrote his own *On Virginity* no earlier than 371 and no later than 378.[50] John Chrysostom's *On Virginity* (*c*. 380–2) in turn borrowed from Gregory and earlier writers.[51] In the Latin West, Ambrose disseminated four works in this genre which originated in sermons, and which were influenced by Athanasius.[52] Jerome's *Letter to Eustochium*, probably sent in 384, fiercely advocated consecrated virginity over marriage, while a brief eulogy of the virgin Asella was explicitly intended to establish her as a model for younger women.[53] Augustine's *On Holy Virginity* (*c*. 401/2) offered a more measured account, and in turn owed a debt to Book One of Ambrose's *On Virgins* as well as earlier African authors, Tertullian and Cyprian.[54] Such works became so common that one version of Gregory's *On Virginity* dismissed many of its predecessors as rhetorical exercises.[55]

John Chrysostom's *On Virginity*, in particular, shared Methodius' aim of advancing the moral superiority of Christianity over its religious and philosophical rivals, but we should recognize the complex purposes and claims advanced through these different works, many of which were written by bishops whose leadership was threatened by doctrinal controversy. Athanasius' *Letter to Virgins*, for example, is 'primarily a polemic against the lures of Arianism'.[56] The anonymous *On Virginity* defended the freedom of young men and women to adopt celibacy against a background of

[48] Athanasius, *Letter to Virgins*, ed. with Fr. tr. by Lefort, 'S. Athanase: sur la virginité', *Muséon* 42 (1929), 197–274, Eng. tr. by D. Brakke, *Athanasius and the Politics of Asceticism* (Oxford: Clarendon Press, 1995), 274–91; *Letter to the Virgins who went to Jerusalem*, ed. with Fr. tr. J. Lebon, 'S. Athanase: lettre à des vierges qui étaient allées prier à Jérusalem et qui étaient revenues', *Muséon* 41 (1928), 169–216, Eng. tr. Brakke, *Athanasius*, 292–302; *On the Incarnation*, 51.

[49] Athanasius (?), *Treatise On Virginity*, ed. with Fr. tr. J. Lebon in *Muséon* 40 (1927), 205–48, Eng. tr. by Brakke, *Athanasius*, 303–9; Ps.-Athanasius, *On Virginity*, PG 28, 251–82.

[50] Gregory of Nyssa, *On Virginity*, 2.2. For his debt to Basil of Ancyra, cf. M. Aubineau, *Grégoire de Nysse, Traité sur la virginité*, SC 119 (1966), 137–42.

[51] John Chrysostom, *On Virginity*, ed. H. Musurillo, *Jean Chrysostome, La Virginité*, SC 125 (1966).

[52] Ambrose, *On Virgins* (by 377), *On Virginity* (*c*. 378), *On the Consecration of a Virgin* (391/2), *Exhortation on Virginity* (*c*. 393–5), ed. F. Gori, *Sant'Ambrogio, Verginità e vedovanza* (Milan and Rome: Città nuova, 1989). For an Eng. translation of *On Virgins*, cf. Boniface Ramsey, *Ambrose* (London and New York: Routledge, 1997), 71–116.

[53] Jerome, *Epp.* 22 and 24, CSEL 54, 143–210 and 214–17.

[54] Augustine, *On Holy Virginity*, ed. P. G. Walsh, *De bono coniugali, De sancta virginitate* (Oxford: Clarendon Press, 2001), 65–147.

[55] Gregory of Nyssa, *On Virginity*, 1.1. The words appear in what has been termed the 'second edition' of the treatise, and scholars dispute whether this should be ascribed to Gregory himself. Among the now lost treatises are works in verse and prose by Pope Damasus referred to by Jerome in *Ep.* 22.22.

[56] Elm, 'Virgins of God', 353.

opposition by fathers or, in the case of slaves, their owners.[57] The author defined the father's role in testing and protecting his child's chosen way of life, and gave value to that role in naming him a new Abraham who did not withhold his child from God as a living sacrifice.[58] Eusebius of Emesa likewise drew on the story of Abraham and Isaac to present the virgin as a sacrificial holocaust; he defended consecrated virginity against men angered at the failure of certain virgins to keep their vow.[59] Augustine, on the other hand, was concerned to relate the spiritual value of virginity to the identity of the Church as virgin bride of Christ, and to secure the good intention of the individual virgin from destructive pride in a state of life higher than that of the ordinary married Christian: the bishop effectively turned a treatise on virginity into a work on humility.[60]

Methodius wrote remarkably little about what form the virginal life should take: the significance of virginity is independent of such considerations as the relations between male and female ascetics, or the path to be negotiated by the female virgin between prayerful seclusion and public activity in worship or charity. These, however, were divisive issues inviting local determination; in contrast to the *Symposium*, many subsequent works sought to relate the inner meaning of virginity to its detailed practice. As a proper diet was generally recognized as an essential prerequisite in the control of sexual appetite, Basil of Ancyra signalled the need to consider *what* one ate as well as *how much*, and warned against taking too much salt.[61] Jerome urged Eustochium to avoid wine like poison.[62] Both writers restricted where a female virgin went, though each identified contrasting dangers. Basil focused on the danger to which virgins were exposed through charitable care of the poor, such as the preparation of corpses prior to burial, and through their service to the clergy. They were to consider what alleyways they were being asked to enter, the time of day, whether they went alone or in company, and their own age. Above all, it was necessary to undertake such activities with a mind dead to the feminine sensuality that was otherwise theirs by nature.[63] Jerome, on the other hand, warned Eustochium against visiting respectable Roman matrons.[64]

Concern that the female virgin avoid male company wherever possible, should stay away from the baths, and that her hands, feet, and head be

[57] Anon., *On Virginity*, II.II and VIII.IIO.   [58] Ibid., II.15–19, 29, and V.61.
[59] Eusebius, *On Virgins*, 3, II, and 25.   [60] Augustine, *On Holy Virginity*, 2, II, and 52.
[61] Basil of Ancyra, *On the Purity of True Virginity*, 8–10. Cf. Teresa M. Shaw, 'Creation, virginity and diet in fourth-century Christianity: Basil of Ancyra's *On the True Purity of Virginity*', *Gender & History* 9.3 (1997), 579–96.
[62] Jerome, *Ep.* 22.8.
[63] Basil of Ancyra, *On the Purity of True Virginity*, 19 and 52.   [64] Jerome, *Ep.* 22.16.

completed hidden from view, implies that female virgins did not always so conduct themselves, and claimed a freedom to move about in public that some at least found objectionable.[65] The charitable ministry of these women was subject to conflicting accounts of the virtues: Basil of Ancyra warned virgins that in some cases it was better to be accused of discourtesy or unkindness than to go about without restriction.[66] Such counsel both restricted the freedom of these women, and secured it through stipulation of conditions for their honourable conduct.

Counsel no doubt served in part to bolster the standing of those who gave it. The exaltation of virginity as superior to marriage by celibate bishops such as Athanasius, Ambrose, and Augustine, enhanced their spiritual authority over married clergy and laity. Stipulation of the ascetic practices and wider conduct to be observed by consecrated virgins articulated a clerical authority over these men and women themselves. Athanasius was explicit about his own authority: he was the servant or steward employed by the virgins' heavenly bridegroom, and as such he was to exhort them to a faithful observance of their ascetic discipline.[67] Such texts, however, also measure just how limited was the authority constructed in this way. The attack on syneisaktism, already seen in Cyprian, is common to a number of these later texts.[68] Yet the repeated denunciations are not simple prohibitions, and their recurrence shows both how long this practice retained its place in urban churches, and its expression of what Basil could only decry as the 'false name of charity (*agape*)'.[69] Where councils prohibited syneisaktism, they, too, were ineffective.[70] The Council of Nicaea restricted its condemnation to clerics who sheltered such women, but even then excepted those 'free from all suspicions'.[71] Likewise, the texts contain

---

[65] Athanasius (?), *Treatise on Virginity*, tr. Brakke, *Athanasius*, 304–5, and 307.

[66] Basil of Ancyra, *On the Purity of True Virginity*, 53, PG 30.776b–c. I take this to be the sense of ἐπὶ τῷ ἀδεξίῳ. Thus, where Susanna Elm thinks that Arius may have given virgins greater public freedom, because of the charges made against his permitting them to roam the streets, I would see a hostile exploitation of an existing ambivalence in the social expectations placed upon these women. Cf. Elm, *Virgins*, 352–3.

[67] Athanasius, *Letter to Virgins*, tr. Brakke, *Athanasius*, 285.

[68] Eusebius of Emesa, *On Virgins*, 20–1; Basil of Ancyra, *On the Purity of True Virginity*, 43; Athanasius, *Letter to the Virgins who went to Jerusalem*, in Brakke, *Athanasius*, 298–301; Gregory of Nyssa, *On Virginity*, XXIII.4; Jerome, *Ep.* 22.14. Outside the genre, further texts against *syneisaktism* include Chrysostom's *Against those who live with Virgins*, tr. E. A. Clark, *Jerome, Chrysostom, and Friends* (New York and Toronto: Edwin Mellon Press, 1979), 164–208.

[69] Basil of Ancyra, *On the Purity of True Virginity*, 43, PG 30, 756b.

[70] Ancyra (AD 314), canon 19, in P.-P. Joannou (ed.), *Discipline générale antique (IVe – Ixe s.)*, 2 vols. (Rome: Pontificia commissione per la redazione del codice di diritto canonico orientale, 1962) vol. 1.2, 70; Carthage (AD 345), in C. Munier (ed.), *Concilia Africae*, A.345–A. 525, CCSL 149 (Turnhout: Brepols, 1974), 5.

[71] Nicaea (325), canon 3, tr. Elm, *Virgins*, 48.

numerous attacks on the abandonment of virginity by women who had married.[72] Councils stigmatized such women by denying them access to the Eucharist.[73] We must presume that for many families preservation of a religious ideal often came second to the economic or other social advantage of marriage at times of need. Yet, if the clerical authority constructed through condemnation did not greatly alter practice in this respect, authors earned moral capital which they spent elsewhere.

Most ascetics dwelt at home, or with an ascetic of the opposite sex contrary to the ideal reflected in many of our texts, but it was also acceptable for a female virgin lacking any family to live with another such woman in mutual companionship and for mutual protection.[74] Occasionally the slaves of a rich ascetic would be manumitted as fellow ascetics who formed a quasi-coenobitic cell within the household. Jerome implies that in such cases it was rare for the social distances between these virgins to be sufficiently transcended for them to eat together.[75] An ascetic household may lie behind two early-fourth-century letters from Egypt which show a certain Didyme and her sisters engaged in various small-scale transactions over sandals, grapes, and an ostrich egg![76] The internal structure of such (probably small) communities of ascetic women is hidden from us, though we occasionally glimpse one of the sisters as the superior.[77] The early texts are silent, however, about large coenobitic communities for men or women which did not exist in the urban churches before the mid fourth century. How many virgins existed in the Christian population, or what proportion of the congregation they comprised in a given place during the late third, fourth, and early fifth centuries is impossible to ascertain. On the rare occasions when numbers are given in our literary sources, they may be subject to exaggeration. All we can conclude is that they formed a growing minority.[78]

At Alexandria female virgins enjoyed sufficient freedom of movement for some to go on pilgrimage to Bethlehem and Jerusalem.[79] There was no

---

[72] Basil of Ancyra, *On the Purity of True Virginity*, 37; Eusebius, *On Virgins*, 5; cf. also, Jerome, *Ep.* 22.6 and 22.13; and Basil (?), *Ep.* 46.

[73] E.g., Council of Elvira (306), canon 13, tr. Elm, *Virgins*, 26.

[74] Eusebius, *On Virgins*, 22.   [75] Jerome, *Ep.* 22.29.

[76] James E. Goehring, 'The origins of monasticism', in H. W. Attridge and G. Hata (eds.), *Eusebius, Christianity, and Judaism* (Leiden: Brill, 1992), 243.

[77] E.g., Athanasius, *Life of Antony*, 54 (Antony's sister in her old age).

[78] Epiphanius claimed that Arius attracted the support of seven hundred virgins at Alexandria (Elm, *Virgins*, 352). Chrysostom (*Homilies on Matthew*, 66.3) counted three thousand widows and virgins at Antioch. Palladius (*Lausiac History*, 67.1) counted some two thousand virgins at Ancyra by the early fifth century.

[79] Athanasius, *Letter to the Virgins who went to Jerusalem*, tr, Brakke, *Athanasius*, 292.

single age at which a girl might be consecrated. At Rome, Asella had been dedicated at the tender age of ten.[80] Basil of Caesarea sought to impose a minimum age of sixteen or seventeen.[81] An older female virgin might train a child in the ascetic discipline expected of her.[82] How the women appeared also varied. Basil of Ancyra encouraged female ascetics to make themselves look more like men.[83] Some wore black; others wore clothing normally worn only by men, and cut short their hair in the male fashion, though these last two practices were anathematized by the Council of Gangra in perhaps 355.[84] The ascetics' prayer lives centred on fasting and the psalms, which the literate might read at home in a Psalter, while at church they regularly attended the late-night vigils.[85] A great many abstained from wine. At Rome, to judge by what Jerome advised Eustochium against doing, but for which he praised Asella, they assiduously visited martyrs' shrines, and attended funerals.[86] Jerome praised Asella for going to the shrines all but invisibly, a neat trick that on paper resolved the tension between conflicting virtues. The status of these consecrated virgins was raised by the custom in some places of naming deceased virgins during the Eucharistic liturgy, though not in the same exalted position as the martyrs.[87] Celibates were not required to embrace total or communal poverty, and many did not.[88] In this, social and economic factors interacted. Many young female virgins depended on the family's wealth for their home and security. Outside the family home, not every ascetic could count on the almsgiving of fellow Christians.

If consecrated virgins did not always live as those who wrote on virginity thought they should, did they share those authors' rarefied understanding of virginity? In previous chapters it was necessary to distinguish between competing readings of common practices. Should we distinguish between more popular beliefs and an elite understanding of virginity located within a broader asceticism which aimed at contemplative assimilation to God? Evidence for a different understanding is surprisingly hard to find. Jerome

---

[80] Jerome, *Ep.* 24.2.   [81] Basil, *Ep.* 199, canon 18.   [82] Jerome, *Ep.* 127.5.
[83] Basil of Ancyra, *On the Purity of True Virginity*, 18.
[84] Jerome, *Ep.* 22.27; Council of Gangra, canons 13 and 17, in Joannou, *Discipline*, vol. 1.2, 94–5 and 96. Cf. also Jerome, *Ep.* 24.3 and 4 (dark and rough clothing). For imperial legislation against women cutting their hair in this way, cf. Elm, *Virgins*, 218.
[85] Anon, *On Virginity*, III.56. Cf also, Athanasius, *Encyclical Letter*, 4; Eusebius, *On Virgins*, 13; Athanasius (?), *Treatise on Virginity*, tr. Brakke, *Athanasius*, 305.
[86] Jerome, *Epp.* 22.17 and 27, and 24.4. For funerals, cf. also Anon., *On Virginity*, II.37.
[87] Augustine, *On Holy Virginity*, 46.
[88] Augustine, *On Holy Virginity*, 46; Jerome, *Ep.* 22.38. For an Egyptian *apotaktikos* who held property, see E. A. Judge 'The earliest use of monachos for "monk" (P. Coll. Youtie 77) and the origins of monasticism', *Jahrbuch für Antike und Christentum* 20 (1977), 72–89, at 82.

described ascetics who 'pretend' to be overcome by sorrow and undertake extensive fasts.[89] Fasting certainly retained its meaning as a sign of mourning and of penitence; but ascetics may have understood such penitence within a larger contemplative picture. When Augustine urges virgins to reflect on the suffering humanity of Christ, and so on his humility, he assumes they are familiar with contemplation of the godhead: 'You are at liberty, and your heart is free from the bonds of marriage. Gaze on the beauty of your lover; contemplate him as equal to the Father and also subject to his mother; as one who while still lord in the heavens became a servant on earth; as one who both created all things and was created among all things.'[90] The rhetorical structure of the passage moves from what is taken for granted to what should be given fresh consideration. Gregory of Nyssa's treatise acknowledged that people commonly saw the virginal life as one of freedom from corruption.[91] The gap between the elite and commonplace is thus narrower than in previous chapters. Virgins understood themselves to be brides of Christ, who by their continence already lived the angelic life of heaven.

ORIGEN AND EGYPTIAN MONASTICISM: I – ANTONY OF EGYPT

At Alexandria, Origen's ascetic teachings and poverty inspired Pierius, head of the catechetical school in the final decades of the third century, whose eloquent preaching, writings, and 'life without possessions' won him the nickname of 'the Younger Origen'.[92] Mid-third- and late-third-century fragments of Origen's homilies and other works have been found at several Egyptian sites, and at least two codices of works by Origen were apparently listed in an Egyptian library catalogue drawn up before 312.[93] At the opening of the fourth century, Origen's asceticism probably influenced Hieracas, a learned Egyptian exegete from Leontopolis in the southern Nile delta, whom Epiphanius loathed as a heretic but considered 'awesome in his asceticism'. Hieracas' followers formed communities in which marriage was refused, syneisaktism practised, and a diet adopted without meat and wine.[94] What influence Origen exercised on

---

[89] Jerome, *Ep.* 22.28.
[90] Augustine, *On Holy Virginity*, 55, tr. P. G. Walsh, *De bono coniugali, De sancta virginitate* (Oxford: Clarendon Press, 2001), 145.
[91] Gregory of Nyssa, *On Virginity*, 1.
[92] Eusebius, *Church History*, VII.32.27; Jerome, *De viris illustribus*, 76.
[93] Cf. C. Roberts, *Manuscript, Society and Belief in Early Christian Egypt* (London: Oxford University Press, 1979), 9, 24, and 63; idem, 'Two Oxford papyri', *ZNW* 37 (1938), 184–8.
[94] Epiphanius, *Panarion* 67.1 and 3. Cf also, Elm, *Virgins*, 339–42.

Egyptian monasticism is highly disputed, but it seems probable, as we shall see, that he profoundly (if indirectly) influenced the semi-anchoretic tradition associated with Antony of Egypt, the so-called 'father of monks'.

In reflecting on Moses' exodus journey, Origen had written that before the soul is perfected, it dwells in the desert 'where it may be trained in the Lord's commandments, and its faith tested by temptations'. Growing in virtue, the soul is led from one test to the next before it finally crosses into the promised land.[95] In around 285, Antony of Egypt took this metaphor literally and withdrew into the desert. He had already adopted an ascetic life which brought him into conflict with demonic forces. Aged twenty or so, in around AD 270, he had given away the substantial part of the family fortune, left his sister to be raised as a dedicated virgin in the care of another virgin, and had adopted near his former home an ascetic life of partial solitude in which he was trained by other nearby ascetics. Athanasius in his *Life of Antony* portrayed him as a docile student who imitated whatever was best in his teachers. From them he learnt the practices of fasting, scriptural meditation, manual labour and prayer, almsgiving, and to reduce his sleep which he took lying on the ground. His first move was to a tomb in the village cemetery.[96] Next, however, Antony left this village world and struck out into the desert some halfway between Lycopolis and Alexandria.[97] We cannot know if he was the first to do so, only that it was as yet uncommon. Antony occupied an abandoned fort near Pispir and remained there for some twenty years in a symbolic isolation which increasingly attracted visitors seeking counsel or other help.[98] Although the solitary left his retreat to visit Alexandria during the persecution by Maximin Daia in around 311–13, he then withdrew to an even more remote area. Here Antony guarded his solitude and issued guidance to other would-be hermits.[99] His growing authority as an interpreter of the ascetic life is attested by letters of instruction which he sent to other solitaries, by Athanasius' *Life*, and by Antony's appearance as a source of authoritative advice in the *Apophthegmata Patrum*, the *Sayings of the Desert Fathers* collected and then redacted in a long process from the early fifth century.[100] This monastic authority, on occasion, extended into wider church affairs.

---

[95] Origen, *Homilies on Numbers*, 27.5.
[96] Athanasius, *Life of Antony*, 3–4, and 7–8.   [97] G. Bartelink, *Vie d'Antoine*, SC 400 (1994), 44.
[98] Athanasius, *Life of Antony*, 12–14.   [99] Ibid., 46, 49, 54–5.
[100] For an introduction to the *Apophthegmata*, cf. Douglas Burton-Christie, *The Word in the Desert: Scripture and the Quest for Holiness in Early Christian Monasticism* (Oxford University Press, 1993), 76–103.

Antony supported the pro-Nicene ascetics of Alexandria by letters to those in power and by visiting the city in AD 337 or 338.[101]

The seven extant letters ascribed to Antony have often been dismissed as inauthentic, but scholars led by Samuel Rubenson now accept their authenticity.[102] *Letter* I appears to address beginners in the solitary or semi-anchoretic life and is of great importance in understanding how Antony saw the ascetic project. All are called to repentance, by the law implanted within us at the creation, by the Mosaic law, and by the sufferings which result from sin. Repentance requires purification, which opens the mind to the wisdom given by the Spirit, and combats the disorder in body and soul. This disorder is largely a matter of sinful desires, which Antony understands as improper motions originating in excessive consumption and demonic temptation.[103] The anthropology owes much to Origen, who had distinguished between the soul's natural drives and the impurities that had to be removed if the soul's proper vitality and virtue were to shine out.[104]

Antony advises the would-be monks on how to tackle the wrongful motions affecting each part of the body. Ears were to be trained not to enjoy malicious gossip. Sinful movements of the soul – pride, hatred, impatience – were tackled through a way of life structured around 'prolonged fasts, vigils, much study of the Word of God and many prayers, as well as the renunciation of the world and human things, humility, and contrition'.[105] Asceticism undoes the fall to return the body to its proper condition, which is also its proper subordination to the spiritual life. Antony twice quotes in *Letter* I Paul's statement 'I keep under my body, and bring it into subjection' (1 Cor. 9:27). The body purified by the Spirit resembles the spiritual body which we shall receive at the resurrection.

The body must be kept in its proper place, because the human person is a 'rational being',[106] and should know himself or herself in his or her intellectual substance or 'spiritual essence'.[107] This directs the believer to God, and to God's will for the creation: 'he who knows himself also knows the dispensations of his Creator, and what he does for his creatures'.[108]

---

[101] Athanasius, *Life of Antony*, 69–71, and 86; *Historia Arianorum*, 14; *Festal Index*, 10. For a discussion of whether Antony's visit was at Athanasius' invitation, cf. Elm, *Virgins*, 364.

[102] For an English translation of the letters as these have been reconstructed from versions in Coptic, Arabic, Latin, and Syriac, see S. Rubenson, *The Letters of St Antony: Monasticism and the Making of a Saint* (Minneapolis: Fortress Press, 1995), 197–231.

[103] Antony, *Letter* I, in Rubenson, *Letters*, 197–9.

[104] Origen, *Homilies on Joshua*, 22.4.   [105] Antony, *Letter* I, tr. Rubenson, *The Letters*, 202.

[106] *Letter* 2, tr. Rubenson, *The Letters*, 203 and 204.

[107] *Letter* 2, tr. Rubenson, *The Letters*, 205. Greek version, οὐσία νοερά.

[108] *Letter* 3, tr. Rubenson, *The Letters*, 206.

Asceticism avails us nothing if we fail to exercise due 'discernment' of the spiritual wars in which we now find ourselves. Christ has won for believers the resurrection of the body from death, but Antony prefers to write of the resurrection of the heart or mind lifted up from the earth.[109] The evidence for Origen's indirect influence on Antony seems strong.[110] Origen had written that 'just as that one well which is the word of God becomes wells and fountains and countless rivers, so the soul of man, which is made to the image of God is capable of containing and producing wells and fountains and rivers. However . . . the wells that are in our souls need someone to dig them out. They have to be cleansed and everything earthly taken away from them that those springs of spiritual sensibility which God has put there may produce pure and wholesome waters.'[111] In this digging out, scripture was a precious aid, and Rubenson has argued that Antony interprets scripture in a manner which owes much to Origen.[112] Antony sees a profound continuity between Old and New Testaments: the Church, the house of truth, is founded by Moses, while he can address his fellow solitaries or monks as 'holy Israelite children'.[113]

In the region of Arsinoë, semi-anchoretic communities sprang up where scattered huts allowed for periods of comparative solitude interspersed with gatherings for prayer in church. Two sites quickly became famous: Nitria and Kellia (*the Cells*). Nitria, sixty kilometres south of Alexandria, was reportedly founded by Amoun, a married man who had decided with his wife that they should go their separate ways in order to lead an ascetic life.[114] The monks assembled from their individual 'cells' for a liturgy on Saturdays and Sundays. In 338 or thereabouts, Amoun, with Antony's blessing, created Kellia in a more remote location, where, according to Rufinus, monks who had previously lived at Nitria could occupy cells further removed from one another, but still meet on Saturdays and Sundays in church. The site was excavated from 1965 and 1990 to reveal that each 'cell' comprised two to four rooms within a sunken courtyard. Each courtyard had its well and

---

[109] *Letters* 2, 3, 6, and 7, in Rubenson, *The Letters*, 204, 207, 222, and 227.

[110] Rubenson, *The Letters*, 60, 66–7, 71, and 76–8; P. Bright, 'The combat of demons in Antony and Origen', in W. A. Bienert and U. Kühneweg, *Origeniana Septima* (Leuven: Peeters, 1999), 339–43; J. Roldanus, 'Origène, Antoine et Athanase; leur interconnexion dans la Vie et les Lettres', *SP* 26 (1993), 389–414.

[111] Origen, *Homilies on Numbers,* 12.1.5, tr. A. Squire, *Asking the Fathers* (London: SPCK, 1973), 107.

[112] Rubenson, *Letters*, 72. Rubenson (ibid., 51) also points out that Antony's regular citation of Proverbs 9:9 (*Give instruction to a wise man, and he will be still wiser*), when apologizing at the end of his letters for what he had omitted, has parallels in Origen, but it is not used by the latter author in the same way. Cf. Antony, *Letters*, 2, 3, 6, and 7, in Rubenson, *Letters*, 205, 209, 224, 229, and 231; Origen, *Homilies on Leviticus*, 1.1 (SC 286, 70), and *Homilies on Numbers*, 14.1 (SC 442, 162).

[113] Antony, *Letters*, 5, and 6, in Rubenson, *Letters*, 212 and 216.   [114] Palladius, *Lausiac History*, 8.

each house a chapel, identified by a niche in the east-facing wall.[115] Near the church, on the site's periphery, was a centre where gifts to the community were stored for distribution to the individual monks or given away to needy pilgrims.

This semi-anchoritic monasticism is also reflected in the *Sayings of the Desert Fathers* which are known to us in various collections organized either alphabetically by the name of the Father whose saying is recorded or systematically by topic.[116] Graham Gould has shown that these sayings witness to the common life that emerged at Scetis in Lower Egypt (the modern Wadi al-Natrun), a site further south than Nitria and Kellia. The sayings highlight the relationship of the *abba* (father) and his pupil. The *abba* first taught him the practicalities of monastic life, but then trained him over a much longer period in self-knowledge, in the virtues, especially humility, and the fear of God. Obedience set the novice in the right direction by countering pride: 'The old men said, 'If you see a young man climbing up to heaven by his own will, grab his foot and pull him down, for this is good for him.''[117] But obedience, though it was demanded, could not be enforced. If the disciple chose not to obey, the *abba* had to live with his disobedience. Gould has reconstructed the type of loose community which the monks struggled to build, with its emphasis on poverty and an individual's manual labour, but characterized also by an interior disposition of charity, non-judgementalism, and restraint of anger. It was remembered that Abba Ammonas, who was Antony's disciple, said 'I have spent fourteen years in Scetis asking God night and day to grant me the victory over anger.'[118] Solitaries shared a common ascetic vision, but the exact form of that asceticism, how strictly to fast, how often to visit a neighbour, when to read, pray, and work, varied from monk to monk.

Soon after 356 an idealized version of this desert asceticism was encapsulated in the figure of Antony created by Athanasius in his *Life* of the saint.[119] Athanasius described Antony in terms which passed on to him the mantle of the Old Testament prophets Moses, Elijah, and Elisha.[120]

---

[115] G. Descoeudres, 'Le désert des Kellia', in *Connaissance des Pères de l'Église* 72 (1998), 31–2.

[116] The principal collections are the *Collectio Graeca Alphabetica* or *Alphabetikon* (GA), PG 65, 72–440, tr. B. Ward, *The Sayings of the Desert Fathers: The Alphabetical Collection* (London and Oxford: Mowbrays, 1975); the *Collectio Graeca Anonyma* (GN), Fr. tr. by L. Regnault, *Les Sentences des Pères du désert: Série des anonymes* (Solesmes, 1985); the *Collectio Graeca Systematica* (GS); and the *Collectio Latina Systematica* (PJ), PL 73, 855–1022.

[117] *Apophthegmata Patrum*, GN 244, tr. Graham Gould, *The Desert Fathers on Monastic Community* (Oxford: Clarendon Press, 1993), 29.

[118] *Apophthegmata Patrum*, GA, Ammonas 3, tr. B. Ward, *The Sayings*, 22.

[119] G. Bartelink, *Vie d'Antoine*, SC 400, 27.   [120] Athanasius, *Life of Antony*, 7, 34, and 54.

The solitary's contest with the demons was a new Christian athleticism and form of martyrdom: Antony was 'daily giving witness (*martyrōn*) in his discernment of right and wrong, and combative in contests for the faith'.[121] The bishop thus endowed the monk with the authority of the prophets and martyrs to witness to the truth of Nicene Christology and condemn Arianism.[122]

The work stressed the wholehearted commitment or zeal of the saint (his *spoudē* and *prothumia*).[123] It was a dedication which Antony taught others; and the author claimed it for himself in answering the request for a *Life* that would inspire others to the same zeal.[124] This virtue was meant to be catching; it was the necessary defence against a like eagerness on the part of the enemy.[125] Athanasius explicitly asserted that 'the life of Antony provides monks with a model of asceticism' and stressed how this model was an inspiration for female virgins as well as men.[126] The *Life* ensured that this model was widely influential across the empire. A Coptic version was read within Egypt. Within five years a Latin translation had been made by Evagrius of Antioch, and it is likely that a second Latin version also circulated. Augustine's *Confessions* suggest just how powerful an inspiration this model proved: two imperial officers chanced upon the book in the house of some ascetics at Trier; as one read 'a change began to occur in that hidden place within him' where only God could see; 'his mind was being stripped of the world'. Not only do both men renounce their careers to embrace the 'glorious combat' of monastic life; the women to whom they were betrothed become consecrated virgins.[127]

ORIGEN IN THE EAST – BASIL OF CAESAREA

We shall see more of Origen's influence on Egyptian monasticism later in the chapter, but I look next at how Origen affected the development of religious life elsewhere in the Graeco-Roman world, through the writings of Basil the Great (*c.* 330–*c.* 378), bishop of Caesarea from 370. Not long

---

[121] Ibid., 12, 46, and 47 (καθ᾽ ἡμέραν μαρτυρῶν τῇ συνειδήσει καὶ ἀγωνιζόμενος τοῖς τῆς πίστεως ἄθλοις), SC 400, 166, 258, and 262.

[122] Ibid., 82.

[123] Ibid., 3, 4, 7, 11, 12, 13, 46, 50, and 93, SC 400, 136, 138, 140, 150, 154, 164, 166, 168, 170, 260, 270, and 372.

[124] Ibid., Prol. 2 and 5; 15, 16, 18, 46, 55, 89, 91, 94. [125] Ibid., 86, 88.

[126] *Life of Antony*, Preface, 3 (ἔστι γὰρ μοναχοῖς ἱκανὸς χαρακτὴρ πρὸς ἄσκησιν ὁ Ἀντωνίου βίος), *Life of Antony*, and 88, SC 400, 126 and 360–2.

[127] Augustine, *Confessions*, VIII.6.15, tr. M. Boulding, *Confessions* (New York: New City Press, 1997), 197.

after completing his literary and philosophical studies at Athens, and after
his baptism in 357, Basil was an enthusiastic visitor to the semi-anchoretic
monks of Egypt and Palestine. A much later letter tells how he admired
their self-control in fasting, their staying awake in prayer, a life eloquent
of sharing in Christ's death so as to be strangers in this world but citizens
of heaven.[128] On return from Egypt, he withdrew to a secluded spot on
his family estate at Annesi. Here, in semi-anchoretic fashion, he could
both pray in solitude and cross the river Iris to the home which his sister
Macrina had turned into a community of female ascetics. Here, too, some-
time between 358 and 365, Basil studied Origen's exegesis with Gregory
Nazianzen.[129] Yet monastic retreat was repeatedly broken by the demands
of a wider Church: Basil was ordained lector, then presbyter, and in 365 he
definitively abandoned the semi-anchoretic life to assist the elderly bishop
of Caesarea. In this he was inspired by Eustathius (b. *c.* 300), an ascetic cleric
at Caesarea and Constantinople who had become bishop of Sebaste by 356
and who visited Basil at Annesi in the years which followed.[130] From this
matrix of Greek philosophy, Christian scriptural reflection, and monastic
experience, Basil developed an ascetic vision both similar to Origen's and
distinctively his own, as he advocated, and legislated for, a monastic life in
close relation to the urban churches.

Before Basil abandoned Annesi he wrote that prayer imprinted 'a clear
understanding of God in the soul' by virtue of which God dwelt there
through 'continual recollection' uninterrupted by 'earthly worries'. The
mind is not 'thrown into confusion by unforeseen passions', and 'the lover
of God, to flee everything, withdraws close to God and banishing those
things that incite us to evil, devotes himself to those practices conducive
to virtue'.[131] It is a view familiar from Platonic philosophy, and from
Origen's ascetic theology.[132] Solitude was valuable for detaching oneself
from mundane pleasures and concerns so as to concentrate on God 'without
ownership, livelihood, or public engagement'. In quiet seclusion, where
sleep was interrupted by periods of prayer, the ascetic could train the

---

[128] Basil, *Ep.* 223.2.
[129] Socrates, *Church History*, IV.26. The Commentary on the Song of Songs was certainly known to
the compilers of the *Philocalia*, traditionally said to be Basil and Gregory Nazianzen, though for
doubts on Basil's authorship, cf. Marguerite Harl, *Origène: Philocalie, 1–20, Sur les Écritures*, SC 302
(1983), 24. For Basil's familiarity with Origen's *Homilies on Numbers*, cf. J. Gribomont, 'Esoterisme
et tradition dans le Traité du Saint-Esprit de saint Basile', in *Oecumenica, an Annual Symposium of
Ecumenical Research* (Minneapolis: Augsburg Press, 1967), 22–58.
[130] Basil, *Ep.* 223.5; Elm, *Virgins*, 107, 125, and 212.   [131] Basil, *Ep.* 2.4.
[132] For this general rather than a specific Neoplatonic background to *Letter 2*, cf. Rist, 'Basil's "Neoplatonism"', 213.

mind with frequent readings from Scripture, the singing of hymns, and prayer which kept the mind focused on God. Humility and penitence were manifest in the ascetic's dishevelled appearance, his shabby clothing with tunic and belt, all of which Basil carefully specifies, and in a simple diet of bread, water, and vegetables eaten at a single daily meal. The companionship which mitigated this solitude was in turn to be disciplined by attention on how and when to speak.[133]

Yet, in his later writings, Basil stressed that such solitude, and the prayer life it enabled, had to be rigorously subordinated to the command of Christ to love one's neighbour. An ascetic life in common with others was thus preferable to isolation: 'the love of Christ does not allow us each to be concerned solely with his own interests . . . Now the solitary life has one aim, the service of the needs of the individual. But this is plainly in conflict with the law of love'.[134] The withdrawal from society which he previously understood as crucial to contemplative prayer had to be interiorized as a metaphorical 'withdrawing from one's own wishes'.[135] This self-abnegation was hard to accomplish without *some* form of actual withdrawal from life 'amid the crowds', but this now meant membership of an appropriate Christian community. Basil urged one group of hermits to band together in community and sent an ascetic to supervise their progress presumably as their superior.[136]

Basil was consulted by numerous ascetics on how best to lead this common life, and many of his letters answered specific questions.[137] These *ad hoc* rulings were collected together and edited, both in Basil's lifetime, and long after his death, to form an influential body of regulations which have held an important place in the formation of Byzantine monks and Western Benedictines. Rufinus translated an early collection into Latin in around 396/7 for Ursacius, an Italian abbot. The regulations survive in two types: very short answers or statements, the so-called *Shorter Rules*, and more elaborate answers, the *Longer Rules*, which may show Basil systematically elaborating on paper what were once shorter oral answers. Both types are found in the two main extant collections, the *Small asceticon*, translated into Latin by Rufinus, and a compendium known as the *Great asceticon*.[138]

---

[133] Basil, *Ep.* 2.3–6.
[134] *Longer Rules*, 7.1, PG 31.928d–929a, tr. A. Holmes, *A Life Pleasing to God: The Spirituality of the Rules of St Basil* (London: Darton, Longman and Todd, 2000), 139.
[135] Basil, *Longer Rules*, 6.1, PG 31.925c, ἡ τῶν θελημάτων ἑαυτοῦ ἀναχώρησις.
[136] *Ep.* 295.   [137] E.g., Basil, *Letter* 22.
[138] P. Rousseau, *Basil of Caesarea* (Berkeley, Los Angeles and Oxford: University of California Press, 1994), 192 and 356–7.

What in Basil's view was an appropriate Christian community for ascetics?[139] Opposing imperatives of withdrawal from distractions and service of the wider community led Basil to favour monastic communities, one for men and one for women, in a given district or suburb from which they could go about their business clearly identified by their distinctive dress.[140] Here they could carry out in a new context the charitable care of the poor we have seen practised by consecrated virgins and which may also have characterized the asceticism promoted by Eustathius.[141] Basil's hostel for the destitute, the *basileiados*, was staffed by monks and located in the suburbs of Caesarea.[142] It was there that a sixth-century commentator found a manuscript containing the *Shorter Rules* (287–313). *Shorter Rule* 155 in turn shows ascetics working as nurses in such an establishment: 'we who serve the sick in the hospital are taught to serve them with such a disposition as if they were brothers of the Lord'. It determines how to respond when the sick behave badly.[143] Since love of neighbour precluded physical isolation, quiet had to be created within the monastic community through restraint over what was said by whom and when.[144]

The proper way to belong to such a community was through voluntary renunciation of wealth.[145] When Basil looked back on his conversion to a life of Christian virtue, he remembered it partly in terms made famous by Athanasius in describing the call of Antony: he read the Gospel call to find perfection in the sale of possessions and their distribution to the needy.[146] Renunciation of private property served a deeper self-denial in the loss of self-determination and in dedication to the service of others. This Basil termed a form of slavery: 'No one should be his own master, but each should think and act in every respect as though given by God into slavery for the brethren who share one same mind, though each in his own allotted place.'[147] Renunciation extended to family ties by the married, but the latter might not separate without the consent of their spouse. They were to be questioned on this before admission into the monastic community.[148]

---

[139] For Basil's monastic goals and rulings, cf. S. Giet, *Les Idées et l'action sociales de Saint Basile* (Paris: J. Gabalda, 1941), 183–216; Thomas Spidlik, 'L'idéal du monachisme basilien', in Fedwick, *Basil*, vol. I, 361–74; Rousseau, *Basil*, 190–232; and Holmes, *A Life Pleasing to God*.

[140] Basil, *Longer Rules*, 22.2 and 3 (dress); ibid., 35.1 (a single community of brothers); *Shorter Rules*, 108–11 (the sisters' superior).

[141] For a community's care of relatives, *Longer Rules*, 32.1; Elm, *Virgins*, 112.

[142] Basil, *Ep.* 150.3, and Gregory Nazianzen, *Or.* 43.63 (location); Basil, *Ep.* 94 (building for those dedicated to God's service).

[143] *Shorter Rules*, 155; Rousseau, *Basil of Caesarea*, 144.   [144] *Shorter Rules*, 208.   [145] Ibid., 85.

[146] Basil, *Ep.* 223.2; Athanasius, *Life of Antony*, 2–3. Elm rightly points out that Basil did not in fact give his money away in a single act of renunciation, but in an extended series of gifts, *Virgins*, 90.

[147] Basil, *Ep.* 22.1.   [148] Basil, *Longer Rules*, 12.

Through extended periods of silence, and detailed instruction, one's very voice was surrendered as the monk learnt to speak in the appropriate manner.[149]

The core of the Basilian communities was to comprise those who had taken a life-long vow to remain, but monasteries might contain suitably segregated children, apprenticed to a particular craft as well as to the monastic life, who were free to leave.[150] Different monks might work at a variety of trades and produce various products, each monk looking after the tools of his trade – providing that the products were not luxury items which would lead the buyer into sin, and that the business did not require heavy involvement in the outside world.[151] Some monasteries also ran a school for children from the neighbourhood.[152] Basil sanctioned the appointment of a superior, and a deputy to govern in the superior's absence.[153] Authority was to be exercized with paternal compassion and fellow-feeling, a doctor's trained eye for another's wellbeing.[154] The number of other office-holders mentioned by the texts – a bursar, a cellarer and his assistant, someone in charge of the boys, someone in charge of common discipline – reveals that some communities at least became sizeable over time, though the lack of division into smaller units overseen by a more senior monk indicates that these larger houses were modest in comparison with the vast Pachomian monasteries of Egypt which we shall examine in the next chapter.[155]

Some houses were double monasteries, where communities of men and women lived in close proximity. Basil legislated for meetings between them: two or three from each community were to attend; total seclusion from the other sex was ruled out 'for the sake of the service which, according to God's command, everyone has a right to expect from his neighbour'.[156] Some of the brethren were to take responsibility for the sisters' material needs, but monks were not to interfere in the government of the women's monastery.[157] *Shorter Rule* 108 instructs a male superior not to give spiritual direction to any of the women without the presence of the women's superior. So, each community enjoyed a real autonomy, though there may have been a major superior, probably male, over both communities. These double monasteries were perhaps a distinctive element in Basil's reform programme, though some argue that here, too, the bishop followed Eustathius of Sebaste.

---

[149] Ibid., 13.   [150] *Longer Rules*, 15 and 36.   [151] Ibid., 39.
[152] *Shorter Rules*, 292.   [153] *Longer Rules*, 24 and 45.
[154] *Shorter Rules*, 99.   [155] Ibid., 141, 142, 149, 156; *Longer Rules*, 15 and 53.
[156] *Longer Rules*, 33, PG 31.997b, tr. Holmes, *A Life*, 213.   [157] *Shorter Rules*, 111.

The ascetics met to pray at dawn, at the third, sixth, and ninth hour, at the day's end, at nightfall, and at midnight.[158] Their diet was similar to that Basil had adopted at Annisa – a single daily meal which thwarted gluttony but met basic needs. While they ate, someone read.[159] There was no detailed prescription of what to eat or not eat – though Basil favoured what was easily and cheaply obtainable in the locality.[160] Laughter was to be sharply restrained. Basil distinguished between smiling, which was acceptable, and 'raucous laughter' with its 'uncontrollable shaking of the body' which was not.[161] Basil pointed out that Jesus in the Gospels was nowhere presented as laughing. The Basilian ascetic was to be moved by recognition of sin to compunction and penitence.

ORIGEN AND EGYPTIAN MONASTICISM: II – EVAGRIUS PONTICUS

The influence of Origen on the semi-anchoretic strand of Egyptian monasticism during the mid fourth century is evident from the writings of Serapion, a monastic leader and bishop of Thmuis to whom Antony had bequeathed one of his two cloaks. Serapion wrote a short letter to, and in praise of, the monks or solitaries (*hoi monazontes*), which shared many essentials of Origen's ascetic vision: the solitaries, in an image reminiscent of Plato's *Phaedrus*, have 'given wings' to their minds and directed them to heaven, where they have 'diligently searched out the good to be won from the lessons God set there'. Not 'swept away by human thoughts (*logismoi*)' they have instead become like angels.[162] 'As though bodiless', the solitaries have 'trampled underfoot hostile pleasures'.[163] Serapion cited the Song of Songs 5:1 ('I have come to my garden, my sister, my bride') to describe each ascetic as an orchard cultivated by God's commandments.[164] Towards the close of the century, writings by Origen and Pierius were among those committed to memory by Ammonius, one of the so-called 'Tall Brothers'.[165] However, the most significant debt to Origen was that of Evagrius Ponticus (*c.* 345–99).

Evagrius hailed from Pontus and was made reader by Basil at Caesarea and then ordained deacon by Gregory Nazianzen. He shared much of their theological vision: a *Letter on the Trinity* now ascribed to Evagrius survived after his posthumous condemnation for heresy as Basil's *Letter* 8. He became a monk under the influence of the Elder Melania in Jerusalem

---

[158] *Longer Rules*, 37.   [159] *Shorter Rules*, 136 and 180.
[160] *Longer Rules*, 19.   [161] *Longer Rules*, 17, PG 31.961b, tr. Holmes, *A Life*, 248.
[162] Athanasius, *Life of Antony*, 91; Serapion, *Letter to the Monks*, 1, PG 40.928a.
[163] Serapion, *Letter to the Monks*, 5.   [164] Ibid., 8.   [165] Palladius, *Lausiac History*, 11.

before moving in 383 to Nitria, where he spent two years, and then on to Kellia where he remained for a further fourteen years and won an increasing reputation as a teacher.[166] Evagrius composed a great many writings addressed to monks, including a trilogy comprising the *Praktikos*, the *Gnostikos*, and the *Kephalaia Gnostika*, a further work *On Prayer*, and a set of proverbs, the *Ad Monachos*.

Evagrius shared Origen's view that God originally created rational beings, pure intellects, who freely clung to the knowledge of God and were united with God in that union of minds. In a letter to the Elder Melania Evagrius explained how these intellects chose to fall away from this contemplative union, and how that fall resulted in human beings comprising body and soul. This plight was reversible through God's providence and human asceticism.[167] The *Praktikos*, which survived its author's condemnation through ascription to Nilus of Ancyra, was concerned, as its name suggests, with the ascetic practice by which vices were removed and virtues instilled within the monk. Its introduction offers a summary of what Evagrian asceticism aimed at: 'The fear of God secures faith, children, and it is secured by self-control, and self-control is made unshakeable by endurance and hope, and from these is born passionlessness (*apatheia*), whose offspring is charity; and charity is the doorway to natural knowledge, which is followed by theology and the ultimate blessedness.'[168] Asceticism enables a freedom from overwhelming emotions that in turn allows one to concentrate on love of God, and in this way cleave to God; asceticism serves the mind's contemplative elevation to God through what God has revealed in the natural world and in Scripture.

Asceticism thus restores man as a rational being to his natural state: 'The rational soul operates naturally when its desiring part desires virtue, and its spirited part (*thumikon*) fights for virtue, and its reasoning part applies itself to the contemplation of creatures' or created things.'[169] But the key state of *apatheia*, or freedom from dominant passions, is only achieved in the difficult business of mastering the thoughts or temptations, the *logismoi*, which arise within the soul. These *logismoi* concern gluttony, sexual immorality, love of wealth, sadness, anger, *acedia* or indifference,

---

[166] D. Chitty, *The Desert a City* (London and Oxford: Basil Blackwell, 1966), 49.

[167] For how Evagrius differs from Origen in his account of mind (*nous*) and soul (*psyche*), cf. Michael O'Laughlin, 'The anthropology of Evagrius Ponticus and its sources', in Charles Kannengiesser and William L. Petersen (eds.), *Origen of Alexandria, His World and His Legacy* (University of Notre Dame Press, 1988), 357–73.

[168] Evagrius, *Praktikos*, prologue, tr. S. Tugwell, *Evagrius Ponticus: Praktikos and On Prayer* (Oxford, Faculty of Theology, 1987), 6.

[169] Evagrius, *Praktikos*, 86, tr. Tugwell, *Evagrius*, 21.

vainglory, and pride. Men and women determine by their free will whether or not these thoughts will sway them from their divine goal: 'Whether these thoughts come to disturb the soul or not is not something which we control; but whether they linger or not, and whether they arouse passions or not; that is subject to our control.'[170] Ascetic practices address or map onto particular temptations. The monk is to grow in discernment and self-discipline, recognizing and fighting off the demons who prompt the different *logismoi* in this 'inner war'.[171] The monk hopes for progress, but must be wary of that progress being wrecked by pride. The greater his progress, the fiercer the demonic opponents who attack.[172]

Evagrius taught that contemplation included the search for *logoi*, the reasons or rational principles within the natural order. This was a matter of uncovering the end for which God had fashioned the world and placed us within it. It involved recognition of our original creation as rational beings fulfilled in knowing the one God as Trinity, the providence of our present condition, and God's mercy in enabling our return to the bliss we were created to enjoy.[173] The goal of contemplation is summed up in two proverbs: 'Contemplations of the worlds expand the heart; the reasons of providence and judgement exalt it'; and 'Knowledge of the incorporeals raises the mind on high and presents it to the Holy Trinity'.[174] Knowledge of the Trinity is found in prayer to God that is itself 'intratrinitarian': prayer to the Father through the Son and in the Spirit. But such prayer, if genuine, requires freedom from anger, a hard-won gentleness of spirit.[175]

ORIGENIST ASCETICISM IN THE LATIN WEST — CASSIAN

In 400, Theophilus, the powerful patriarch of Alexandria, moved, for reasons I will not explore here, against a number of monks associated with Origen's theology. Many, among them the famed Tall Brothers, fled from Nitria to Jerusalem and Palestine. In the Latin-speaking churches Jerome savaged Origen and those whom he saw as the exegete's latter-day disciples.

---

[170] Ibid., 6, tr. Tugwell, *Evagrius*, 7.
[171] Evagrius, *Praktikos*, 48, SC 171, 608 (ὁ κατὰ διάνοιαν πόλεμος), tr. Tugwell, *Evagrius*, 15.
[172] Ibid., 59.
[173] J. Driscoll OSB, *Evagrius Ponticus: Ad Monachos*, Ancient Christian Writers 59 (New York and Mahwah: Paulist Press, 2003), 14–15.
[174] Evagrius, *Ad Monachos*, 135 and 136, tr. R. Sinkewicz, *Evagrius of Pontus: The Greek Ascetic Corpus* (Oxford University Press, 2003), 131.
[175] Driscoll, *Evagrius*, 27.

Origen's ascetic legacy, however, now reached a new Latin audience suitably disguised through the pen of Cassian (*c.* 360–*c.* 435).[176]

Cassian's monastic life began in perhaps the early 380s when with an older friend, Germanus, he entered a monastery near the Cave of the Nativity in Bethlehem.[177] The two were soon drawn to Egypt, to Panephysis, a monastery near the mouth of the Nile, but then to Scetis and Kellia. From there Cassian moved soon after 399 to Constantinople, where he served as a deacon. Fluent in Greek and Latin, he served on Chrysostom's diplomatic staff, taking letters at the time of his master's downfall in 404 to Pope Innocent at Rome.[178] By 419 he was a priest in Marseilles, active in founding or directing two religious communities – one a monastery (perhaps Saint Victor), and the second a convent of nuns (perhaps the later Saint Saviour's).[179] Here Cassian articulated for local bishops and monks, such as Castor, bishop of Apta Julia, an account of monastic life which was deeply indebted to Evagrius, and which also explicitly acknowledged the teachings of Basil and Jerome.[180] This he did in the *Institutes* and the *Conferences*, both written in the 420s and which form an extended account of monastic life.[181]

The *Institutes*, dedicated to Castor, begins in Books I–IV with external observances: the correct monastic habit and its symbolic meanings; the hours of communal prayer and psalms to be sung; who is to sing; the posture of those at prayer; and how to deal with novices. Cassian then turns to the inner discipline required of the monks. The remainder of the *Institutes*, Books V–XII, analyzes the eight faults which a monk must combat within himself if he is to achieve, by grace, the perfection to which he is called. These eight faults are Evagrius' *logismoi*: the spirit of gluttony, the spirit of fornication, or sexual impurity, love of money, or avarice, the spirit of anger, sadness, sloth, vanity, and pride. Cassian exposes the origins of these faults within the monk, for example, in an imperfect renunciation

---

[176] For a detailed account of Cassian's life, see C. Stewart, *Cassian the Monk* (Oxford University Press, 1998), 4–24 and 141 n.10.

[177] Cassian, *Institutes*, 3.4; *Conferences* I.I.   [178] Palladius, *Dialogue*, 3.

[179] For the date, cf. Stewart, *Cassian*, 16. Identification of the houses cannot be dated earlier than the eleventh century. See C. Leyser, *Authority and Asceticism from Augustine to Gregory the Great* (Oxford: Clarendon Press, 2000), 42.

[180] Cassian, *Institutes*, Preface, 5. Cassian quoted Jerome's *Letter to Eustochium* in his *De incarnatione*, VII.26. For the view that Cassian had read the *Life of Antony* and perhaps Antony's letters, cf. Stewart, *Cassian*, 36.

[181] For the view that the works also show a changing view of the relative worth given to the anchoretic and the cenobitic life, in which Cassian finally sees the latter as the only practical form of monasticism, see Philip Rousseau, *Ascetics, Authority, and the Church in the Age of Jerome and Cassian* (Oxford University Press, 1978), 182. For a rather different assessment, cf .Stewart, *Cassian*, 30–2.

of the world on entering religious life. He describes their pathology, how they corrupt a monk where they have taken hold, how they manifest themselves, and then how such faults may be overcome. The vices are tackled in order of gravity or depravity, linked in that only by tackling the first can the last be conquered. The monk starts by addressing his own gluttony and ends by seeking to eradicate pride.

Conferences I–X looks closely at the virtues and ascetic practices which the monk must cultivate in order to make progress. Later conferences are concerned with specific issues such as friendship in XVI, and generally look in greater detail at topics already raised. Throughout, Cassian took pains to relate ascetic practices to their spiritual goals, and to subordinate those practices to their goals. The practices must never hinder what they were meant to foster. He severely criticized monks whose inflexibility compromised fraternal charity: 'what is gained by fasting is less than what is spent on anger, and the fruit that is obtained from reading is not so great as the loss that is incurred by contempt for one's brother'.[182] A central virtue was thus discretion, the ability to judge and act wisely with respect to the thoughts which welled up within the mind. Some thoughts come from God, some from within oneself, and yet others come from demons. Cassian analyzed the distractions which beset prayer. He also set out a dynamic of progressive renunciation: the giving up of external goods led to a more intimate surrender, the loss of that part of oneself which is vitiated by sin. The monk was led to the ultimate renunciation of this world in contemplation of the divine. Charity made for peace, and purity of heart allowed the ascetic to be illuminated by God's divine light.

In this process, there was need for experiential wisdom, on the part of the teacher and pupil: 'just as these things cannot be put across except by someone of proven experience, so likewise they cannot even be seen, or understood, except by the man who has worked hard to comprehend them with the same sweat and effort.'[183] What had been learnt was easily lost, unless recalled through spiritual conferences. The dialogues in which Cassian imparted his monastic theology exemplified the teaching practices to be adopted.

Monks could only grow spiritually if they disclosed their thoughts to the elders. Sinful desires were excised through being confessed. And growth in wisdom came from obedience to what the Fathers enjoined. Cassian understood obedience, however, not simply as docility, but also as a mortification

---

[182] Cassian, *Conferences*, 1.7, tr. B. Ramsey, *John Cassian, The Conferences*, Ancient Christian Writers 57 (New York: Paulist Press, 1997), 46.

[183] *Institutes*, Preface, 4–5.

of the will. Through monastic obedience selfish desire was 'crucified': 'Just
as someone who has been crucified can no longer move or turn his limbs as
he wishes, so we, too, should direct our desires and wishes, not according
to what delights us at the time by its pleasantness, but according to God's
law, wherever that pins us down.'[184] Capricious desires were to be forcibly
restrained, so that the monk was not deflected from the path mapped out
by God's law. The imagery of crucifixion was not only graphic, it made
a theological point: monastic obedience conformed the monk to Christ
crucified.

Scripture secured purity of thought. Texts were to be committed to
memory, where they furnished material for a reflective process that inter-
nalized the biblical message: 'Holy Scripture must be diligently committed
to memory and ceaselessly reviewed.' This bestows 'a double fruit'. First,
because preoccupied, the mind 'cannot be taken captive in the entrap-
ments of harmful thoughts'. Second, 'things that we have not been able
to understand because our mind was too busy at the time' are understood
afterwards: 'while we are at rest and as it were immersed in the stupor of
sleep, there will be revealed an understanding of hidden meanings'.[185]

The need to strive for progress required there to be some way to measure
progress. One such was the frequency of the monk's nocturnal emissions.
These were stimulated not only by how much a monk ate and drank, but
by his daytime thoughts. Though not sinful, nocturnal emissions served
as an index of the ascetic's relative purity of mind. For the virtuous monk,
they might occur only once every couple of months or some three times a
year.[186] They kept him from undue spiritual pride.[187] Absolute chastity, a
purity of heart in which the ascetic already lived the angelic life of heaven,
where sexual desire and activity no longer had any place, could be achieved
only by a very few in the context of eremitical contemplation.

Like Evagrius, Cassian saw contemplation of God as the pinnacle of
human existence. In *Conference* XXIII Cassian's mouthpiece, the *abba*
Theonas, looks at Romans 7:19–23, where Paul reflects on 'the good that I
want I do not do, but the evil that I hate, this I do'. Theonas denies that
these verses apply to ordinary sinners: the latter do evil all too willingly.
Paul describes rather the condition which afflicts those who are already far
advanced in the spiritual life. The good which even a saintly apostle cannot
accomplish, despite his other virtues, is 'theoria, or the contemplation of
God, whose dignity is greater than all the dignity of righteousness and all

---

[184] Ibid., 4.35. [185] *Conferences*, 14.10, tr. Ramsey, *John Cassian*, 514–15.
[186] *Institutes*, 3.20, and *Conferences*, 2.23. [187] *Conferences*, 4.15.

the zeal for virtuousness'. For 'all the dignity of holiness, which not only is good and beneficial for the present but also obtains the gift of eternity, will nonetheless be considered commonplace and as it were saleable if it is compared with the dignity of divine contemplation'.[188] Cassian envisages the soul bathed in the divine light, absorbed by that light, and taken up into the divine life.

Cassian adeptly hid his discredited source, Evagrius. First, he chose Latin translations which avoided controversy: where Evagrius wrote of freedom from the passions (*apatheia*), Cassian wrote about purity of heart. Second, in the *Conferences* he put Evagrius' ideas on the lips of famous desert fathers that were not from the now suspect centres of Nitria and Kellia.[189] The *Conferences* appear to report conversations held with the great monks of Scetis. Furthermore, although much of what Cassian taught concerns the invisible life of the mind, he made his teaching accessible through memorable images. Spiritual discrimination is compared with the work of a 'money-changer' who has to judge the value of different coins. The continual working of the mind is compared to a water mill, the millstones of which are never still, but which can be fed variously with corn, barley, or darnel. The monk's need for continual effort if he is not to regress under pressure from sinful inclinations, is expressed in the image of rowing upstream.[190]

Cassian's writings were not without detractors. This in part reflects his criticism of existing Gallic monasteries inspired by Martin of Tours (d. 397).[191] Furthermore, Augustine's anti-Pelagian teaching won fervent admirers in Gaul, some of whom found Cassian seriously wanting. He had argued (*Conference* XIII) that God's grace is essential in allowing the monk to begin the ascetic project, and that without grace the monk cannot hope to win perfection, but it seemed to his enemies that Cassian portrayed a free will independent of grace as the monk strove to advance. They complained without success to the pope and in 432 one of them, Prosper, attacked *Conference* XIII in his *Contra collatorem*.

Cassian's writings nonetheless proved influential locally in the monasteries of Lérins, the monks of which became bishops in southern Gaul; they were also admired more widely, principally in the West.[192] Later in the fifth century Eucherius of Lyons composed an epitome of his work.[193]

---

[188] Ibid., 23.3.1–2, tr. Ramsey, *John Cassian*, 791–2.
[189] Stewart, *Cassian*, 11–12.   [190] Cassian *Conferences*, 1.18; 1.20; and 6.14.
[191] Stewart, *Cassian*, 17.   [192] Dunn, *The Emergence of Monasticism*, 83; Stewart, *Cassian*, 24–5.
[193] The *Epitomes operum Cassiani* attributed to Eucherius of Lyons (PL 50.867–94) may not in fact be this work; cf. Stewart, *Cassian*, 157 n.222.

A similar work was produced in North Africa.[194] Cassian's thought shaped the monastic legislation of bishop Caesarius at Arles (*c.* 470–542), who sent his sister to be educated in the monastic life of Cassian's nunnery at Marseilles before making her the head of his new convent at Arles. Cassiodorus (*c.* 485–*c.* 580) recommended the *Institutes* to his monks at Viviarium in southern Italy.[195] Pope Gregory the Great (*c.* 540–604) used Cassian's description of the eight principal faults as the basis of his writing on the seven deadly sins. Above all, St Benedict's *Rule*, probably composed in the mid-sixth century, would recommend the reading of both the *Institutes* and the *Conferences*, thereby securing Cassian's place among the monastic authorities of medieval Europe.[196]

CONCLUSION

This chapter has shown how Origen's ascetic teaching was adapted and promoted by men who sought to shape both ascetic life in the urban churches of the fourth century and the new forms of monasticism, semi-anchoretic and cenobitic, which developed outside the cities. Origen offered a compelling reading of the Old Testament which made Biblical texts the window onto, and arms for, a Christian psychomachy. In that battle, asceticism, together with scriptural meditation, purified the soul and thus enabled contemplation of God. A single theological vision made sense, for these clerics, of consecrated virginity by men and women in the urban churches and of the monastic asceticism practised by solitaries and cenobites. There are few indicators that the ascetics who listened to and read the sermons, letters, and treatises of these figures thought this vision alien to their own understanding. Authors such as Origen, Antony, Basil, Evagrius, and Cassian, were honoured as experienced ascetics.[197] Likewise, Nilus of Ancyra, who drew extensively on Origen's homilies and *Commentary on the Song of Songs* in composing his own commentary on that book around the beginning of the fifth century, was an ascetic writing for fellow monks and ascetics.[198]

In Cappadocia, Basil promoted a contemplative love of God described in terms drawn from Greek philosophy, but shaped and tested by the love of neighbour understood in scriptural terms. There was no escape from the Christian community, only the search for a type of community where

---

[194] Cassiodorus, *Institutiones*, 29.2.   [195] Ibid.   [196] *Rule of St Benedict*, 42 and 73.
[197] Athanasius was counted as an ἀσκητής by his fellow Alexandrians according to his *Defence against the Arians* (*Apologia secunda*), 6.5, in Opitz, *Athanasius*, II.1, 92; cf. Brakke, *Athanasius*, 7.
[198] Marie-Gabrielle Guérard (ed.), *Nil d'Ancyre, Commentaire sur le Cantique des Cantiques*, SC 403 (1994), 23, 61 and 84.

love of neighbour was properly articulated, whether in the mutual respect of superior and subordinate, fraternal correction, or the monks' external charity. Monks in the Greek east, but also in parts of Syria and Armenia, would regard Basil as a central authority in the ensuing centuries.[199] In Egypt, Antony, Athanasius, and Evagrius did not neglect love of neighbour, but stressed the need to train the mind assailed by demonic temptation.

Origen's teaching was transmitted westwards through multiple channels, not least a network of educated ascetics that centred upon the Elder Melania, and included Rufinus and Evagrius. The monasteries of Melania and Rufinus on the Mount of Olives were centres in the early fifth century for transmitting ideas through their role as hostels for the visiting 'bishops, solitaries, and virgins' who came to the city as pilgrims; and Evagrius, whom Melania had encouraged to adopt the monastic life, corresponded with their members.[200] Rufinus' translations of Origen's sermons and treatises in the early fifth century, as well as of writings by Evagrius, were read by elite Latin Christians.[201] Much was thereby preserved which is now lost in the original Greek. It was also Rufinus' translation of Basil's rulings that would become recommended reading for Benedictine monks in the final chapter of their own Rule.[202] However, of equal or even greater importance in the West were the monastic writings of John Cassian through whose pen Evagrian ideas were successfully disguised and disseminated. Origen's ascetic legacy, though invisible, was all-pervasive.

---

[199] Holmes, *A Life*, xix–xx.
[200] Palladius, *Lausiac History*, 38.8 and 46.5. For Evagrius' correspondence, cf. Driscoll, *Ad Monachos*, 35–6.
[201] Rufinus is known to have translated Evagrius' *Sententiae ad virgines* and *Sententiae ad monachos*, but remarks by Jerome (*Ep.* 133.3) suggest that he translated other treatises as well which reached a wide readership. On Rufinus' translations of Origen and Evagrius, cf. C. P. Hammond, 'The last ten years of Rufinus' life and the date of his move south from Aquileia', *Journal of Theological Studies* ns 28 (1977), 372–429.
[202] *Rule of St Benedict*, 73.

CHAPTER 5

Cavemen, cenobites, and clerics

Theodoret (b. *c*. 393), bishop of Cyrrhus from 423 to 449, looked back on a childhood in Antioch during which he was taken by his mother to be blessed by the renowned Persian monk Aphraate and sent each week to be blessed by another monk, Peter, who inhabited a tomb outside the city.[1] His visits testify to the reputation monks could win for protecting Christians from the evils to which they believed themselves exposed. A monk could be recognized as a holy man through whom the saving power of God was manifested. Peter made a belt for Theodoret from his own, which was then used to heal the child, and others, of sickness.[2] These connections with individuals and families in the cities from which the monks only partially distanced themselves, partly explain the value and thus the rise of much monastic life which emerged in the course of the fourth century. They also point to its variety.

Aphraate and Peter do not obviously belong in the Origenist tradition charted in the last chapter; nor were they the only monks around Antioch with its large Christian population. By AD 386 a 'black-robed tribe' of 'cave-dwellers' had incurred the deep hostility of Libanius (314–*c*. 393), the pagan teacher of rhetoric, who decried their attacks on rural shrines, and their appearance each summer in the city.[3] Already, in the late 360s, the young Chrysostom had persuaded two friends to join in him in learning the ascetic life from Carterius and Diodore, the heads of local monastic communities (*askētēria*).[4] He later spent four years away from the city under the guidance of a solitary, followed by two years alone in a cave.[5] Theodoret himself grew up to be a monk, in conformity with a vow

---

[1] Theodoret, *Historia religiosa*, 8.15 and 9.4.   [2] Ibid., 9.15.   [3] Libanius, *Orr.* 30.8–9, and 45.26.

[4] Socrates, *Church History*, VI.3, Hansen, *Sokrates, Kirchengeschichte*, 314. D. G. Hunter who follows the text of PG 67, 665b, sees a single 'seminary', *A Comparison Between a King and a Monk / Against the Opponents of the Monastic Life: Two Treatises by John Chrysostom* (Lewiston/Queenston and Lampeter: Edwin Mellen Press, 1988), 8–9.

[5] Hunter, *A Comparison*, 10.

made by his parents long before his birth, but in a cenobitic community at Nikertai, thereby showing how readily monasticism won adherents, the role that parents might take in shaping a vocation, and perhaps how quickly fashions changed within monasticism.[6] Just as it would be an error to underestimate the importance of Origen in monastic development, so it would be a mistake to underplay the multiplicity of forms this development took, or to ignore the socio-economic factors which conditioned it. These factors were not always benign. Chrysostom defended the wish of young men to adopt the ascetic life from Christian parents who apparently took legal action against the monks.[7] A prosperous family might divide over a son's future – the mother supportive of an ascetic life, the father eager to see the boy adopt a military career.[8] Chrysostom's defence indicates the support given by leading preachers. From further down the social scale, among the great mass of poor or *penetes*, came the 'sons of farmers and craftsmen'.[9] Evidence from elsewhere in the empire suggests that some would find in the monasteries either a higher standard of living, or greater security from want in times of scarcity. In this chapter, I survey some of the major features in this wider landscape of emerging monasticism.

PACHOMIUS

The semi-anchoretic desert monasticism of Antony's pupils was constrained by its nature to sites close enough to the urban communities that would buy the products of each monk's individual labour in return for other goods and supplement their income by almsgiving. At Nitria, monks wove linen; Evagrius worked as a copyist. A virgin sent fruit to Macarius the Alexandrian in thanks for his healing of her paralysis. Dorotheus, a Theban cave-dweller, wove ropes from date-palm leaves by night. Pambo was working with palm leaves at the visit of Melania, and boasted that he had only lived on what he had worked for. The same boast is reported of Chronius and made by the anchorite Philoromus in Cappadocia.[10] Yet this boast, precisely as such, permits us to see behind an ideal which Palladius promotes to a more usual 'mixed economy' in which meagre earnings were supplemented by alms.

---

[6] Theodoret, *Epp.* 80, 81, and 119. Two monasteries at Nikertai were founded in *c.* 380. Cf. Theodoret, *Historia religiosa*, 3.4. For families dedicating children to the ascetic life, cf. P. Escolan, *Monachisme et église. Le Monachisme syrien du IVe au VIIe siecle: un monachisme charismatique* (Paris: Beauchesne, 1999), 181. For one three-year-old, cf. Theodoret, *Historia religiosa*, 26.4. For monks as 'sources of benefaction', cf. Rowan Greer, 'Pastoral care and discipline', *CHC2*, 575.

[7] Chrysostom, *Against the Opponents of the Monastic Life*, i., 2–3.

[8] Ibid., III.12.   [9] Ibid., II.8, PG 47.344, tr. Hunter, *A Comparison*, 114.

[10] Palladius, *Lausiac History*, 7, 38, 18, 2, 10, 47, and 45.

Fourth-century Egypt saw other ascetic teachers who chose a common life in monasteries which permitted a different economy and thus location, either close to the Nile in areas bordering the desert or in the towns. Some monasteries belonged to the Meletian church which had separated from the Catholic Church of Alexandria, and these may have inherited an Origenist asceticism. Remains of an archive dated to the 330's have survived from a Meletian monastery called Hathor in the Kynopolite nome.[11] Other communities further south owed allegiance to the charismatic figure of Pachomius. By the late fourth century, the literature associated with these monasteries shows marked hostility to Origen, and while this suggests paradoxically how widely Origen was read, he seems not to have been a direct influence on Pachomius.[12]

When Antony courted martyrdom at Alexandria during the persecutions, in around 312, Pachomius, a pagan conscript of about twenty, was billeted in Thebes and became deeply impressed by the charitable works of the city's Christians.[13] On release from the army, Pachomius was baptised at Chenoboskion, a village close to the Nile north of Thebes in the diocese of Diospolis, where, after a few years he adopted a solitary ascetic life close to the village similar to that practised by the young Antony. At first under the supervision of an older hermit, Pachomius in turn became a respected ascetic teacher with followers who settled nearby. Some time between 320 and 323 Pachomius founded a walled monastery near the deserted village of Tabennesi, also close to the Nile. It was a difficult decision which caused a rift between Pachomius and his brother John, who had joined him in the ascetic life. Would-be monks, who recognized Pachomius as their 'father',[14] were clothed in a monastic habit and instructed in a common way of life characterized by mutual respect articulated in regulations concerning how they were to eat, sleep, pray, and work. Palladius' *Lausiac History* (32) tells how Pachomius received a vision of an angel who dictated a Rule for his monks; the detailed *Rule* we now have evolved more slowly, but the story reveals the regard in which it was widely held.[15] Sources probably downplay

---

[11] E. A. Judge, 'The earliest use', 84.
[12] E.g., *First Greek Life of Pachomius*, 31 and *Paralipomena* 4.7, tr. Armand Veilleux, *Pachomian Koinonia*, 3 vols. (Kalamazoo: Cistercian Publications, 1980–2), vol. I, 318 and vol. II, 28–9. For the late-fourth-century origin of these episodes, and a maximalist reading of Origen's influence, cf. S. Rubenson, 'Origen in the Egyptian monastic tradition in the fourth century', in Bienert and Kühneweg, *Origeniana Septima*, 330. For a minimalist reading, cf. Graham Gould, 'The influence of Origen on fourth-century monasticism', in G. Dorival, A. Le Boullec, *et al.* (eds.), *Origeniana Sexta* (Leuven: Peeters, 1995), 591–8.
[13] *Bohairic Life of Pachomius*, 7.   [14] Ibid., 20, tr. Veilleux, *Pachomian Koinonia*, vol. I, 43.
[15] P. Rousseau, *Ascetics, Authority, and the Church*, 74.

the shaky start of this community, and we cannot recover with certainty the exact nature of the primitive settlement at Tabennesi, but Pachomius hit upon a form of monastic life which expanded rapidly. By 330 Pachomius had founded a second monastery at Phbow, closer to Chenoboskion. Each became home within Pachomius' lifetime to a thousand or more monks.[16] Seven other male houses were either founded or placed under Pachomius' authority before his death in 346, as well as two convents of women.

The success of these monasteries can be attributed to various factors. Men or boys could join who were not yet baptized: catechumens travelled to Phbow for baptism at Easter.[17] The houses were federated in a single fellowship (*koinonia*) which formed a single, more productive, monastic economy overseen by an official who redistributed the goods produced by each monastery, to match needs and surplus.[18] Large numbers facilitated production. Many were involved in farming, and its related skills of carpentry and metalworking, but others were bakers, makers of baskets, ropes, and mats from rushes, or shoemakers, etc.[19] Stable government was ensured through the oversight of Pachomius and his successors, who sent deputies to visit the houses, and by holding twice-yearly assemblies.[20] Most houses were relatively close to at least one other house: Phbow was only two miles from Tabennesi; when Pachomius moved to Phbow and appointed Theodore as superior at Tabennesi, Theodore visited him daily.[21] Early houses were mainly located in two adjacent dioceses; close to the Nile, they could communicate and transfer goods by boat (there were regulations for monks on-board ship, an indication of the commercial interaction of the Pachomian monasteries with the wider world).[22] Houses also interacted economically with neighbouring villages, as happened at Phbow, a formerly deserted village, so that the monastery formed part of local society subject to taxation. A tax list from the Hermopolite nome dated 367–8 records the payment of land taxes by Anoubion for the Tabennesi monastery.[23] By the end of the fourth century, these houses held perhaps seven thousand members.[24]

[16] Idem., *Pachomius: The Making of a Community in Fourth-Century Egypt* (Berkeley: University of California Press, 1985), 74.
[17] *Bohairic Life of Pachomius*, 81.   [18] Ibid., 71.
[19] Palladius, *Lausiac History*, 32.   [20] *Bohairic Life of Pachomius*, 71 and 78.
[21] Ibid., 73.   [22] Jerome, *Rule of Pachomius*, 118–19, PL 23, 76.
[23] J. Goehring, 'The world engaged: the social and economic world of early Egyptian monasticism', in J. Goehring, C. W. Hedrick, J. T. Sanders, and H. D. Betz (eds.), *Gnosticism and the Early Christian World* (Sonoma: Polebridge Press, 1990), 142.
[24] Rousseau, *Pachomius*, 74.

Yet the enclosing wall of each monastery also created a symbolic space apart from the outside world, and a porter controlled who might visit the monks. A bakery increased the independence of the monks from the villagers outside. News was filtered: monks returning to the house were to pass on only those messages approved by the superior.[25] Inside, Pachomius translated the more informal relationship of an individual master and disciple into 'a carefully planned hierarchy of offices'.[26] The day's work was allotted by a more senior monk. A monk's cell might be part of a larger block housing twenty men under a superior. Unlike the conditions in semi-anchoretic communities, obedience was enforced. The *Rule* (translated by Jerome in the early fifth century) specifies faults for public rebuke, a few for punishment by solitary isolation, the most serious by whipping or expulsion. The virtue of this command structure was not primarily its efficiency: it secured the peaceable order in which to pray. The monastery was 'a school of self-knowledge and self-improvement'.[27]

Everyone gathered together at dawn for prayer, which was described in regulations attributed to Pachomius' successor Horsesios: the monks listened to scriptural readings which were interspersed with time for silent meditation, and perhaps chanted psalms.[28] Certain jobs, such as preparing food and serving meals, rotated on a weekly basis: a monk was not identified by what he did. Whatever the job he was working upon, he prayed by reciting scriptural texts. The midday meal of bread and vegetables was eaten in silence. The evening saw another modest vegetarian meal (extremes of fasting were avoided), prayers, and a catechetical instruction given either by the abbot or by the monk in charge of each house. This was then discussed. At some point in the day, or on certain days, there was time to read, and all monks were expected to be able to read. As Wednesdays and Fridays were fast days for Christians generally, they were also kept as such by the monks. Sundays were marked by celebration of the Eucharist. While there was a common dietary regimen, individuals could also keep a more austere fast.[29]

In fact, there was some controversy within the early Pachomian communities about the correct level of communal fasting. That is the likely background to the story that Theodore had once consulted Pachomius on why their total fast in Holy Week was limited to the Friday and Saturday and not extended back throughout the week, a suggestion which

[25] *Bohairic Life of Pachomius*, 104.   [26] Brakke, *Athanasius*, 85.   [27] Rousseau, *Pachomius*, 95.
[28] Bryan D. Spinks, 'The growth of liturgy and the church year', *CHC2*, 609. Rousseau, *Pachomius*, 79–80.
[29] *Bohairic Life of Pachomius*, 26.

Pachomius rejected 'so that we might still have the strength to accomplish without fainting the things we are commanded to do, namely, unceasing prayer, vigils, reciting of God's law, and our manual labour about which we have orders in the holy Scriptures and which ought to permit us to hold our hands to the poor'.[30] Integrating the different strands of ascetic practice was not easy. In the Syriac East a way to avoid this problem would be found which led to a very different ethic and thus a different relation to the ordinary Christian world.

SYRIAC MONASTICISM AND MESSALIANISM

If the success of Pachomian monasticism outlined above can be traced to the intersection of economic and religious factors, we can also explain the distinctive form of much Syriac monasticism in terms of a similar intersection, though the factors involved prove very different. Here, we must attend to (i) scriptural interpretation; (ii) pagan religious traditions and persecution; and (iii) the geography of the region.

The *Letter to the Hebrews* told how some of the faithful in past ages 'went about in skins of sheep and goats, destitute, afflicted, ill-treated . . . wandering over deserts and mountains, and in dens and caves of the earth' (RSV Hebrews 11:37–8). St Paul had avowed how 'to the present hour we hunger and thirst, we are ill-clad and buffeted and homeless' (RSV 1 Cor. 4:11). The author of the Pseudo-Macarian homilies, probably composed in northern Syria or Mesopotamia during the 380s, cited both these texts in teaching the humility proper to the Christian life, and in urging imitation of the apostles and prophets.[31] That such imitation held a privileged place in the monasticism of the Syriac East by the late fourth century is evident from various texts. Chrysostom's congregation at Antioch associated monks with 'seizing hold of the mountains'. The preacher reminded them of how the monks' sackcloth, chains, fasting, and window-less enclosures prepared them for death.[32] The Syriac *Liber Graduum* (or *Book of Steps*), probably written in the mid to late fourth century, describes ascetics (the 'Perfect') who, like the apostles, 'travel to many places, speak to each one the word that is helpful to him and leave them for another

---

[30] Ibid., 35, tr. Veilleux, *Pachomian Koinonia*, vol. 1, 59–60.

[31] Ps.-Macarius, *Homily* 12.4, ed. H. Dörries, *Die 50 Geistlichen Homilien des Makarios* (Berlin: de Gruyter, 1964), 109. For the date and provenance, cf. C. Stewart, '*Working the Earth of the Heart.*' *The Messalian Controversy in History, Texts, and Language to AD 431* (Oxford: Clarendon Press, 1991), 70–1; Caner, *Wandering, Begging Monks*, 106–7.

[32] Chrysostom, *Homilies on Matthew*, 7.7, PG 57, 81; *On the Statues*, 6.3.

place'.[33] It likewise ascribed to the apostles and Perfects one and the same diet: 'the apostles ate no meat at all; they fasted until the ninth hour and then they consumed just bread, salt, herbs, and olives'.[34] In all this they followed the example of Christ who 'walked on the earth as a stranger and alien'.[35]

Theodoret's *Religious History* highlighted heroes who variously embodied these ideals of extreme solitude and harsh diet, exposure to the elements, and periods of wandering from place to place. Before becoming bishop of Nisibis in the early fourth century, James was said to have wandered in the mountains, slept in the open, and kept to a diet of wild plants eaten raw.[36] Abrahames avoided cooked food including bread, and maintained this diet despite being made a bishop.[37] Julian Saba lived in a cave; though he then attracted disciples who built a monastery around him, he would escape on long walks of up to ten days through the desert.[38] A pilgrim to the Holy Land discovers an ascetic occupying a hole in the Sinai desert; only his hands stretched up in prayer were visible from outside.[39] After years in the mountains exposed to the elements Eusebius has limbs so wasted that he appears mummified, his face wrinkled and weather-beaten.[40] John, Moses, Antiochus, and Antoninus mortify the body with the extreme cold on the mountain tops.[41] Another James, of Theodoret's generation, is said to have progressed from living in a tiny cell to complete exposure to the elements on a mountain thirty stades from Cyrhus.[42] A further mortification stressed by Theodoret was to be weighed down by chains.[43] According to the Pseudo-Macarian homilies, an ascetic renounced family and wealth to become a poor 'stranger' or 'wanderer', but others made a point of immobility.[44] The abandonment in 363 of Roman forts along the former border with Persia led recluses to adopt some as ascetic retreats by the early fifth century.[45] Many solitaries prayed raucously 'like coxwains who exhort the rowers to keep time'. Though the writer of the homilies thought such noise unhelpful, the *Liber Graduum* suggests that it imitated the 'powerful shout' which

---

[33] *Liber Graduum*, Memra 19.31, *TBS*, 203. On the date and likely provenance in the Persian Empire, Kitchen and Parmentier, *TBS*, l. For a more cautious dating, cf. Escolan, *Monachisme*, 15–16.

[34] *Liber Graduum*, Memre 5.17 and 19.6 (where 'vegetables' are named instead of 'herbs'), *TBS*, 56 and 187.

[35] Ibid., Memra 20.10, *TBS*, 219.   [36] Theodoret, *Historia religiosa*, 1.2.   [37] Ibid., 17.6.

[38] Ibid., 2.2 and 4.   [39] Ibid., 6.7–9.   [40] Ibid., 18.1.   [41] Ibid., 23.1–2.

[42] Ibid., 21.3–5.   [43] Theodoret, *Historia religiosa* 4.6, 10.2, 11.1, 15.2, and 23.1.

[44] Ps.-Macarius, *Homily* 49.1, in Dörries, *Die 50 Geistlichen Homilien*, 315 (ξένος).

[45] I. Pena, P. Castellana, and R. Fernandez, *Les Reclus Syriens: Recherches sur les anciennes formes de vie solitaire en Syrie* (Milan: Franciscan Printing Press, 1980), 54 and 83.

Christ himself supposedly uttered in his agony at Gethsemane.[46] This fits
with the changes made in the Syriac *Life of Antony* that identify its hero
as a Christ-like figure.[47] Fidelity to a scriptural model probably interacted
here with pagan religious traditions which claimed the mountains for their
own deities. Theodoret noted among the signs of Christian victory over
paganism 'stops for ascetics that make holy the peaks of the mountains and
colonize the uninhabited wilderness'.[48]

Fidelity to Scripture was not straightforward. Some passages were pri-
oritized over others, interpreted and harmonized in a matrix unlike that
found in Origenist monasticism. St Paul's account of his sufferings to the
Corinthians related in verse 11 how 'we labour, working with our own
hands', but the author of the Pseudo-Macarian homilies stopped short of
this boast. The omission reflects a further feature of the Syrian monasticism
which had developed by the late fourth century: abstention from physical
labour. For those who aspire to perfection, the *Liber Graduum* presents
work as motivated by a concern for bodily satisfaction which is incompatible with a vocation inspired by Matthew 6:25: 'Do not be anxious about
what you shall eat or what you shall drink. That means: do not work for the
sake of your own belly.'[49] Agriculture, like marriage, entered human life
at the fall, which the monk sought to reverse.[50] Manual labour is replaced
by dependency on God, 'begging food and clothing like a poor person',
and by the spiritual work of prayer and teaching: 'one who feeds the sheep
of Christ is not able to go guide the plough and work the visible land'.[51]
Romans 12:12 inspired the monk to be 'constant in prayer and intercession,
in ministering and studying, in applying himself to God's truth and to have
it interpreted'.[52] Such a lifestyle was facilitated by its geographical setting.
The Syrian landscape permitted a solitary to withdraw into isolation and yet
remain at close proximity to relatively prosperous centres of population.[53]
The town or villages which benefited from his prayers and healings could
afford alms. From this perspective monasticism which included physical
labour seemed a perverse conflation of two different Christian lifestyles.

---

[46] Ps.-Macarius, *Homily* 6.3, tr. G. Maloney, *Pseudo-Macarius: The Fifty Spiritual Homilies and The
Great Letter* (New York and Mahwah: Paulist Press, 1992), 76; *Liber Graduum*, Memra 20.8, *TBS*,
216. Cf. also Luke 22:44.

[47] F. Takeda, 'The Syriac version of the *Life of Antony: A meeting point of Egyptian monasticism with
Syriac native asceticism*', in R. Lavenant (ed.), *Symposium Syriacum* VII (Rome: Pontificio Istituto
Orientale, 1998), 191–2.

[48] Theodoret, *Cure for Greek Maladies*, 6.87; cf. also 9.29 and 10.52.

[49] *Liber Graduum*, Memra 2.5, *TBS* ,17. Cf. also, Memre 19.13 and 20.1, *TBS*, 192 and 211.

[50] Ibid., Memra, 15.8.

[51] *Liber Graduum*, Memra 12.6, *TBS*, 124–5.   [52] Ibid., Memre 20.2 and 3.7, *TBS*, 212 and 28.

[53] Pena, Castellana, and Fernandez, *Les Reclus Syriens*, 71.

Likewise, from this perspective the ascetic should have no possessions from which to give alms or practise hospitality; the call for him to do so was heard as a demonic temptation, whereas other monastic traditions were more open to monks giving alms from their surplus income or acting as conduits for the alms of others.[54]

The monastic practice of the Syrian East was not confined to the above ideals, and Theodoret's portrayals cannot be taken as so many windows on what was typical. Solitude was further compromised in so far as the holy man was expected to visit others and instruct them.[55] Whilst some refused all cooked food, a diet based upon bread and salt was common.[56] Monastic communities grew up in the shadows of more solitary and footloose heroes, whose images they constructed, and whose teachings they communicated. Less advanced monks worked to support the perfect who did not. The Pseudo-Macarian homilist writes of monasteries containing thirty monks, some devoted to prayer for more of the day than others, who perhaps spend only an hour in prayer, but all of whom seek the Spirit; it is the Spirit who calms the passions and inspires in them the profound contemplation of Christ. The *Great Letter*, a treatise from the same period and milieu as the homilies, exhorts the monastic superior to lead the community with all due humility, and to instruct those brethren whose prayers remain distracted.[57]

Theodoret in fact reveals a monasticism tensed between two poles – the solitary and the cenobitic monks – so that the young Simeon Stylites could both be expelled from an ascetic community for a dangerous rigorism, and then re-embraced as the community recognized the holiness of its banished member. The stylite can even be thought of as mediating between ideals, isolated upon the pillar in extreme deprivation, and surrounded at close quarters by an attendant community. He parallels the mountain-top ascetics surrounded by villages and towns. Theodoret related, while Simeon was still alive, how this holy man stood night and day upon his pillar, repeatedly bowing profoundly in prayer, and eating only once a week.[58] He also shows the community which came into existence round him.

---

[54] *Liber Graduum*, Memra 25.5. For monastic almsgiving in the Graeco-Roman world, cf. my *Almsgiving in the Later Roman Empire*, 90–9.

[55] Ps.-Macarius, *Homily* 40.6.

[56] Pena, Castellana, and Fernandez, *Les Reclus Syriens*, 94. The ascetics' diet was similar to that of local peasantry, cf. Escolan, *Monachisme*, 135.

[57] Ps.-Macarius, *Great Letter*, tr. Maloney, *Pseudo-Macarius*, 261–3, and 268. The earliest monastery seems to have been founded by Asterius at Gindaros, some fifty km from Antioch, perhaps before the death of Constantine, though later writers projected monastic origins back into a legendary past. Cf. Theodoret, *Historia religiosa*, 2.9. For monasteries before the fifth century, cf. I. Pena, P. Castellana, and R. Fernandez, *Les Cénobites Syriens* (Milan: Franciscan Printing Press, 1983), 22–7.

[58] Theodoret, *Historia religiosa*, 26.22.

What solitaries and cenobites shared was an ideal of completely renouncing wealth, which was to be given to the poor. This form of entry into ascetic life is repeatedly described by the Pseudo-Macarian homilist.[59] It was modelled upon the self-denial of Job and Abraham.[60] The monks were 'pilgrims without possessions'.[61] The ideal was to have only the clothing one wore and food to survive the day.[62]

How Syrian monks understood their ascetic practices shared much with ascetics we have met elsewhere. The Pseudo-Macarian homilies and *Liber Graduum* set frequent prayer and fasting, almsgiving, and the renunciation of wealth and marriage, within the familiar pattern of a graced psychomachy in which the monk quelled his disordered passions against demonic temptation or possession: 'when we cut off all our visible sins we shall rise up in the struggle against the Sin that dwells in us internally, because they are the evil thoughts that Sin devises in the heart'.[63] The monk set heart and mind on God firmly, though humbly, through contemplation. The Pseudo-Macarian homilist in particular adapted an Origenist account of the ascetic life to interpret Syrian monastic traditions for a Greek-speaking audience.[64]

Yet, the Pseudo-Macarian homilies also show a distinctive concern with how asceticism prepares the monk to receive the Holy Spirit, and thereby experiential knowledge (even among the uneducated) of 'hidden mysteries' revealed in inspired visions. The perfect Christian is a 'participator' in the Spirit, and shares in the 'secrets of the heavenly King'.[65] The Syriac *Life* of Simon Stylites, unlike Theodoret's account, emphasizes the holy man's reception of visions.[66] In the *Liber Graduum* the Spirit finally brings the Perfect to a point where he knows the whole truth and can teach others from a pure heart.[67] In this latter work the author insists on the humility required of each person who makes progress in the spiritual life, and which is expressed in prescinding from judgementalism.[68] This refusal to condemn others for their sins belongs with imitation of Christ in not repaying others for the sufferings they inflict.[69] Ascetic practices are the outer expression and training for a 'hidden renunciation of the heart' of which suffering

---

[59] Ps.-Macarius, *Homilies* 11.6–7; 27.10 and 14; and 32.7.   [60] Ibid., 5.6.
[61] Ibid., 27.18, tr. Maloney, *Pseudo-Macarius*, 181.   [62] *Liber Graduum*, Memre 13.7 and 16.7.
[63] Ibid., Memre 18.3, *TBS*, 179. Cf. also, Ps.-Macarius, *Homilies* 32.9 and 37.8–9.
[64] Stewart, *'Working the Earth'*, 69, 119 and 124–6. Stewart rejects influence by Evagrius Ponticus.
[65] Ps.-Macarius, *Homilies* 1.2, 17.2 , and 26.5, tr. Maloney, *Pseudo-Macarius*, 38, 136, and 165. Cf. Stewart, *'Working the Earth'*, 150.
[66] Escolan, *Monachisme*, 111.   [67] *Liber Graduum*, Memre 1.2, 3.14, 20.7, and 28.2.
[68] *Liber Graduum*, Memra 16.7.   [69] Ibid., Memra 17.

without recourse to vengeance is an essential element.[70] This spirituality suited Christian missionary endeavour (the Perfect may associate with pagans), and was reinforced by the persecution that was unleashed within the Persian Empire from AD 340 onwards. The influence, however, of this spirituality extended well beyond the borders of that Empire.[71]

Syrian monastic traditions not only won admirers within the Graeco-Roman world, but aroused opposition among bishops against ascetics whom they labelled 'Messalians' (from the Syriac for 'those who pray'). Theodoret, for example, understood them as teaching that baptism was of no real value to its recipients, because it was unable to cut out the root of evil which could only be removed through ascetic commitment and prayer.[72] This opposition may have been strengthened by the threat which Syrian monasticism posed to the bishops' authority. Ephrem and Aphrahat suggest that in the early fourth century Syrian clerics belonged to an ascetic elite distinct from the non-ascetics, whether the latter were baptized or catechumens, but in the latter part of the century the urban clergy found themselves split from the ascetic elite through their ministerial engagement: the *Liber Graduum* does not count church leaders 'managing the congregations' among the Perfect, because of their function as judges dispensing justice.[73] They cannot 'enter that joy of our Lord' reserved for the Perfect in the bridal chamber.[74] The author urged the 'leaders' not to complain about the Perfect, and not to 'chase us away for nothing from the ministry in which it is right for us to walk – going to everyone, instructing and teaching', a measure of how often the monks as teachers met with hostility from local churchmen.[75] The period between 370 and 460 saw literary denunciations of 'Messalians' by Ephrem, Epiphanius of Salamis, and Theodoret, as well as condemnations by synods: at Antioch in what was probably the 380s; at Side in Pamphylia under Amphilocius of Iconium; at Constantinople in 426 under Sisinnius; and at Ephesus in 431 when the *Asceticon*, a work with close links to the Pseudo-Macarian texts, was condemned. 'Messalians' stood accused of refusing to work, of teaching that baptism was incapable of freeing the soul from the grip of evil demons, that prayer alone could achieve this liberation, and that the presence of the Holy Spirit within the soul was perceptible to the one thus graced. These charges do not finger a unified ascetic group, but witness to ideas more or less current among Syrian teachers. These ideas were influential beyond

---

[70] Ibid., Memra 12.1, *TBS*, 119.
[71] Ibid., Memra 30.4.   [72] Theodoret, *Haeret. fab. compendium*, IV.11, PG 83.429b.
[73] *Liber Graduum*, Memra 19.24, *TBS*, 199; Escolan, *Monachisme*, 4–5, and 23–4.
[74] *Liber Graduum*, Memra 19.36, *TBS*, 206.   [75] Ibid., Memra 19.31, *TBS*, 203.

the Syriac-speaking world, but did not win uncritical acceptance in the Graeco-Roman churches. The Pseudo-Macarian *Great Letter* would, for example, by drawn upon and adapted by Gregory of Nyssa's *De instituto* in the mid 390s even as Gregory rejected its account of religious experience.

It is in this cultural borderland between empires and ecclesiastical traditions that we may place Alexander the Sleepless (*Akoimetes*), his appeal, and the opposition he encountered. According to the Greek *Life* (probably composed in the early sixth century, but drawing upon an earlier Syriac account), Alexander had grown up in Asia Minor in the decades after 350, receiving at Constantinople the literary education which marked out the elite.[76] However, the young man entered the Syrian monastery of Elias, the reputation of which had spread westwards, only to leave after four years in search of a more faithful adherence to the Gospel injunction that he take no thought for tomorrow (Matthew 6:34). Alexander spent twenty years as a solitary in the hills close to the Euphrates, where he attracted, according to his *Life*, four hundred men whom he organized into a monastery. The holy man then launched out with a band of disciples on a missionary journey along the border between the Roman and Persian empires. From Palmyra the ascetics reached Antioch, from where they were twice evicted in a contest for authority with the city's bishop. The holy man made a further foundation at Constantinople near the martyrium of St Menas; he was expelled from here, too, probably in the late 420s, when he briefly found refuge in the monastery of Hypatius at Rouphinianes. His remaining few years were spent in another new monastery nearby, the Akoimete.[77]

Alexander's asceticism shows the stamp of his Syrian monastic formation: his journeys during which he constantly taught the importance of almsgiving to the poor by ordinary Christians; his dependence on alms, but the acceptance by his monks of only enough food for a single day; and the celebration in his monasteries of continual prayer.[78] In the Mesopotamian house he introduced seven daily and seven nightly offices. At Antioch his monks devoted themselves to perpetual psalmody in a former set of baths;

---

[76] *Life of Alexander*, 5, ed. E. De Stoop, *Vie d'Alexandre l'Acémète*, PO 6 (Paris, 1911), 660. For the composition, and Alexander's likely chronology (b. *c.* 355–60), cf. Caner, *Wandering, Begging Monks*, 249–50 and 252 n.25. For Eng. translation and commentary, cf. ibid., 250–80.

[77] *Life of Alexander* 6, 27, 32–3, 35, 37–8, 41, 43; Callinicus, *Life of Hypatius*, 41. For Alexander's itinerary cf. A. Vööbus, *History of Asceticism in the Syrian Orient*, 3 vols. (Louvain: CSCO, 1958, 1960, and 1988), vol. II, 187; Pierre-Louis Gatier, 'Un moine sur la frontière: Alexandre l'Acémète en Syrie', in A. Rousselle (ed.), *Frontières terrestres, frontières célestes dans l'antiquité* (Paris: Presses Universitaires de Perpignan, 1995), 435–57. Gatier for unspecified reasons (plausibility?) reduces the Euphrates community from 400 to 40.

[78] Gatier, 'Un moine', 439, argues that the journeys are 'simples voyages d'un point à l'autre et non vagabondages', but this overlooks their preaching character.

and the monks at Constantinople were divided up for perpetual prayer into six choirs of Latins, Greeks, and Syriac speakers.[79] The same background explains both his popular appeal and the opposition he encountered from church authorities: moral teaching, especially in urging the laity to greater generosity towards the poor, could be understood as the construction of spiritual authority in rivalry with local bishops. Furthermore, abstention from work for the sake of continual prayer, with the consequent need to secure alms for several hundred monks, could be understood as a major burden on churches which contravened the Pauline injunction to earn one's living. A pattern of dependence acceptable among communities who funded individual ascetics could not easily be translated to serve large monastic communities, except perhaps in the empire's few metropolises. Alexander's practice in this regard was sharply attacked by Nilus of Ancyra.[80] It is plausibly suggested that Alexander was expelled from Constantinople as 'a Messalian heretic'.[81]

AUGUSTINE AND ROMAN NORTH AFRICA

We have seen how geography, economics, and demography could favour different types of monasticism in conjunction with different readings of the Scriptures. In the final part of this chapter, I turn to Roman North Africa to demonstrate the difference which Church politics could also make to the development of Christian asceticism.

When St Augustine (354–430) established a quasi-monastic community with friends on the family property at Thagaste after his return to Africa as a baptized Christian, it may have been the nearest thing to a cenobitic monastery in Roman North Africa at this time.[82] Augustine later claimed that he wrote his treatise *On the Work of Monks* (normally dated by scholars to c. AD 400) at the time when monasteries first appeared at Carthage.[83] Other evidence suggests that what was true of Carthage was indicative of the late development of cenobitic monasticism in the African provinces generally. This is best explained in terms of Church politics: most North African Christians were Donatists, whose separation from the Catholics in the early fourth century had isolated them from changing fashions in asceticism. In a polemical letter of 402 the Donatist bishop Petilian

[79] Ibid., 27, 28, 30, 33, 38, 43.   [80] Nilus of Ancyra, *On Voluntary Poverty*, PG 79, 997a.

[81] Caner, *Wandering, Begging Monks*, 128.

[82] For this community, cf. Possidius, *Life of Augustine*, 3.

[83] Augustine, *Retractions*, II.21. The Council of Carthage in 397, canon 44, had already permitted female virgins to live together after the death of their parents (CCSL 149.186).

defended his church's claim to be the true and ancient African church by attacking the establishment of monasteries as an unwarranted innovation by Augustine. The Catholics dismissed his charge as a pretended or wilful ignorance of the practice in the universal Church.[84] To judge by a sermon of Augustine, the Donatists rejected cenobitic monasticism as without Biblical warrant: 'show us where the name of these monks appears in Scripture' (*ostendite ubi scriptum sit nomen Monachorum*).[85]

This does not mean that Donatism lacked an ascetic movement. Where the Donatists challenged Catholics over scriptural warrant for '*monachi*', Augustine challenged them to provide a like warrant for the '*Agonistici*', the 'Fighters' or circumcellions whose peregrinations around the martyrs' shrines was one element of an ascetic preparation for the martyrdom they actively sought in conflict with pagans or Catholic authorities.[86] According to Augustine's biographer Possidius, circumcellions could be found in practically every Donatist church 'on the march as though bound by the vow of those who profess chastity'.[87] The Donatist literature which circulated in fourth- and fifth-century Africa celebrated these new martyrs. Parmenian, Donatist bishop of Carthage from 363 to 391, was a sharp polemicist who wrote popular catechetical psalms and a five-volume condemnation of the Catholic party.[88] The focus in such literature was on the holiness of the Church united around its bishops; the literature thus militated against the formation of novel monastic communities internal to the churches as much as against withdrawal into semi-anchoretic communities or complete solitude. Although we cannot ascertain how far monastic literature originating outside North Africa, like the *Life of Antony*, circulated within Donatist churches, we may presume that it had less penetration and less impact there than elsewhere.

The monasticism which Augustine then developed in North Africa needs to be understood partly as an expression of Christian unity promoted in opposition to Donatist separatism. The *Confessions* avow that he had once 'pondered flight into the wilderness' (*in solitudinem*) only to be forbidden by God: he was to live not for himself but for Christ who had died for all.[89]

---

[84] *Against the Writings of Petilian*, III.40.48.   [85] *En. in Ps.*, CXXXII.6, CCSL 40, 1930.
[86] W. H. Frend, *The Donatist Church: A Movement of Protest in Roman North Africa* (Oxford: Clarendon Press, 1971), 172–7.
[87] Possidius, *Life*, 10, ed. A. Bastiaensen, in C. Mohrmann, A. Bastiaensen, L. Canali, and C. Carena (eds.), *Vita di Cipriano, Vita di Ambrogio, Vita di Agostino* (Milan: Fondazione Lorenzo Valla/A. Mondadori, 1975), 152 ('velut sub professione continentium ambulantes').
[88] Frend, *The Donatist Church*, 193–5.
[89] Augustine, *Confessions*, X.43.70, ed. J. O'Donnell, *Augustine, Confessions*, 3 vols. (Oxford: Clarendon Press, 1992), vol. 1, 146–7.

Any Christian asceticism was to be located within, and perhaps identified with, this fundamental re-orientation of the human person away from a disordered and dissipating self-love to a single-minded love of God which embraced Christ's self-sacrificing and generous love of others. Augustine's return in baptism to his childhood Catholicism in 387 had thus meant a break with the self-seeking ambitions of his career as an orator at the imperial court in Milan. The circle of friends and family whom Augustine gathered round him at Cassiciacum in the weeks before the baptism, together with the round of discussions, prayers, and reading which they followed, anticipated the common life he would soon enter and foster.[90]

The second way in which Church politics impinged on monastic development was through Augustine's forcible ordination at Hippo, which left him little option but to found the new house in a 'garden' or plot of land belonging to the church there.[91] The location and Augustine's new clerical identity required him to develop a monastic vision in close relationship to the urban church in which it was set. While at some point a convent for women was also established nearby under the authority of Augustine's sister, the trajectory of this urban monasticism would be expressed most clearly in the creation, on his becoming bishop, of a third and clerical monastery in the bishop's residence. The house was described in 426 as containing 'priests, deacons, subdeacons', as well as Augustine's nephew Patrick.[92]

Augustine's monasticism can be reconstructed from various sources. *On the Work of Monks* required manual labour of the able-bodied who were not otherwise occupied by 'church business or instruction in holy doctrine'.[93] Alms supplied what was lacking for a common life partially described by Augustine in the short *Rule* (of 387 lines) which he composed probably for the so-called 'garden monastery' in around 397.[94] The work provides no detailed prescriptions for daily routine although Augustine refers to set times for prayer and certain psalms to be sung not given in the *Rule* itself.[95] The concern is rather for the general spirit or intention with which things are done.

Augustine stressed the fraternal charity which secured unity, and his *Rule* addressed areas of the common life where that unity was at risk. Other

---

[90] *On Order*, 1.2.5.   [91] Augustine, *Serm.* 355.2.
[92] *Serm.* 356.3.   [93] *On the Work of Monks*, XVI.19.
[94] Unlisted by Augustine among his works, the *Rule*'s internal style secures the traditional attribution. For when it was written and for whom, see G. Lawless, *Augustine of Hippo and his Monastic Rule* (Oxford: Clarendon Press, 1987), 148–52.
[95] Augustine, *Rule*, 2.1.

monasteries might internalize the divisive class structures that featured so strongly in Late Antique society: at Bethlehem Paula divided her sisters at work and at table into three classes, 'noble, middle et lower', though she then brought them together to pray.[96] While Augustine catered for the 'weakness' of aristocratic monks unsuited for heavy labour and used to good food and clothes, there was no separation into distinct classes. Indeed, those who were poor in the world were not to grow proud 'because they *socialise* with those whom they would not dare to approach outside'. And those who once enjoyed wealth were not to glory in their family status but 'in the company (*societas*) of their poor brethren'.[97] The significance of this in a stratified world of patrons and clients, family estates, and elites should not be underestimated.

Fraternal charity required the monk to abjure private property: 'Do not call anything your own; possess everything in common'.[98] Augustine glossed the words of Scripture that 'Love is not self-seeking' as meaning that 'the common good takes precedence over the individual good'.[99] The monk was called to shared ownership based upon need. For some this would mean an escape from poverty not its adoption.[100] Goods must not be privatized, nor gifts 'pocketed on the sly'; the distribution of goods must not foster a divisive jealousy, resentment, or pride.[101] The clothes were to be stored in a common room or wardrobe and what was given to one person might be handed to another later; no one had a right to any particular article. Clothes were distributed to each according to need given the season. Bedding and food was likewise to be distributed according to need with an eye to the weakness of individual brothers.[102]

The centrality attached to renunciation of private property, and the distinction between this and poverty, is indicated by the action Augustine took in the winter of 425–26. A priest and monk of Hippo, Januarius, had died leaving a will in which he left a sum of money to the church. Augustine ordered each member of the clerical monastery to reveal his financial affairs and choose between the monastery and any money they claimed for themselves.[103] Augustine had approved Januarius' management of a fund set aside in case a daughter should not remain a nun, but he abhorred Januarius' belief that the money was *his own* to dispose of, while the will put Augustine in an awkward position whether he accepted or rejected the bequest.

[96] Jerome, *Ep.* 108.19, CSEL 55, 334.   [97] Augustine, *Rule*, 1.6 and 1.7, tr. Lawless, *Augustine*, 82.
[98] Ibid., 1.3, tr. Lawless, *Augustine*, 81.   [99] Ibid., 5.2, tr. Lawless, *Augustine*, 95.
[100] Ibid., 1.5 and 1.7.   [101] Ibid., 5.3, tr. Lawless, *Augustine*, 95.
[102] Ibid., 5.1 and 3.4.   [103] *Serm.* 355.6.

Augustine believed, on the basis of Acts 4, that the voluntary dispossession of private property was an apostolic witness which communicated the faith: 'How many thousands believed, my brethren, when they placed at the Apostles' feet the proceeds from the sale of their possessions . . . they truly became the Temple of God; it was not so much that they each became a Temple of God, but all together a Temple of God.'[104] Renunciation of private wealth was thus a key element of the individual's integration into an apostolic life where common ownership served a common purpose. The *Rule* opens with an allusion to Psalm 67:7 and Acts 4:32a: 'the reason why you have been brought together as one is to live with one mind (*unianimes*) in the house and for you to have one mind and heart set on God' (1.2). Before 399 or so Augustine usually thought that to be of one mind in prayer, to be *unianimis*, meant enjoying an inner unity of soul, being single-minded in the contemplation of the One God. The bishop, however, came to see that to be *unianimis* was about sharing a common mind and love for God that found voice in prayer, and the *Rule* may well show him using the word in this new sense. In chapter 1 of the *Rule* he sums up a section on the attitudes of the monks towards wealth and common property with an allusion to the temple that draws on 2 Corinthians 6:16: 'You are, thus, all to be of one mind and heart in your life together (*Omnes ergo unianimiter et concorditer vivite*); honour in one another the God whose temples you have become.'[105] So important for Augustine was this link between common ownership and purpose that in the 'Januarius affair', when the bishop reported back to the congregation what his priests had revealed, he had the deacon chant the text from Acts 4 and then read it out a second time himself.[106]

The sermons preached by Augustine in response to Januarius' will and the bishop's public investigation into the affairs of his clerical monks, suggest for us the importance of the relationship between those monks and the lay congregation, and help us to specify that relationship. The clerical monks were supported by the congregation's offerings, but were meant, in turn, to offer that congregation a model of what it should be as a church. The apostolic life was both missionary *and* communal, and missionary *because* communal. Petilian's attack on Augustine's monasteries, already mentioned, was not unmotivated. In the same year (402), Augustine presented the monasteries of Egypt as an embodiment of perfection. The Catholic Church of the Egyptian monks, and not the Donatist church of Africa, was the bride of Christ spoken of in the Song of Songs

---

[104] *En. in Ps.*, 131.5.   [105] *Rule*, I.8.   [106] *Serm.* 356.1.

(1:6) as lying in the South. The verse alluded to the peace of the monks'
holy society (*sancta societas*) as opposed to the unholy violence wrought
by the Circumcellions.[107] This reinterpretation of Scripture undermined
Donatist ecclesiology. It also suggested that the monastic life was, in Augustine's view, a pre-eminent expression of the Church's life. The common life
of the monks was the hem perfecting the garment of the Church worn by
Christ.[108] Augustine therefore adapted Jerome's etymology of the *monachus*
as solitary in favour of that of the *monachus* as one-with-others. He commented on verse one of Psalm 132 (*how good and how pleasant it is for
brothers to dwell in unity*) that 'it is from what is spoken in this psalm that
monks take their name'.[109]

The apostolic character of Augustinian monasticism explains why his
monks were not forbidden to see women outside of the house.[110] It also
provides a theological grounding for the clerical monasteries which the
bishop advocated in sharp contrast to the stated views of Jerome. The
latter polemicist wrote to Paulinus of Nola in around 395: 'If you wish to
exercise the office of priest . . . then live in the cities and the towns (*castellis*)
and make the salvation of others benefit your own soul. But if you wish
to be what you are called, a monk – that is, one who is solitary – what are
you doing in the cities, which are not at all the places inhabited by those
who are solitary, but by the many?'[111] Augustine rejected this division, with
its underlying definition of the monk as solitary, and for a time at least
ordained only those at Hippo who would be both clerics and monks in his
community.[112] His clerical monasticism was in turn promoted by his most
able pupils: clerical monasteries were set up by former monks of Hippo
when they became bishops of other African churches: Profuturus at Cirta,
Possidius himself at Calama, Severus at Milevis, Evodius at Uzalis, Novatis
at Sitifis, ten in all.[113] Augustine imagined Christ knocking at the door of
the contemplative's cell: 'Open to me, preach about me . . . How will they
be able to listen without a preacher?'[114]

The apostolic nature of Augustine's clerical monastery largely explains
not only whom monks could meet, but their diet. Hospitality not austerity
was the key virtue, with meat and wine on the table to offer the visiting

---

[107] *Letter to the Catholics Against the Donatists*, 16.41.   [108] *En. in Ps.*, 132.9.
[109] *En. in Ps.*, 132.3, CCSL 40, 1927 (*ex voce huius psalmi appellati sunt et monachi*).
[110] *Rule*, 4.4.   [111] Jerome, *Ep.* 58.5, CSEL 54, 533.
[112] Augustine, *Serm.* 355.6. The Januarius affair forced him to allow clerics the option of retaining their
status as such but of ceasing to be monks.
[113] Possidius, *Life of Augustine*, 11.   [114] Augustine, *Tractates on John*, 57.4.

clerics, officials, and lay people who sought out the bishop and theologian. Augustine may also have thought it prudent to avoid abstention from meat and wine that might be mistaken for a Manichaean asceticism.[115] Possidius cited the *Confessions* and 1 Timothy 5:23 to explain that Augustine located evil not in specific foods, but in an immoderate or wrongful desire.[116]

How influential was Augustine's monastic vision? It is reflected in a second rule, the *Ordo monasterii*, used by Caesarius of Arles and ascribed to Augustine in later centuries, but which cannot now be ascribed to Augustine with any certainty.[117] Yet Augustinian monasticism was by no means the only sort to develop in Roman North Africa in the early fifth century. The monastery at Carthage which occasioned his *On the Work of Monks* was clearly inspired by ideas current in Syrian traditions. One of the priests at Hippo, Leporius, founded a lay monastery for his former household, but it is unknown whether the monks followed Augustine's *Rule*.[118] In 411 the younger Melania founded a convent at Thagaste for one hundred and thirty women, and a monastery for eighty manumitted men. There is no reason to think that these former estate slaves led a monastic life informed by Augustine's understanding.[119] The growth of clerical monasteries in North Africa was then cut short by the Vandal invasions. The bishop's *Rule* would find a place in Western collections of monastic legislation, but only much later in the medieval period would it acquire new importance, especially for canons and friars again concerned to integrate monastic life within an urban clerical mission.

BISHOPS AND THEIR CHURCHES

Augustine's clerical monasticism, with his dual identity as a monk and bishop, finally raises the question about how monks interacted more widely with the church communities which gave rise to them. We have already glimpsed the significance for them of bishops' support or opposition, the significance of alms and markets, and the value of a monk's prayers or relics. Discussion of the monastic life adopted by many Late Antique Christians should not occlude the wider impact of that monasticism on their churches.

---

[115] J. D. BeDuhn, *The Manichaean Body in Discipline and Ritual* (Baltimore and London: Johns Hopkins University Press, 2002), 31, and 33–5.

[116] Possidius, *Life of Augustine*, 22; *Confessions*, x.31.46.

[117] Cf. Lawless, *Augustine*, 167–71; A. Zumkeller, *Augustine's Ideal of the Religious Life* (New York: Fordham University Press, 1986), 285–7. For part authorship of the *Ordo* by Alypius, cf. L. Verheijen, *La Règle de saint Augustin*, 2 vols. (Paris: Études Augustiniennes, 1967), vol. II, 125–74.

[118] Augustine, *Serm.* 356.10.   [119] Gerontius (?), *Life of Melania*, 22.

At the start of the fifth century most bishops (and other clergy) within the empire were married men.[120] Consecrated male virgins and ascetics were frequently passed over in episcopal elections, in some places because a bishop supported one of his married relatives, or because a married man brought to the office wealth or valuable social connections.[121] It was not until Justinian that imperial law restricted the episcopate to the unmarried, to widowers, or men who had separated from their wives. However, from the late fourth century onwards, ideals and practices began to alter under the influence of monasticism. Already, in the fourth century, it was generally expected that bishops would abstain from sexual relations. African church legislation attempted with imperfect results to require abstinence of bishops, priests, and deacons.[122] Though Ambrose acknowledged that the ideal was not universally observed in what he dismissed as backwaters, Jerome insisted: 'You surely admit that he cannot be a bishop who during his episcopate fathers sons.'[123]

From the mid fourth century onwards ascetic celibate bishops increasingly appear in our sources, initially in close proximity to monastic centres in Egypt and Palestine. Serapion, recipient of the dying Antony's second sheepskin, was both monk and bishop.[124] Three monks, Dracontius, Isidore, and Dioscorus, served in turn from the early 350s as bishop of the diocese in which Nitria was located.[125] Two brothers, both monks, Melas and Solon, were bishops of Rhinocorura in Sinai during the Arian controversy.[126] The Palestinian monk Epiphanius was made bishop of Salamis in 367.[127] According to Mark the Deacon, Porphyry was a monk at Scetis before he was later forcibly elected bishop of Gaza in the late fourth century.[128] Pachomian literature related the founder's disapproval of monks being ordained possibly because they might be made bishop and lost to the monastery.[129] A monk might cut off an ear to ensure he would avoid this fate.[130] In Egypt this pattern of monastic bishops may be traced to

[120] Jerome, *Ep.* 69.2.
[121] *Against Jovinian*, 34. For clerical dynasties in Italy, cf. C. Sotinel, 'Le recrutement des évêques en Italie aux IVe et Ve siècles: essai d'enquête prosopographique', in *Vescovi e pastori in epoca teodosiana*, 2 vols. (Rome: Institutum Patristicum Augustinianum, 1997), vol. 1, 199–200.
[122] C. Munier (ed.), *Concilia Africae*, A.345–A. 525, CCSL 149, 201.
[123] Ambrose, *On Duties*, 1.50, 258; Jerome, *Against Jovinian*, 34. Cf. also, Socrates, *Church History*, v.22.
[124] Athanasius, *Life of Antony*, 91; *Ep.* 49.7.
[125] Socrates, *Church History*, vi.7; Chitty, *The Desert*, 32.
[126] Sozomen, *Church History*, vi.31. For Sozomen's motives, cf. A. H. Merrills, 'Monks, monsters, and barbarians: re-defining the African periphery in Late Antiquity', *JECS* 12.2 (2004), 233–4.
[127] Sozomen, *Church History*, vi.32.   [128] Mark the Deacon, *Life of Porphyry*, 4.
[129] Cf. Rousseau, *Pachomius*, 169–70.   [130] Socrates, *Church History*, IV.23.

Athanasius' alliances with monks whose support he valued against Meletian and Arian rivals.[131] In the Western empire, Martin of Tours is the first known monk to be made a bishop (in 371), while a number of ascetics associated with the monasteries at Marseilles, Lérins, and the Stoechadic islands became bishops of Gallic towns in the early fifth century.[132] The phenomenon is to be traced here to a network of powerful families and friends.

We may thus distinguish between factors promoting the rise of monastic bishops of smaller dioceses, and the rise to prominence of ascetic bishops in the major churches of the East. Here, the high standing of the ascetic was increasingly desirable for bishops whose spiritual authority had to be deployed in relation to rival claimants for their title, imperial dignitaries, and monastic leaders. Socrates describes a number of ascetics chosen as Novatian bishop of Constantinople from the second half of the fourth century.[133] An ascetic outsider might also appear an attractive candidate at court for the Catholic bishopric of Constantinople to avoid ceding power to factions within the presbyterate: a relatively high number of ascetics appear as its bishop from the late fourth century: Gregory Nazianzen, Chrysostom, and Nestorius. Another, Atticus, was seemingly trained as an ascetic in the Macedonian sect before becoming Catholic.[134] Elsewhere, Athanasius at Alexandria, Ambrose in the imperial capital of Milan, Basil, and Theodoret, contributed by their reputation to the slow rise of the ascetic bishop as holy man. While these long remained a minority, they indicate the degree to which some of the most talented figures and writers were drawn to asceticism and then chosen for high office.

A bishop found himself in a complex relationship to monks who resided within or visited his diocese. I have written elsewhere about how monastic almsgiving allowed monks to enter into competition with bishops for spiritual authority, as well as to assist bishops with the care of the urban destitute in hostels.[135] To some extent monks were useful allies and assistants. An imperial law of 398 permitted bishops to ordain monks to minister as clerics where there would otherwise be a shortage, which may indicate the growth of the Church in less heavily populated areas, or the difficulties facing Nicene bishops whose clergy were tainted by Arianism.[136] Ambrose gained control of a see which had previously been held by an Arian bishop, and it is

---

[131] C. W. Griggs, *Early Egyptian Christianity: From its Origins to 451 CE* (Leiden: Brill, 1990), 146–8; Brakke, *Athanasius*, 99–102.

[132] Dunn, *The Emergence of Monasticism*, 73–4, and 83; Stewart, *Cassian*, 16–18.

[133] Socrates, *Church History*, IV.9 and VII.46. [134] Sozomen, *Church History*, VIII.27.

[135] Finn, *Almsgiving*, 98, and 210–12. [136] *Theodosian Code*, XVI.2.

noticeable that his treatise *On Duties* was written for celibate presbyters.[137]
Monks, however, did not simply form a pool of obedient ministers. In
North Africa, synods acted in 401 and 402 to prevent monks from one
area being accepted for ordination as clerics in a different diocese, and to
stop clerics abandoning one diocese for a monastery in another.[138] Behind
the earlier legislation probably lay Augustine's irritation with monks disobedient to his authority who sought clerical employment in their home
district.[139] At Antioch, Chrysostom portrayed the monks as intervening
to protect citizens from the wrath of the imperial commissioners after the
statues had been pulled down.[140] However accurate his account, the monks
became figures who embodied for his congregation the courageous speech
of the apostles where pagan philosophers had failed.[141]

Monks could be used in attacks on pagan cult, whether to destroy shrines
or neutralize them by occupying their sites. Martin reportedly founded
monasteries (perhaps cells?) during the late fourth century at some of the
shrines he destroyed in rural Gaul.[142] Libanius bitterly complained in 385
about the damage wrought by monks in the countryside round Antioch.
They were active at Beroea and Edessa.[143] To what extent monks acted at
the request of a bishop, or with the tacit blessing of civil authorities, is
often unclear and no doubt varied.[144] In the early fifth century Hypatius
apparently acted independently when cutting down and burning sacred
trees in Bithynia.[145] From Constantinople Chrysostom sent monks on a
mission to convert pagans in Phoenicia. Words mattered as much as deeds.
Where Libanius and Julian had used monks to denigrate Christianity,
Chrysostom's Antiochene *Comparison Between a King and a Monk* reapplied
to monks the ascetic virtues Libanius gave to Socrates.[146]

The value of monks as a source of support in the doctrinal wars of
the fourth and fifth centuries may be measured by the violence unleashed
against monks favourable to Athanasius.[147] By the early decades of the

---

[137] Ambrose, *On Duties,* 1.50.258.
[138] C. Munier (ed.), *Concilia Africae,* A.345–A. 525, CCSL 149, 204.
[139] Augustine, *Ep.* 60; cf. C. Munier, 'Problèmes monastiques et conciles Africains (a. 345–427)', in
     Augustinianum 39.1 (1999), 149–68.
[140] Chrysostom, *On the Statues,* 17.3–4.
[141] D. G. Hunter, 'Preaching and propaganda in fourth-century Antioch: John Chrysostom's *Homilies
     on the Statues*', in D. G. Hunter (ed.), *Preaching in the Patristic Age: Studies in Honor of Walter J.
     Burghardt, S.J.* (New York: Paulist Press, 1989), 126–30.
[142] Sulpicius Severus, *Life of Martin,* 13.   [143] Libanius, *Or.* 30, 8–9, 21–3, and 44–5.
[144] Ibid., 30. For monks used by bishops as 'a form of "deniable" violence', cf. P. Garnsey and
     C. Humfress, *The Evolution of the Late Antique World* (Cambridge: Orchard Academic, 2001), 149.
[145] Callinicus, *Life of Hypatius,* 30.1.
[146] Hunter, *A Comparison,* 24–7.   [147] Socrates, *Church History,* IV.23.

fifth century Eastern monks had become a powerful factor in the ever difficult business of determining orthodoxy. They were instruments, but also players. Some 500 monks from Nitria supported Cyril in his dispute with the imperial Prefect Orestes in AD 415 when they mobbed the latter's chariot.[148] Theodoret complained in 434 of the pressure he came under from three 'holy monks' to settle his dispute with John of Antioch after count Flavius Titus had written to them. Despite the complaint, the dispute was soon resolved.[149]

One bishop's instrument was thus another man's threat and source of disorder. It is this which explains both the law of 390 which theoretically exiled monks from the cities of the East (after riots at Constantinople were blamed on them), and the law of 392 which revoked the ban.[150] Authorities were also worried by the attraction which monasteries posed to runaway slaves. The law might allow for their enforced return and punishment, but a powerful abbot could drawn on a spiritual authority that faced down demands for the law to be upheld.[151] The desire on the part of bishops to control monks led to the legislation by the Council of Chalcedon in 451 which prohibited the foundation of monasteries outside the bishop's control.[152] We have no reason to believe the legislation resolved the problems it addressed.

I have only sketched some of the changes which monasticism brought to urban churches. The rise of cenobitic monasticism also contributed, for example, to the slow decline in syneisaktism. Finally, it is likely that monasticism contributed indirectly to the growth of Lent in Late Antiquity as a penitential season of fasting for lay Christians. In the mid fifth century Socrates claimed that there was a three-week fast before Easter at Rome, except on Saturdays and Sundays, while in Greece and at Alexandria there was a six-week fast known as the 'forty days'. Elsewhere, he reported that the 'forty days' began earlier but with longer intermissions. What Christians fasted from also varied: from red meat, from birds or fish as well, from eggs and fruit; some fasted from all food until the ninth hour, and were then at liberty to eat what they wished.[153] His details may be wrong, but he was surely right about the variety of practice.

When had Lenten fasting extended backwards from the fasting imme-diately before Easter discussed in Chapter 3? Dionysius of Alexandria in a letter to a fellow bishop Basilides before AD 265 indicates a holy week fast that varied between two and six days, with no commonly agreed hour for

---

[148] Ibid., VII.14.   [149] Theodoret, *Epp.* IV.27.
[150] *Theodosian Code*, XVI.3.1 and 2.   [151] Callinicus, *Life of Hypatius*, 21.
[152] Chalcedon, canon 4, Joannou, *Discipline*, vol. I, 72–4.   [153] Socrates, *Church History*, V.22.

it to conclude, but he is silent on what, if anything, preceded holy week.[154] An early third-century 'church order', the *Didascalia*, which established ideals of Church practice, likewise contains nothing about a Lenten fast before Holy Week.[155] The *Apostolic Constitutions*, however, compiled in or at Antioch in the mid fourth century advocate a more extensive pattern of periodic fasting. The forty days of Lent are to be kept as a fast from Mondays to Fridays.[156] This is followed in Holy Week by a fast of increasing intensity, beginning on the Monday with a diet of bread, salt, and vegetables, leading to a total fast on Good Friday and Holy Saturday until cock-crow early on the Sunday morning.[157] The octave of Pentecost is then followed by a week of fasting which is linked with petitionary prayer.[158] This is not a straightforward window on universal practice, but indicates the clerical promotion of Lenten fasting. The festal letters of Athanasius suggest that at roughly the same time in the mid fourth century the Alexandrian church and its Egyptian satellites switched from a six- to a forty-day fast.[159]

CONCLUSIONS

Much monasticism developed independently from the Origenist ascetic tradition, and these forms of monasticism are to be explained by the interaction of both socio-economic and religious factors. They involved not only different ways of life for practitioners, and understandings of that life, but differing relations with ordinary Christians. The Syriac monastic tradition emphasized a radical personal asceticism in which constant prayer prevented manual labour but won for the holy man access to divine power on behalf of the disciples and lay followers, who both interrupted, and supported through almsgiving, his otherwise solitary devotions. This monasticism in which individuals effectively competed in public for support was at odds first with the Pachomian vision of a common enterprise largely secluded from public gaze. Within the federated monasteries detailed legislation realized an ideal of self-sufficiency through manual labour both by organizing industry and agricultural production on a large scale, and by controlling the relations between the producers and their markets. Syriac monasticism was likewise at odds with the semi-anchoretic tradition in Egypt, which generally favoured monastic labour, and where

---

[154] Dionysius of Alexandria, *Ep.* 14.   [155] *Didascalia*, v.12–13.   [156] Ibid., v.13.3.
[157] Ibid., v.18–19.   [158] *Apostolic Constitutions*, v.13.3, v.18–19, and v.20.14–17.
[159] T. D. Barnes, Review of the *Histoire acéphale*, *JThS* 37.2 (1986), 583.

an ascetic virtue of working to support oneself was partly at odds with the lay Christian's virtue in giving alms to ascetics.[160] In North Africa, Augustine championed a more moderate urban and clerical monasticism which located the essence of asceticism in commitment to the common good and Christian unity.

As monasticism developed, bishops found new allies in their campaigns against pagan cult and heresy. However, these allies soon became rivals for moral authority, and bishops sought to control the monks with limited success. The promotion of monasticism by church leaders would also have far-reaching consequences for the churches they led. Over time bishops would increasingly be chosen from among ascetics. Ordinary church members not only turned to the monks for spiritual and practical help; they found the monks held up to them as examples of dedication to the Gospel and the truly Christian life. This in turn shaped the development of lay piety.

[160] Palladius, *Lausiac History*, 47. Cf. my *Almsgiving*, 93–5.

Final Thoughts

Arthur Vööbus, the pioneering scholar of much Eastern monasticism, wrote that 'ideas have legs'.[1] This book has demonstrated how ideas about abstention from food, drink, sleep, and wealth, could travel between religions as well as between far distant places in the Graeco-Roman world, though they were often much changed on the journey. Widely varying practices concerning food and sex could be given a new home in Porphyry's philosophical asceticism. Neoplatonist ideas about training for contemplation of the divine could then be deployed in Philo's redescription of Jewish practices originally meant to uphold the priestly purity of Israel. From there, amongst other places, they crossed into service within a Christian psychomachy. Within Christianity communal fasts were taken over from Judaism only to be partly turned against their original practitioners. Origen's ascetic theology travelled far across the empire, so that purely regional accounts of monasticism obscure the exegete's profound influence. Regional cultures, on the other hand, proved more or less hospitable to different ascetic ideas. The idea of prayer without work found it hard to get a foothold in urban communities likely to be burdened by its presence. Semi-anchoretic monasticism could only travel a certain distance from the communities which sustained it. Some ideas proved extremely hard to budge, despite the best efforts of eloquent Christian preachers: widowed Christians continued to remarry; while celibate men and women continued to live together for something like two hundred years after we first find them denounced for so doing.

Some ascetic ideas could not find a space within the pages of this book: Manichaean abstention has been the most notable absentee. So many ideas jostling for attention should give us pause before we speak of even Christian 'asceticism' *tout court*. It has been argued that 'asceticism began as a method for men and women to transcend as virgins of God, the

[1] Vööbus, *History of Asceticism*, vol. II, 139.

limitations of humanity in relation to the divine'.[2] This is true only if we discount the asceticism by which Jews and Christians also accepted their limited humanity in humble fasting. The same author has written that asceticism 'slowly changed into a way for men as men and for women as women to symbolize the power of the Church to surpass human weakness', a change which 'coincided with the establishment of Christianity as the religion of the Roman Empire'. Yet in the late second century, if not earlier, Hermas shows that virgins were already becoming signs of the angelic life which characterized the Church. Ambrose wrote much later that 'the character of our mind may be perceived in the attitude of our body'.[3] He was thinking about the modesty and decorum shown in how we deport ourselves. The notion certainly oversimplifies the ways in which pagans, Jews, and Christians used bodily abstention to work upon the mind, and to work upon each other, to lower themselves before God or raise themselves up to Him, but Ambrose's half truth directs us to the importance of bodily abstention if we are to know better the mind of pagans, Jews, and Christians in the Graeco-Roman world.

[2] Elm, *Virgins*, 384.   [3] Ambrose, *On Duties*, 1.18.71.

Bibliography

I. ANCIENT TEXTS

Texts appear under the name of their author where known, otherwise by title only.

1 Clement, ed. A. Jaubert, SC 167 (1971).

2 Baruch, tr. A. F. Klijn, *OTP*, vol. I, 615–52.

2 *Clement*, ed. M. W. Holmes, J. B. Lightfoot, and J. R. Harmer, *The Apostolic Fathers*, 3rd edn (Grand Rapids: Baker Book House, 2007), 132–65.

4 Ezra, tr. B. M. Metzger, *OTP*, vol. I, 517–59.

Acts of Andrew, ed. with Eng. tr., Dennis R. MacDonald, *The Acts of Andrew and The Acts of Andrew and Matthias in the City of the Cannibals* (Atlanta: Scholars Press, 1990).

Acts of John, ed. K. Schäferdiek, *NTA*, vol. II, 152–212.

Acts of Paul (including the *Acts of Paul and Thecla*), ed. W. Schneemelcher, *NTA*, vol. II, 213–70.

Acts of Peter (including the *Actus Vercellenses*) ed. W. Schneemelcher, *NTA*, vol. II, 271–321.

Acts of Peter and the Twelve Apostles, tr. H.-M. Schenke, *NTA*, vol. II, 420–4.

Acts of Thomas tr. A. F. J. Klijn, *The Acts of Thomas: Introduction, Text, and Commentary*, 2nd rev. edn (Leiden: Brill, 2003).

Ambrose, *On Duties* (*De officiis*), ed. M. Testard, *Les Devoirs*, 2 vols. (Paris: Les Belles Lettres, 1984 and 1992).

    On Virgins, On Virginity, On the Consecration of a Virgin, Exhortation on Virginity, ed. with It. tr. in F. Gori, *Sant'Ambrogio, Verginità e vedovanza* (Milan and Rome: Città nuova, 1989).

Antony of Egypt, *Letters*, tr. S. Rubenson, *The Letters of St Antony: Monasticism and the Making of a Saint* (Minneapolis: Fortress Press, 1995).

Apocalypse of Zephaniah, tr. O. S. Wintermute, *OTP*, vol. I, 497–512.

The Apocryphon of John, tr. F. Wisse, *NHL*, 104–23.

Apophthegmata Patrum, Collectio Graeca Alphabetica or *Alphabetikon* (GA), PG 65, 72–440, tr. B. Ward, *The Sayings of the Desert Fathers: The Alphabetical Collection* (London and Oxford: Mowbrays, 1975); the *Collectio Graeca Anonyma* (GN), Fr. tr. L. Regnault, *Les Sentences des Pères du désert: Série des anonymes* (Solesmes, 1985); and the *Collectio Latina Systematica* (PJ), PL 73, 855–1022.

Apostolic Constitutions, ed. M. Metzger, *Les Constitutions apostoliques*, SC 320, 329, 336 (1985–7).

Apostolic Tradition, ed. B. Botte, *Hippolyte de Rome, La Tradition apostolique*, SC 11 bis (1984).

Apuleius, *Metamorphoses*, ed. J. Gwyn Griffiths, *Apuleius of Madauros, The Isis-Book (Metamorphoses, Book XI)* (Leiden: Brill, 1975).

Athanasius, *Festal Index*, ed. M. Albert, in A. Martin and M. Albert (eds.), *Histoire 'Acephale' et Index Syriaque des lettres festales d'Athanase d'Alexandrie*, SC 317 (1985).

 Letter to Virgins, ed. with Fr. tr. Lefort, 'S. Athanase: sur la virginité', *Muséon* 42 (1929), 197–274.

 Letter to the Virgins who went to Jerusalem, ed. with Fr. tr. J. Lebon, 'S. Athanase: Lettre à des vierges qui étaient allées prier à Jérusalem et qui étaient revenues', *Muséon* 41 (1928), 169–216.

 Life of Antony, ed. G. Bartelink, *Vie d'Antoine*, SC 400 (1994).

 On the Incarnation, ed. R. W. Thomson, *Athanasius: Contra Gentes and De Incarnatione* (Oxford: Clarendon Press, 1971).

 Works, in H. G. Opitz (ed.), *Athanasius Werke* (Berlin and Leipzig: de Gruyter, 1934–41).

Athanasius (?), *Treatise On Virginity*, ed. with Fr. tr. J. Lebon in *Muséon* 40 (1927), 205–48.

Athenagoras, *Embassy*, ed. W. Schoedel, *Legatio and De Resurrectione* (Oxford: Clarendon Press, 1972).

Augustine, *Against the Writings of Petilian*, ed. A. Lombardi, *Polemica con I Donatisti, Opere di Sant' Agostino XV.2* (Rome: Città Nuova, 1999).

 Confessiones, ed. J. O'Donnell, 3 vols. (Oxford: Clarendon Press, 1992).

 Enarrationes in Psalmos, ed. D. Dekkers and J. Fraipont, 2 vols., CCSL 39 and 40 (1956).

 Letter to the Catholics Against the Donatists, ed. A. Lombardi, *Polemica con I Donatisti, Opere di Sant' Agostino XV.2* (Rome: Città Nuova, 1999).

 Letters, ed. A. Goldbacher, *S. Aurelii Augustini Hipponensis Episcopi*.

 Letters, I–LV, ed. K. Daur, CCSL 31 (2004).

 Letters, ed. A. Goldbacher, *S. Aurelii Augustini Hipponensis Episcopi Epistulae* CSEL 34 (1 and 2), 44, 57 and 58 (Prague, Vienna and Leipzig: Tempsky, 1895–1923).

 On Holy Virginity, ed. P. G. Walsh, *De bono coniugali, De sancta virginitate* (Oxford: Clarendon Press, 2001), 65–147.

 On Order, ed. J. Doignon, *L'Ordre*, Bibliothèque Augustinienne, Oeuvres de saint Augustin, 4/2 (Paris: Institut d'Études Augustiniennes, 1997).

 On the Work of Monks, ed. J. Zycha, CSEL (1900), 531–96.

 Retractions, ed. A. Mutzenbecher, CCSL 57 (1984).

 Tractates on John, ed. R. Willems, CCSL 36 (1954).

Aulus Gellius, *Attic Nights*, ed. R. Marache and Y. Julien, *Aulu-Gelle, Les Nuits attiques*, 4 vols. (Paris: Les Belles Lettres, 1967–98).

Authoritative Teaching, tr. G. MacRae, *NHL*, 304–10.

Basil of Ancyra, *On True Purity of Virginity*, PG 30, 669–810.

Basil of Caesarea, *Letters*, ed. Y. Courtonne, *Saint Basile, Lettres*, 3 vols. (Paris: Les Belles Lettres, 1957–66).

Longer Rules, PG 31, 889–1052.

Shorter Rules, PG 31, 1079–306.

Benedict, *Rule of St Benedict*, ed. J. Neufville and A. de Vogüé, *La Règle de saint Benoît*, SC 181–6 (1971–2).

Callinicus, *Life of Hypatius*, ed G. Bartelink, *Callinicos, Vie d'Hypatios*, SC 177 (1971).

Cassian, *Conférences*, ed. E. Pichery, *Jean Cassien: Conférences*, SC 42, 54 and 64 (1955–9), tr. B. Ramsey, *John Cassian, The Conferences*, Ancient Christian Writers 57 (New York: Paulist Press, 1997).

De incarnatione, ed. M. Petschenig, *Cassianus, De institutis coenobiorum, De incarnatione contra Nestorium*, CSEL 17 (Vienna, 2004).

Institutes, ed. Jean-Claude Guy SJ, *Jean Cassien, Institutions cénobitiques*, SC 109 (1965).

Cassiodorus, *Institutiones*, ed. R. A. B. Mynors, *Cassiodori Senatoris Institutiones* (Oxford: Clarendon Press, 1937).

Cercidas, *Fragments*, in J. Powell. (ed.), *Collectanea Alexandrina* (Oxford: Clarendon Press, 1925).

Cicero, *De officiis*, ed: M. Winterbottom, *M. Tulli Ciceronis, De Officiis* (Oxford: Clarendon Press, 1994).

Clement of Alexandria, *Works*, ed. O. Stählin, L. Früchtel and U. Treu, *Clemens Alexandrinus*, 4 vols., GCS (1970–85).

Crates, *Fragments*, in G. Giannantoni. (ed.), *Socraticorum reliquiae*, 2 vols. (Rome: Ateneo, 1983).

Cyprian, *Letters*, ed. G. F. Diercks, *Sancti Cypriani Episcopi Epistularum* 1–57, CCSL 3b (1994).

On the Dress of Virgins, ed. G. Hartel, CSEL 3 (Vienna, 1868).

Didache, ed. W. Rordorf and A. Tuilier, *La Doctrine des douze apôtres (Didachè)*, SC 248 bis (1998).

Dio Chrysostom, *Orations*, ed. J. De Arnim, *Dionis Prusaensis quem vocant Chrysostomum quae extant omnia*, 2 vols. (Berlin: Weidmann, 1893–6).

Diogenes Laertius, *Lives of Eminent Philosophers*, ed. M. Marcovich, *Diogenes Laertius, Vitae Philosophorum*, 2 vols. (Stuttgart and Leipzig: Teubner, 1999).

Dionysius of Alexandria, *Letters*, ed. C. Lett Feltoe, *The Letters and Other Remains of Dionysius of Alexandria* (Cambridge University Press, 1904).

Elenchos, ed. M. Marcovich, *Hippolytus, Refutatio Omnium Haeresium*, (Berlin and New York: de Gruyter, 1986).

Ephrem, *Commentary on the Diatessaron*, ed. L. Leloir, *Éphrem de Nisibie, Commentaire de l'évangile concordant ou diatessaron*, SC 121 (1966).

Epictetus, *Discourses*, ed. J. Souilhé and A. Jagu, *Epictète: Entretiens* (Paris: Belles Lettres, 1949–75).

Epicurus, *Works*, ed. G. Arrighetti, *Epicuro, Opere*, 2nd edn (Turin: Giulio Einaudi, 1973).

Epiphanius, *Panarion*, ed. J. Drümmer, *Epiphanius*, vol. III, GCS (Berlin: Akademie Verlag, 1985), tr. F. Williams, *The Panarion of Epiphanius of Salamis*, 3 vols. (Leiden, New York, and Cologne: Brill, 1987–94).

Epistle of Barnabas, ed. P. Prigent and R. Kraft, *Épître de Barnabé*, SC 172 (1971).

Euripides, *Cretans*, 19–20, ed. and tr. C. Collard, M. J. Cropp, and K. H. Lee, *Euripides, Selected Fragmentary Plays*, vol. I (Warminster: Aris and Phillips, 1995).

Eusebius of Caesarea, *Church History*, ed. G. Bardy, *Eusèbe de Césarée, Histoire ecclésiastique*, SC 31, 41, 55, and 73 (1952–60).

Eusebius of Emesa, *On Virgins*, in É. M. Buytaert, *Eusèbe d'Emèse, Discours conservés en latin, textes en partie inédits*, 2 vols. (Louvain: Spicilegium Sacrum Lovaniense, 1953 and 1957).

Evagrius Ponticus, *Ad Monachos*, tr. J. Driscoll OSB, *Evagrius Ponticus, Ad Monachos*, ACW 59 (New York and Mahwah: Paulist Press, 2003); also R. Sinkewicz, *Evagrius of Pontus: The Greek Ascetic Corpus* (Oxford University Press, 2003).

Praktikos, ed. A. Guillaumont and C. Guillaumont, SC 170 and 171 (1971), tr. S. Tugwell, *Evagrius Ponticus: Praktikos and On Prayer* (Oxford, Faculty of Theology, 1987).

Gerontius (?), *Life of Melania*, ed. Denys Gorce, *Vie de Sainte Mélanie*, SC 90 (1962).

Gospel of the Ebionites, ed. P. Vielhauer and G. Strecker, *NTA,* vol. I, 166–71.

Gospel of the Egyptians, ed. W. Schneemelcher, *NTA*, vol. I, 209–15.

Gospel of the Hebrews, ed. P. Vielhauer and G. Strecker, *NTA*, vol. I, 172–8.

Gospel of Peter, ed. C. Maurer, *NTA*, vol. I, 216–27.

[*Coptic*] *Gospel of Thomas*, ed. T. O. Lambdin, *NHL*, 124–38.

Gregory Nazianzen, *Oratio* 43, ed. J. Bernardi, *Grégoire de Naziance, Discours 42–43*, SC 384 (1992).

Gregory of Nyssa, *On Virginity*, ed. M. Aubineau, *Grégoire de Nysse, Traité sur la virginité*, SC 119 (1966).

Gregory Thaumaturgus, *Address of Thanksgiving*, PG 10, 1052–104.

History of the Rechabites, tr. J. H. Charlesworth, *OTP*, vol. II, 443–61.

Iamblichus, *On the Pythagorean Life*, tr. G. Clark (Liverpool University Press, 1989).

Ignatius, *Letters*, ed. M. W. Holmes, J. B. Lightfoot, and J. R. Harmer, *The Apostolic Fathers*, 3rd edn (Grand Rapids: Baker Book House, 2007), 166–271.

Irenaeus, *Against the Heresies*, ed. A. Rousseau, L. Doutreleau, and C. Mercier, *Irénée de Lyon, Contre les hérésies*, SC 100, 152, 153, 210, 211, 263, 264 (1965–79).

Jerome, *De viris illustribus*, ed. A. Ceresa-Gastaldo, *Gerolamo, Gli Uomini Illustri* (Florence: Nardini, 1988).

Letters, ed. I. Hilberg, *Sancti Eusebii Hieronymi Epistulae*, CSEL 54–6 (Vienna, 1996).

Rule of Pachomius, PL 23, 61–78.

John Chrysostom, *Against those who live with Virgins*, ed. J. Dumortier, *Saint Jean Chrysostome: Les Cohabitations suspectes; comment observer la virginité* (Paris:

Les Belles Lettres, 1955), tr. E. A. Clark, *Jerome, Chrysostom, and Friends* (New York and Toronto: Edwin Mellon Press, 1979), 164–208.

Against the Opponents of the Monastic Life, PG 47, 519–386, tr. D. G. Hunter, *A Comparison Between a King and a Monk / Against the Opponents of the Monastic Life: Two Treatises by John Chrysostom* (Lewiston/Queenston and Lampeter: Edwin Mellen Press, 1988).

Homilies on Matthew, PG 57, 13–PG 58, 794.

On the Statues, PG 49, 15–240.

On Virginity, ed. H. Musurillo with introduction by B. Grillet, *Jean Chrysostome, La Virginité*, SC 125 (1966).

Joseph and Aseneth, tr. C. Burchard, *OTP*, vol. ii, 177–247.

Jubilees, tr. O. S. Wintermute, *OTP*, vol. ii, 35–142.

Julian, *Orations*, ed. G. Rochefort, *L'Empereur Julien: Oeuvres completes, vol. 2.1: Discours de Julien empereur* (Paris: Belles Lettres, 1963).

Justin, *Dialogue with Trypho*, ed. P. Bobichon, *Justin Martyr, Dialogue avec Tryphon*, 2 vols. (Fribourg: Academic Press, 2003).

First Apology, ed. A. Wartelle, *Saint Justin, Apologies* (Paris: Études augustiniennes, 1987).

Libanius, *Orations* 30, and 45, tr A. F. Norman, *Libanius: Selected Works*, vol. ii (Cambridge, Mass. and London: Heinemann, 1977).

Liber Graduum tr. Robert A. Kitchen and Martien Parmentier *The Book of Steps: The Syriac Liber Graduum* (Kalamazoo: Cistercian Publications, 2004).

Life of Alexander, ed. E. De Stoop, *Vie d'Alexandre l'Acémète*, PO 6 (Paris, 1911), 641–705.

(*Bohairic*) *Life of Pachomius*, tr. A. Veilleux, *Pachomian Koinonia*, 3 vols. (Kalamazoo: Cistercian Publications, 1980–2), vol. i, 23–295.

(*First Greek*) *Life of Pachomius*, tr. A. Veilleux, *Pachomian Koinonia*, 3 vols. (Kalamazoo: Cistercian Publications, 1980–2), vol. i, 297–423.

Livy, *Histories*, XXXVI–XL, ed. P. G. Walsh, *Titi Livi, Ab urbe condita*, vol. vi (Oxford: Clarendon Press, 1999).

Lucian, *Works*, ed. M. D. Macleod, *Luciani Opera*, 4 vols. (Oxford: Clarendon Press, 1972–87).

Mark the Deacon, *Life of Porphyry*, ed. H. Grégoire and M.-A. Kugener, *Marc le diacre, Vie de Porphyre, évêque de Gaza* (Paris: Les Belles Lettres, 1930).

Menander, *Fragments*, ed. A. Koerte and A. Thierfelder, *Menandri quae supersunt*, 2nd edn, 2 vols. (Leipzig: Teubner 1955–9).

Methodius, *Symposium*, ed. H. Musurillo with Fr. tr. by V.-H. Debidour, *Méthode d'Olympe, Le Banquet* SC 95 (1963).

Minucius Felix, *Octavius*, ed. B. Kytzler, *M. Minuci Felicis Octavius* (Leipzig: Teubner, 1982).

Musonius, *Discourses*, ed. and tr. C. Lutz, *Musonius Rufus, 'The Roman Socrates'*, Yale Classical Studies 10 (New Haven: Yale University Press, 1947), 3–147.

Nilus of Ancyra, *Commentary on the Song of Songs*, ed. Marie-Gabrielle Guérard, *Nil d'Ancyre, Commentaire sur le Cantique des Cantiques*, SC 403 (1994).

On Voluntary Poverty, PG 79, 968–1060.

On the Origin of the World, tr. H.-G. Bethge and B. Layton, *NHL*, 170–89.

On Virginity, ed. D. Armand and M.-C. Moons, 'Une curieuse homélie grecque inédite sur la virginité adressée aux pères de famille', *RB* 63 (1953), 18–69.

Origen, *Commentary on Matthew*, Books X–XVII, PG 139, 836–1600; and ed. R. Girod, *Origène, Commentaire sur l'évangile selon Matthieu X–XI*, SC 162 (1970).

    Commentary on the Song of Songs, ed. L. Brésard, H. Crouzel, and M. Borret, *Origène, Commentaire sur le Cantique des Cantiques*, vol. 1, SC 375 (1991).

    Homilies on Exodus, ed. M. Borret, *Origène, Homélies sur l'Exode*, SC 321 (1985).

    Homilies on Genesis, ed. L. Doutreleau, *Origène, Homélies sur la Genèse*, SC 7 bis (1985).

    Homilies on Jeremiah, ed. P. Nautin, *Origène, Homélies sur Jérémie*, with Fr. trans. by P. Husson and P. Nautin, SC 232 and 238 (1976 and 1977).

    Homilies on Joshua, ed. Annie Jaubert, *Origène, Homélies sur Josué*, SC 71 (1960).

    Homilies on Judges, ed. P. Messié, L. Neyrand and M. Borret, *Origène, Homélies sur les Juges*, SC 389 (1993).

    Homilies on Leviticus, ed. M. Borret, *Origène, Homélies sur le Lévitique*, SC 286 and 287 (1981).

    Homilies on Numbers, ed. L. Doutreleau SJ, *Origène, Homélies sur les Nombres*, SC 415, 442, and 461 (1996–2001).

    Philocalia, 1–20, ed. Marguerite Harl, *Origène, Philocalie, 1–20, Sur les Écritures*, SC 302 (1983).

Palladius, *Dialogue*, ed P. R. Coleman-Norton, *Palladii Dialogus De Vita S. Joannis Chrysostomi* (Cambridge University Press, 1928).

    Lausiac History, ed. C. Mohrmann, G. Bartelink, and M. Barchiesi, *Palladio, La storia Lausiaca* (Verona: Arnolda Mondadori, 1974).

Philo, *The Contemplative Life*, ed. F. Daumas and P. Miquel, *De vita contemplativa* (Paris: Éditions du Cerf, 1963).

    Life of Moses, ed. R. Arnaldez, C. Mondésert, J. Pouilloux, P. Savinel, *De vita Mosis* (Paris: Éditions du Cerf, 1967).

    Works, tr. C. D. Yonge, 2nd edn (Peabody, Mass.: Hendrickson, 1993).

Philostratus, *Life of Apollonius*, ed. C. P. Jones, *The Life of Apollonius of Tyana I–IV* (Harvard University Press, 2005).

Plutarch, *Numa*, ed. C. Lindskog and K. Ziegler, 2nd edn (Leipzig: Teubner, 1973).

Polycarp, *Letter to the Philippians*, ed. M. W. Holmes, J. B. Lightfoot, and J. R. Harmer, *The Apostolic Fathers*, 3rd edn (Grand Rapids: Baker Book House, 2007), 272–97.

Porphyry, *On Abstinence*, ed. J. Bouffartigue (ed.), *Porphyre: De l'abstinence*, with introduction by J. Bouffartigue and M. Patillon, (Paris: Belles Lettres, 1977–); Eng. tr. by G. Clark, *On Abstinence from Killing Animals* (London: Duckworth, 2000).

    Letter to Marcella, ed. E. Des Places, *Porphyre, Vie de Pythagore, Lettre à Marcella* (Paris: Belles Lettres, 1982).

Life of Plotinus, ed. P. Henry and H.-R. Schwyzer, *Plotini Opera*, vol. 1 (Paris and Brussels: Desclée de Brouwer, 1951), 1–41.

Life of Pythagoras, ed. E. Des Places, *Porphyre, Vie de Pythagore, Lettre à Marcella* (Paris: Belles Lettres, 1982).

Possidius, *Life of Augustine*, ed. A. A. R. Bastiaensen, in C. Mohrmann, A. A. R. Bastiaensen, L. Canali, and C. Carena (eds.), *Vita di Cipriano, Vita di Ambrogio, Vita di Agostino* (Milan: Fondazione Lorenzo Valla / A. Mondadori, 1975), 130–240.

Protevangelium of James, ed. O. Cullmann, in *NTA*, vol. 1, 421–39.

Ps.-Anacharsis, *Letters*, tr. A. McGuire, in A. Malherbe, *The Cynic Epistles: A Study Edition* (Missoula: Scholars Press, 1977), 36–51.

Ps.-Athanasius, *On Virginity*, PG 28, 251–82.

Ps.-Crates, *Letters*, tr. R. Hock, in A. Malherbe, *The Cynic Epistles: A Study Edition* (Missoula: Scholars Press, 1977), 53–89.

Ps.-Diogenes, *Letters*, tr. B. Fiore, in A. Malherbe, *The Cynic Epistles: A Study Edition* (Missoula: Scholars Press, 1977), 91–183.

Ps.-Lucian, *The Cynic*, ed. M. D. Macleod, *Luciani Opera*, 4 vols. (Oxford: Clarendon Press, 1972–87), vol. IV, 134–46.

Ps.-Macarius, *Homilies*, ed. H. Dörries, *Die 50 Geistlichen Homilien des Makarios* (Berlin: de Gruyter, 1964), tr. G. Maloney, *Pseudo-Macarius: The Fifty Spiritual Homilies and The Great Letter* (New York and Mahwah: Paulist Press, 1992).

Ptolemaeus, *Letter to Flora*, ed. G. Quispel, *Ptolémée, Lettre à Flora*, SC 24 bis (1966).

The Pythagorean Golden Verses, ed. J. C. Thom (Leiden: Brill, 1995).

Seneca, *De Beneficiis*, ed. F. Préchac, *Sénèque, Des bienfaits* (Paris: Les Belles Lettres, 1927–61).

Moral Letters, ed. L. D. Reynolds, *L. Annaei Senecae ad Lucilium Epistulae Morales* (Oxford: Clarendon Press, 1965).

Serapion, *Letter to the Monks*, PG 40, 925–41.

Shepherd of Hermas, ed. R. Joly, *Hermas, Le Pasteur*, SC 53 (1958).

Silius Italicus, *Punica*, ed. J. Delz, *Silius Italicus, Punica* (Stuttgart: Teubner, 1987).

Socrates, *Church History*, ed. G. Hansen, *Sokrates, Kirchengeschichte*, GCS (1995).

Sulpicius Severus, *Life of Martin*, ed. J Fontaine, *Sulpice Sévère, Vie de saint Martin*, SC 133, 134, 135 (1967–9).

(Palestinian) Talmud, ed. J. Neusner, *The Talmud of the Land of Israel: A Preliminary Translation and Commentary* (Chicago and London: University of Chicago Press, 1982–).

Tatian, *Oration*, ed. M. Whittaker, *Tatian, Oratio ad Graecos and Fragments* (Oxford: Clarendon Press, 1982).

Teles, *A Comparison of Poverty and Wealth*, ed. O. Hense, *Teletis Reliquiae*, 2nd edn (Tübingen: P. Siebeck, 1909).

Tertullian, *Works*, ed. D. Dekkers, *Tertulliani Opera*, CCSL 1 and 2 (1954).

Against Marcion, ed. and tr. E. Evans, *Tertullian, Adversus Marcionem*, 2 vols. (Oxford: Clarendon Press, 1972).

The Testaments of the Twelve Patriarchs: A Commentary, ed. and tr. H. W. Hollander and M. de Jonge (Leiden: Brill, 1985).

Testimony of Truth, tr. S. Giversen and B. A. Pearson, *NHL*, 448–59.

Themistius, *Oratio* 20, tr. Robert J. Penella, *The Private Orations of Themistius* (Berkeley, Los Angeles, and London: University of California Press, 2000).

Theodoret of Cyrrhus, *Cure for Greek Maladies*, ed. P. Canivet, *Théodoret de Cyr, Thérapeutique des maladies helléniques*, SC 57, 2 vols. (1958).

   Historia religiosa, ed. P. Canivet and A. Leroy-Molinghen, *Théodoret de Cyr, Histoire des moines de Syrie*, SC 234 and 257 (1977 and 1979).

   Letters, ed. Y. Azéma., *Théodoret de Cyr, Correspondence*, SC 40, 98, 111 and 429 (1955–98).

Xenophon, *Works*, ed. E. C. Marchant, *Xenophontis Opera omnia*, 5 vols. (Oxford: Clarendon Press, 1900).

2. MODERN SCHOLARSHIP

Alviar, J. José, *Klesis: The Theology of the Christian Vocation According to Origen* (Blackrock: Four Courts Press, 1993).

Aune, D., *Revelation 1–5*, Word Biblical Commentary, vol. LII (Dallas: Word Books, 1997).

Avigad, N., 'The Burial vault of a Nazirite family on Mount Scopus', *Israel Exploration Journal* 21 (1971), 185–200.

Baarda, T., '2 Clem 12 and the sayings of Jesus', in J. Delobel (ed.), *Logia, Les Paroles de Jésus – The Sayings of Jesus* (Leuven: Leuven University Press, 1982), 529–56.

Baarda, T., '*If you do not sabbatize the Sabbath . . .* The Sabbath as god or world in Gnostic understanding (Ev. Thom., Log. 27)', in R. Van Den Broek, T. Baarda, and J. Mansfeld (eds.), *Knowledge of God in the Graeco-Roman World* (Leiden: Brill, 1988), 178–201.

Barclay, J., *Jews in the Mediterranean Diaspora: From Alexander to Trajan (323 BCE–117 CE)* (Edinburgh: T&T Clark, 1996).

Barnes, Timothy D., *Constantine and Eusebius* (Cambridge, Mass. and London: Harvard University Press, 1981).

   'Methodius, Maximus, and Valentinus', *JThS* 30 (1979), 47–55.

   Review of the *Histoire acéphale*, *JThS* 37.2 (1986), 576–89.

   Tertullian (Oxford: Clarendon Press, 1985).

Beard, M., North, J., and Price, S., *Religions of Rome* (Cambridge University Press, 1998).

Beckwith, Roger, *The Old Testament Canon of the New Testament Church and its Background in Early Judaism* (Grand Rapids: Eerdmans, 1985).

BeDuhn, J. D., *The Manichaean Body in Discipline and Ritual* (Baltimore and London: Johns Hopkins University Press, 2002).

Behr, J., *Asceticism and Anthropology in Irenaeus and Clement* (Oxford University Press, 2000).

Bell, C., *Ritual Theory, Ritual Practice* (New York and Oxford: Oxford University Press, 1992).

Boismard, M.-É., *Le Diatessaron: De Tatien à Justin* (Paris: Librarie Lecoffre, 1992).

Bowie, E. L., 'Apollonius of Tyana: tradition and reality', *ANRW* II.16.2 (1978), 1652–99.

Boyarin, D., *Carnal Israel: Reading Sex In Talmudic Culture* (Berkeley, Los Angeles and Oxford: University of California Press, 1993).

   Dying for God (Stanford University Press, 1999).

Brakke, David, *Athanasius and the Politics of Asceticism* (Oxford: Clarendon Press, 1995).

Brent, Allen, *Hippolytus and the Roman Church in the Third Century: Communities in Tension before the Emergence of a Monarch-bishop* (Leiden and New York: Brill, 1995).

Bright, P., 'The combat of demons in Antony and Origen', in W. A. Biernert and U. Kühneweg, *Origeniana Septima* (Leuven: Peeters, 1999).

Brown, Peter, *Authority and the Sacred: Aspects of the Christianization of the Roman World* (Cambridge University Press, 1995).

   The Body and Society: Men, Women and Sexual Renunciation in Early Christianity (London and Boston: Faber, 1989).

   'The Rise and Function of the Holy Man in Late Antiquity', *JRS* 61 (1971), 80–101.

   'The Saint as Exemplar in Late Antiquity', *Representations* 2 (1983), 1–25.

Burkert, W., *Greek Religion: Archaic and Classical*, tr. J. Raffan (Oxford: Blackwell, 1985).

Burton-Christie, Douglas, *The Word in the Desert: Scripture and the Quest for Holiness in Early Christian Monasticism* (Oxford University Press, 1993).

Caner, D., 'The practice and prohibition of self-castration in Early Christianity', *VC* 51 (1997), 396–415.

   Wandering, Begging Monks: Spiritual Authority and the Promotion of Monasticism in Late Antiquity (Berkeley, Los Angeles, London: University of California Press, 2002).

Chepey, Stuart, *Nazirites in Late Second Temple Judaism* (Leiden: Brill, 2005).

Chesnutt, R. D., *From Death to Life: Conversion in Joseph and Aseneth* (Sheffield Academic Press, 1995).

Chitty, D., *The Desert a City* (London and Oxford: Basil Blackwell, 1966).

Clark, E. A., *Reading Renunciation: Asceticism and Scripture in Early Christianity* (Princeton University Press, 1999).

Clark, G., 'Philosophic Lives and the Philosophic Life: Porphyry and Iamblichus', in T. Hägg and P. Rousseau (eds.), *Greek Biography and Panegyric in Late Antiquity* (Berkeley, Los Angeles, and London: University of California Press, 2000), 29–51.

Clark Smith, John, *The Ancient Wisdom of Origen* (London and Toronto: Associated University Presses, 1992).

Clay, D., 'Lucian of Samosata: Four Philosophical Lives (Nigrinus, Demonax, Peregrinus, Alexander Pseudomantis)', *ANRW* II.36.5 (1992), 3406–50.

Coggins, R. J., *Haggai, Zechariah, Malachi* (Sheffield Academic Press, 1987).

Coggins, R. J., and Re'emi, S. Paul, *Israel Among the Nations* (Grand Rapids and Edinburgh: Eerdmans, 1985).

Cohen, Shaye J. D., *From the Maccabees to the Mishnah* (Philadelphia: Westminster Press, 1987).

Conick, A. De, and Fossum, J., 'Stripped before God: a new interpretation of Logion 37 in the Gospel of Thomas', *VC* 45 (1991), 123–50.

Conybeare, C., 'Tertullian on flesh, spirit, and wives', *Sev*, 430–9.

Cox [Miller], P., *Biography in Late Antiquity: A Quest for the Holy Man* (Berkeley: University of California Press, 1983).

Davies, S., *The Gospel of Thomas Annotated and Explained* (London: Darton, Longman and Todd, 2002).

de Faye, E., *Origène, sa vie, son oeuvre, sa pensée*, 3 vols. (Paris: E. Leroux, 1927–8).

de Mendieta, David Amand, 'La virginité chez Eusèbe d'Emèse et l'ascéticisme familial dans la première moitié du IVe siècle', *Revue d'Histoire Ecclésiastique* 50 (1955), 777–820.

Dechow, Jon F., *Dogma and Mysticism in Early Christianity: Epiphanius of Cyprus and the Legacy of Origen* (Macon, Ga.: Mercer University Press, 1988).

Descoeudres, G., 'Le désert des Kellia', in *Connaissance des Pères de l'Église* 72 (1998), 30–8.

Desprez, V., 'Jewish Ascetical groups at the time of Christ: Qumran and the Therapeuts', *American Benedictine Review* 41.3 (1990), 291–311.

Detienne, M., *The Gardens of Adonis: Spices in Greek Mythology* (Princeton University Press, 1994).

Diamond, E., *Holy Men and Hunger Artists: Fasting and Asceticism in Rabbinic Culture* (Oxford University Press, 2004).

Dillon, J., 'Iamblichus of Chalcis', *ANRW* II.36.2 (1987), 863–909.

Dillon, J., and Hershbell, J., *Iamblichus: On the Pythagorean Way of Life* (Atlanta: Society of Biblical Literature, 1991).

Dillon, M., *Pilgrims and Pilgrimage in Ancient Greece* (London and New York: Routledge, 1997).

Doran, R., '2 Maccabees', in J. Barton and J. Muddiman (eds.), *The Oxford Bible Commentary* (Oxford University Press, 2001), 734–50.

Douglas, M., *Leviticus as Literature* (Oxford University Press, 1999).

Natural Symbols (Harmondsworth: Penguin, 1973).

Purity and Danger (Harmondsworth: Penguin, 1970).

Downing, F. G., *Cynics and Christian Origins* (Edinburgh: T&T Clark, 1992).

Drijvers, H. J. W., *Bardaisan of Edessa* (Assen: Van Gorcum, 1966).

Drijvers, H., 'Christ as warrior and merchant – aspects of Marcion's Christology', *SP* XXI (1989), 73–85.

Dudley, D., *A History of Cynicism: From Diogenes to the 6th Century AD*, 2nd edn (Bristol Classical Press, 1998).

Dunn, G., 'Infected sheep and diseased cattle, or the pure and holy flock: Cyprian's pastoral care of virgins', *JECS* 11.1 (2003), 1–20.

Dunn, M., *The Emergence of Monasticism* (Oxford: Blackwell, 2000).

Elm, S., *'Virgins of God': The Making of Asceticism in Late Antiquity* (Oxford: Clarendon Press, 1994).

Escolan, P., *Monachisme et église. Le Monachisme syrien du IVe au VIIe siecle: un monachisme charismatique* (Paris: Beauchesne, 1999).

Fear, Andrew, 'A journey to the end of the world', in Jaś Elsner and Ian Rutherford (eds.), *Pilgrimage in Graeco-Roman and Early Christian Antiquity: Seeing the Gods* (Oxford University Press, 2005), 319–31.

Feldman, L. H., and Reinhold, M. (eds.), *Jewish Life and Thought Among Greeks and Romans: Primary Readings* (Edinburgh: T&T Clark, 1996).

Festugière, A.-J., 'Sur une nouvelle edition du *"De vita Pythagorica"* de Jamblique', *Revue des Études Grecques* 50 (1937), 470–94.

Finn, R. D., *Almsgiving in the Later Roman Empire: Christian Promotion and Practice (313–450)* (Oxford University Press, 2006).

'Almsgiving for the pure of heart: continuity and change in early Christian teaching', *Sev*, 419–29.

Fishbane, M., *Biblical Interpretation in Ancient Israel* (Oxford: Clarendon Press, 1985).

Fitzmyer, J., 'The Oxyrhynchus *logoi* of Jesus and the Coptic Gospel according to Thomas', in *Theological Studies* 20.4 (1959), 505–60.

Fitzmyer, J., *Tobit* (Berlin and New York: de Gruyter, 2003).

Foucault, M., *The Use of Pleasure: The History of Sexuality*, vol. II, tr. R. Hurley (Harmondsworth: Penguin, 1986).

Fraade, Steven D., 'Ascetical aspects of ancient Judaism', in A. Green (ed.), *Jewish Spirituality*, vol. I, *From the Bible Through the Middle Ages* (London: Routledge, 1986), 253–88.

Francis, James A., *Subversive Virtue: Asceticism and Authority in the Second-Century Pagan World* (Pennsylvania State University Press, 1995).

Frankfurter, D., 'Beyond "Jewish Christianity": continuing religious sub-cultures of the second and third centuries and their documents', in Annette Yoshiko Reed and Adam H. Becker (eds.), *The Ways that Never Parted: Jews and Christians in Late Antiquity and the Early Middle Ages* (Tübingen: Mohr Siebeck, 2003), 131–43.

Frend, W. H., *The Donatist Church: A Movement of Protest in Roman North Africa* (Oxford: Clarendon Press, 1971).

Gamble, H. Y., *Books and Readers in the Early Church: A History of Early Christian Texts* (New Haven and London: Yale University Press, 1995).

Garnsey, P., 'Pythagoras, Plato and communality: a note', *Hermathena* 179 (2005), 77–87.

Garnsey, P. and Humfress, C., *The Evolution of the Late Antique World* (Cambridge: Orchard Academic, 2001).

Gatier, Pierre-Louis, 'Un moine sur la frontière: Alexandre l'Acémète en Syrie', in A. Rousselle (ed.), *Frontières terrestres, frontières célestes dans l'antiquité* (Paris: Presses universitaires de Perpignan, 1995), 435–57.

Geiger, J., 'Sophists and Rabbis: Jews and their past in the Severan age', in *Sev*, 440–8.

Giet, S., *Les Idées et l'action sociales de Saint Basile* (Paris: J. Gabalda, 1941).

Goldberg, Abraham, 'The Palestinian Talmud', in S. Safrai (ed.), *The Literature of the Sages*, First Part (Assen and Philadelphia: Van Gorcum and Fortress Press, 1987), 303–22.

Goehring, James E., 'The origins of monasticism', in H. W. Attridge and G. Hata (eds.), *Eusebius, Christianity, and Judaism* (Leiden: Brill, 1992), 235–55.

'The world engaged: the social and economic world of early Egyptian monasticism', in J. Goehring, C. W. Hedrick, J. T. Sanders, and H. D. Betz (eds.), *Gnosticism and the Early Christian World* (Sonoma: Polebridge Press, 1990), 134–44.

Goldstein, J. A., *1 Maccabees* (New York: Doubleday, 1976).

Gould, Graham, *The Desert Fathers on Monastic Community* (Oxford: Clarendon Press, 1993).

'The influence of Origen on fourth-century monasticism', in G. Dorival, A. Le Boullec, *et al.* (eds.), *Origeniana Sexta* (Leuven: Peeters, 1995), 591–8.

Goulet-Cazé, M.-O., *L'Ascèse cynique: Un commentaire de Diogène Laërce* VI 70–71 (Paris: Vrin, 1986).

'Le cynicisme à l' époque impériale', *ANRW* II.36.4 (1990), 2720–833.

Greer, Rowan, 'Pastoral care and discipline', *CHC*2, 567–84.

Gribomont, J., 'Esoterisme et tradition dans le Traité du Saint-Esprit de saint Basile', in *Oecumenica, an Annual Symposium of Ecumenical Research* (Minneapolis: Augsburg Publishing, 1967), 22–58.

Griffith, S. H., 'Asceticism in the Church of Syria: the hermeneutics of early Syrian monasticism', in V. L. Wimbush, and R. Valantasis (eds.), *Asceticism* (Oxford and New York: Oxford University Press, 1995), 220–45.

Griggs, C. W., *Early Egyptian Christianity: From its Origins to 451 CE* (Leiden: Brill, 1990).

Grimm, Veronika E., *From Feasting to Fasting, The Evolution of a Sin: Attitudes to Food in Late Antiquity* (London and New York: Routledge, 1996).

Guarducci, M., *Epigrafia Greca*, vol. IV (Rome: Instituto Poligrafico dello Stato, 1978).

Hadot, Pierre, *Philosophy as a Way of Life: Spiritual Exercises from Socrates to Foucault*, ed. Arnold I. Davidson (Oxford: Blackwell, 1995).

Hägg, T., *The Novel in Antiquity* (Berkeley and Los Angeles: University of California Press, 1991).

Hajjar, Youssef, *La Triade d'Héliopolis-Baalbek: iconographie, théologie, culte et sanctuaires* (University of Montreal, 1985).

Hammond, C. P., 'The last ten years of Rufinus' life and the date of his move south from Aquileia', *JTS* ns 28 (1977), 372–429.

Harland, P., *Associations, Synagogues, and Congregations: Claiming a Place in Ancient Mediterranean Society* (Minneapolis: Fortress Press, 2003).

Harrington, H. K., *Holiness: Rabbinic Judaism and the Graeco-Roman World* (London and New York: Routledge, 2001).

The Purity Texts (London and New York: T&T Clark, 2004).

Hay, D. M., 'Things Philo said and did not say about the Therapeutae', *SBLSP* 31 (1992), 673–84.

Heine, R. (ed.), *The Montanist Oracles and Testimonia* (Belgium and Macon, Ga.: Peeters and Mercer University Press, 1989).

Hoffmann, R. J., 'Women in Marcionite churches of the second century', *SP* 18.3 (1989), 161–71.

Holmes, A., *A Life Pleasing to God: The Spirituality of the Rules of St Basil* (London: Darton, Longman and Todd, 2000).

Hunt, E. J., *Christianity in the Second Century: The Case of Tatian* (London and New York: Routledge, 2003).

Hunter, D. G., *A Comparison Between a King and a Monk / Against the Opponents of the Monastic Life: Two Treatises by John Chrysostom* (Lewiston/Queenston and Lampeter: Edwin Mellen Press, 1988).

'Preaching and propaganda in fourth-century Antioch: John Chrysostom's *Homilies on the Statues*', in D. G. Hunter (ed.), *Preaching in the Patristic Age: Studies in Honor of Walter J. Burghardt, S.J.* (New York: Paulist Press, 1989), 119–38.

Inwood, B., *Ethics and Human Action in Early Stoicism* (Oxford: Clarendon Press, 1985).

Jenkins, P., *Hidden Gospels, How the Search for Jesus Lost its Way* (Oxford University Press, 2001).

Joannou, P.-P. (ed.), *Discipline générale antique (IVe–Ixe s.)*, 2 vols. (Rome: Pontificia commissione per la redazione del codice di diritto canonico orientale, 1962–3).

Johnson, Luke Timothy, *The First and Second Letters to Timothy* (New York and London: Doubleday, 2001).

Judge, E. A., 'The earliest use of monachos for "monk" (P. Coll. Youtie 77) and the origins of monasticism', *Jahrbuch für Antike und Christentum* 20 (1977), 72–89.

Kahn, C. H., *Pythagoras and the Pythagoreans: A Brief History* (Indianapolis: Hackett, 2001).

Karasszon, I., 'Heroism in the Acts of Paul and in the Bible', in J. Bremmer (ed.), *The Apocryphal Acts of Paul and Thecla* (Kampen: Pharos, 1996), 179–90.

Klawans, J., *Impurity and Sin in Ancient Judaism* (Oxford University Press, 2000).

Koester, H., *Ancient Christian Gospels: Their History and Development* (London: SCM, 1990).

Koltun-Fromm, Naomi, 'Zipporah's Complaint: Moses is not conscientious in the deed! Exegetical traditions of Moses' celibacy', in Reed and Becker (eds.), *The Ways that Never Parted*, 283–306.

König, Jason, 'Sympotic dialogue in the first to fifth centuries CE', in S. Goldhill (ed.), *The End of Dialogue in Antiquity* (Cambridge University Press, 2009), 85–113.

Konstan, D., 'Acts of love: a narrative pattern in the apocryphal acts', *JECS* 6.1 (1998), 15–36.

Kraemer, D., 'The Mishnah', in *CHJ4*, 299–315.

Kraemer, R., *When Aseneth Met Joseph* (Oxford University Press, 1998).

Krause, Jens-Uwe, *Witwen und Waisen im Römischen Reich*, 4 vols., (Stuttgart: Steiner, 1994–5).

Kugel, James, *Traditions of the Bible: A Guide to the Bible As It Was at the Start of the Common Era* (Cambridge, Mass.: Harvard University Press, 1998).

Lalleman, P., *The Acts of John: A Two-Stage Initiation into Johannine Gnosticism* (Leuven: Peeters, 1998).

Lampe, P., *From Paul to Valentinus: Christians at Rome in the First Two Centuries*, tr. M. Steinhauser (London: T&T Clark, 2003).

Lawless, G., *Augustine of Hippo and his Monastic Rule* (Oxford: Clarendon Press, 1987).

Leyser, C., *Authority and Asceticism from Augustine to Gregory the Great* (Oxford: Clarendon Press, 2000).

Levenson, J. D., *Esther* (London: SCM Press, 1997).

Levine, A.-J., 'Judith', in J. Barton and J. Muddiman (eds.), *The Oxford Bible Commentary* (Oxford University Press, 2001).

Lieu, J., *Christian Identity in the Jewish and Graeco-Roman World* (Oxford University Press, 2004).

Lightfoot, J. L. (ed.), *Lucian: On the Syrian Goddess* (Oxford University Press, 2003).

'Pilgrims and ethnographers: in search of the Syrian goddess', in Jaś Elsner and Ian Rutherford (eds.), *Pilgrimage in Graeco-Roman and Early Christian Antiquity: Seeing the Gods* (Oxford University Press, 2005), 333–52.

Lightstone, J., *The Rhetoric of the Babylonian Talmud, Its Social Meaning and Context* (Waterloo, Ontario: Wilfred Laurier University Press, 1994).

MacDonald, D., *Christianizing Homer* (New York and Oxford: Oxford University Press, 1994).

Malherbe, A., *The Cynic Epistles: A Study Edition* (Missoula: Scholars Press, 1977).

Mandel, P, 'The Tosefta', *CHJ* 4, 316–35.

Markschies, C., *Gnosis: An Introduction*, tr. J. Bowden (London and New York: T&T Clark, 2003).

McGowan, Andrew, *Ascetic Eucharists: Food and Drink in Early Christian Ritual Meals* (Oxford: Clarendon Press, 1999).

'Marcion's love of creation', *JECS* 9.3 (2001), 295–311.

Meeks, W. A., 'The image of the androgyne: some uses of a symbol in earliest Christianity', *History of Religions* 13 (1974), 165–208.

Ménard, J.-É., *L'Évangile selon Thomas* (Leiden: Brill, 1975).

Merrills, A. H., 'Monks, monsters, and barbarians: re-defining the African periphery in Late Antiquity', *JECS* 12.2 (2004), 217–44.

Metzger, B. M., *The Canon of the New Testament: Its Origin, Development, and Significance* (Oxford: Clarendon Press, 1987).

Miller, R. H., 'Liturgical materials in the *Acts of John*', *SP* 13 (1975), 375–81.

Moles, J., ' "Honestius Quam Ambitiosius"? An exploration of the Cynic's attitude to moral corruption in his fellow men', *JHS* 103 (1983), 103–23.

Mondésert, C., *Clément d'Alexandrie: Introduction à l'étude de sa pensée religieuse à partir de l'Écriture* (Paris: Aubier, 1944).

Moore, C. A., *Daniel, Esther and Jeremiah: The Additions* (New York: Doubleday, 1977).

'Why wasn't the Book of Judith included in the Hebrew Bible?', in J. VanderKam (ed.), *'No One Spoke Ill of Her': Essays on the Book of Judith* (Atlanta: Scholars Press, 1992), 61–71.

Muddiman, J., 'Fast, fasting', in N. Freedman (ed.), *Anchor Bible Dictionary*, vol. ii (New York and London: Doubleday, 1992), 773–6.

Munier, C., (ed.), *Concilia Africae*, A.345–A. 525, CCSL 149 (1974).

'Problèmes monastiques et conciles Africains (a. 345–427)', in *Augustinianum* 39.1 (1999), 149–68.

Murphy O'Connor, J., 'Philo and 2 Cor. 6:14–7:1', *Revue Biblique* 45 (1988), 55–69.

Murray, R., *Symbols of Church and Kingdom: A Study in Early Syriac Tradition*, 2nd edn (London and New York: T&T Clark, 2004).

Naeh, Shlomoh, 'Freedom and celibacy: a Talmudic variation on tales of temptation and fall in Genesis and its Syrian background', in J. Frishman and L. Van Rompay (eds.), *The Book of Genesis in Jewish and Oriental Christian Interpretation* (Louvain: Peeters, 1997), 73–89.

Naiden, Fred, '*Hiketai* and *Theoroi* at Epidauros' in Jaś Elsner and Ian Rutherford (eds.), *Pilgrimage in Graeco-Roman and Early Christian Antiquity: Seeing the Gods* (Oxford University Press, 2005), 73–95.

Nautin, Pierre, *Origène, sa vie et son oeuvre* (Paris: Beachesne, 1977).

Neusner, J., *The Mishnah: A New Translation* (Yale, New Haven, and London: Yale University Press, 1988).

Niederwimmer, K., *Die Didache* (Göttingen: Vandenhoeck and Ruprecht, 1989).

Nikiprowetzky, V., 'Le *De vita contemplativa* revisité', in J. Leclant (ed.), *Sagesse et religion: colloque de Strasbourg (octobre 1976)* (Paris: Presses universitaires de France, 1979), 105–25.

O'Laughlin, Michael, 'The anthropology of Evagrius Ponticus and its sources', in Charles Kannengiesser and William L. Petersen (eds.), *Origen of Alexandria, His World and His Legacy* (University of Notre Dame Press, 1988), 357–73.

Osiek, C., *Shepherd of Hermas, A Commentary* (Minneapolis: Fortress Press, 1999).

'The Widow as altar: the rise and fall of a symbol', *The Second Century* 3 (1983), 159–69.

Parker, Robert, *Miasma: Pollution and Purification in Early Greek Religion* (Oxford: Clarendon Press, 1983).

Polytheism and Society at Athens (Oxford University Press, 2005).

Patterson, L. G., *Methodius of Olympus: Divine Sovereignty, Human Freedom, and Life in Christ* (Washington: Catholic University of America, 1997).

Pena, I., Castellana, P., and Fernandez, R., *Les Cénobites Syriens*, Studium Biblicum Franciscanum, Collectio Minor 28 (Milan: Franciscan Printing Press, 1983).

Les Reclus Syriens: Recherches sur les anciennes formes de vie solitaire en Syrie, Studium Biblicum Franciscanum, Collectio Minor 23 (Milan: Franciscan Printing Press, 1980).

Petersen, W., *Tatian's Diatessaron: Its Creation, Dissemination, Significance, and History in Scholarship* (Leiden: Brill, 1994).

Petsalis-Diomidis, Alexia, 'The body in space: visual dynamics in Graeco-Roman healing pilgrimage', in Jaś Elsner and Ian Rutherford (eds.), *Pilgrimage in Graeco-Roman and Early Christian Antiquity: Seeing the Gods* (Oxford University Press, 2005), 183–218.

Price, S., *Religions of the Ancient Greeks* (Cambridge University Press, 1999).

Rituals and Power, The Roman Imperial Cult in Asia Minor (Cambridge University Press, 1984).

'Latin Christian Apologetics: Minucius Felix, Tertullian, and Cyprian', in M. Edwards, M. Goodman, and S. Price (eds.), *Apologetics in the Roman Empire: Pagans, Jews, and Christians* (Oxford University Press, 1999), 105–29.

Prigent, P., *Commentary on the Apocalypse of St John*, tr. W. Pradels (Tübingen: Mohr Siebeck, 2004).

Procopé, J. F., 'Morality and manners in Clement's *Paidagogos*', *SP* 26 (1993), 313–17.

Quispel, G., 'The study of encratism: a historical survey', in U. Bianchi (ed.), *La tradizione dell'enkrateia* (Rome: Edizioni dell'Ateneo, 1982), 35–81.

Ramsey, Boniface, *Ambrose* (London and New York: Routledge, 1997).

Rankin, D., *Tertullian and the Church* (Cambridge University Press, 1995).

Reed, A. Yoshiko and Becker, A. H., 'Introduction: traditional models and new directions', in idem (eds.), *The Ways that Never Parted: Jews and Christians in Late Antiquity and the Early Middle Ages* (Tübingen: Mohr Siebeck, 2003).

Riaud, J., 'Quelques réflexions sur les Thérapeutes d'Alexandrie à la lumière de *De Vita Mosis* II, 67', in E. Hilgert, D. T. Runia, D. Hay, and D. Winston (eds.), *Heirs of the Septuagint: Philo, Hellenistic Judaism and Early Christianity, Studia Philonica Annual* 3 (Atlanta: Scholars Press, *c.* 1991), 184–91.

Rist, J., 'Basil's "Neoplatonism": its background and nature', in P. Fedwick (ed.), *Basil of Caesarea: Christian, Humanist, Ascetic*, 2 vols. (Toronto: Pontifical Institute of Medieval Studies, 1981), vol. i, 137–220.

Roberts, C., *Manuscript, Society and Belief in Early Christian Egypt* (London: Oxford University Press, 1979).

'Two Oxford papyri', *ZNW* 37 (1938), 184–8.

Roitman, A. D., 'Achior in the Book of Judith: his role and significance', in J. VanderKam (ed.), *"No One Spoke Ill of Her": Essays on the Book of Judith* (Atlanta: Scholars Press, 1992), 31–45.

Roldanus, J., 'Origène, Antoine et Athanase: leur interconnexion dans la Vie et les Lettres', *SP* 26 (1993), 389–414.

Rordorf, W., 'Quelques jalons pour une interpretation symbolique des *Actes de Paul*', in D. Warren, A. Brock, and D. Pao (eds.), *Early Christian Voices In Texts, Traditions, and Symbols* (Boston and Leiden: Brill, 2003), 251–65.

'Terra incognita: recent research on Christian apocryphal literature, especially on some Acts of Apostles', *SP* 25 (1993), 142–58.

Rousseau, P., *Ascetics, Authority, and the Church in the Age of Jerome and Cassian* (Oxford University Press, 1978).

Basil of Caesarea (Berkeley, Los Angeles and Oxford: University of California Press, 1994).

Pachomius: The Making of a Community in Fourth-Century Egypt (Berkeley: University of California Press, 1985).

Rubenson, S., *The Letters of St Antony: Monasticism and the Making of a Saint* (Minneapolis: Fortress Press, 1995).

'Origen in the Egyptian monastic tradition in the fourth century', in W. A. Bienert and U. Kühneweg (eds.), *Origeniana Septima* (Leuven: Peeters, 1999), 319–37.

Runia, D., *Philo in Early Christian Literature: A Survey* (Assen and Minneapolis: Van Gorcum and Fortress Press, 1993).

Sanders, James A., 'The canonical process', *CHJ4*, 230–43.

Sawyer, D., *Women and Religion in the First Christian Centuries* (London and New York: Routledge, 1996).

Schneider, P. G., *The Mystery of the Acts of John: An Interpretation of the Hymn and the Dance in the Light of the Acts' Theology* (San Francisco: Mellen Research University Press, 1991).

Sfameni Gasparro, Giulia, 'Asceticism and anthropology: *Enkrateia* and "double creation" in Early Christianity', in V. L. Wimbush and R. Valantasis (eds.), *Asceticism* (Oxford and New York: Oxford University Press, 1995), 127–46.

Shaw, T. M., *The Burden Of The Flesh: Fasting And Sexuality In Early Christianity* (Minneapolis: Fortress Press, c. 1998).

'Creation, virginity and diet in fourth-century Christianity: Basil of Ancyra's On the True Purity of Virginity', *Gender & History* 9.3 (1997), 579–96.

Simon, E., *Festivals of Attica: An Archaeological Commentary* (Madison, Wisc.: University of Wisconsin Press, 1983).

Simonetti, M. (ed.), *Ippolito: Contro Noeto* (Bologna: EDB, 2000).

Siniossoglou, N., *Plato and Theodoret: The Christian Appropriation of Platonic Philosophy and the Hellenic Intellectual Resistance* (Cambridge University Press, 2008).

Smith, J. Z., *Drudgery Divine: On the Comparison of Early Christianities and the Religions of Late Antiquity* (University of London, 1990).

Sotinel, C., 'Le recrutement des évêques en Italie aux IVe et Ve siècles: essai d'enquête prosopographique', in *Vescovi e pastori in epoca teodosiana*, 2 vols. (Rome: Institutum Patristicum Augustinianum, 1997), vol. i, 193–204.

Spidlik, Thomas, 'L'idéal du monachisme basilien', in P. J. Fedwick (ed.), *Basil of Caesarea: Christian, Humanist, Ascetic*, 2 vols. (Toronto: Pontifical Institute of Mediaeval Studies, 1981), vol. i, 361–74.

Spinks, Bryan D., 'The growth of liturgy and the church year', *CHC2*, 601–17.

Stewart, C., *Cassian the Monk* (Oxford University Press, 1998).

'Working the Earth of the Heart.' The Messalian Controversy in History, Texts, and Language to AD 431 (Oxford: Clarendon Press, 1991).

Tabory, J., 'Jewish festivals in late antiquity', in S. Katz (ed.), *CHJ4*, 556–72.

Takeda, F., 'The Syriac version of the *Life of Antony: A meeting point of Egyptian monasticism with Syriac native asceticism*', in R. Lavenant (ed.), *Symposium Syriacum* VII (Rome: Pontificio Istituto Orientale, 1998), 185–94.

Thomas, C. M., *The Acts of Peter, Gospel Literature, and the Ancient Novel: Rewriting the Past* (Oxford University Press, 2003).

Thompson, J. A., *The Book of Jeremiah* (Grand Rapids: Eerdmans, 1980).

Thornton, T., 'Problematical Passovers: difficulties for Diaspora Jews and early Christians in determining Passover dates during the first three centuries AD', *SP* 20 (1989), 402–8.

Tissot, Y., 'L'encratisme des *Actes de Thomas*', *ANRW* 25.6 (1988), 4415–30.

Trebilco, P., *Jewish Communities in Asia Minor* (Cambridge University Press, 1991).

Trevett, C., *Montanism: Gender, Authority and the New Prophecy* (Cambridge University Press, 1996).

Turcan, R., *The Cults of the Roman Empire*, tr. A. Nevill (Oxford: Blackwell, 1996).

  The Gods of Ancient Rome: Religion in Everyday Life from Archaic to Imperial Times, tr. A. Nevill (Edinburgh University Press, 2000).

Uro, R., 'Is *Thomas* an encratite gospel?', in R. Uro (ed.), *'Thomas' at the Crossroads: Essays on the 'Gospel of Thomas'* (Edinburgh: T&T Clark, 1998), 140–62.

  '*Thomas* and oral gospel tradition', in R. Uro (ed.), *'Thomas' at the Crossroads: Essays on the 'Gospel of Thomas'* (Edinburgh: T&T Clark, 1998), 8–32.

Valantasis, R., 'Is the Gospel of Thomas ascetical? Revisiting an old problem with a new theory', *JECS* 7.1 (1999), 55–81.

  'Constructions of power in asceticism', *JAAR* 63 (1995), 775–821.

  The Gospel of Thomas (London: Routledge, 1997).

  'Nag Hammadi and asceticism: theory and practice', *SP* 35.4 (2001), 172–90.

Verheijen, L., *La Règle de saint Augustin*, 2 vols. (Paris: Études Augustiniennes, 1967).

Vermes, G., *The Complete Dead Sea Scrolls in English* (London: Penguin, 1997).

Vööbus, A., *History of Asceticism in the Syrian Orient*, 3 vols. (Louvain: CSCO, 1958, 1960, and 1988).

Walzer, R., *Galen on Jews and Christians* (London: Oxford University Press, 1949).

Williams, M., *Rethinking Gnosticism: An Argument for Dismantling a Dubious Category* (Princeton University Press, 1996).

Williams, R., *Why Study the Past? The Quest for the Historical Church* (London: Darton, Longman and Todd, 2005).

Wills, L. M., *The Jewish Novel in the Ancient World* (Ithaca and London: Cornell University Press, 1995).

Wilson, R. McL., 'Alimentary and sexual encratism in the Nag Hammadi tractates', in U. Bianchi (ed.), *La tradizione dell'enkrateia: motivazioni ontologiche e protologiche* (Rome: Edizioni dell'Ateneo, 1985), 317–39.

Wilson, S. G., *Related Strangers, Jews and Christians 70–170 CE* (Minneapolis: Fortress Press, 1995).

Wimbush, V. L., 'The ascetic impulse in early Christianity: some methodological challenges', *SP* 25 (1993), 462–78.

Wimbush, V. L., and Valantasis, R. (eds.), *Asceticism* (Oxford and New York: Oxford University Press, 1995).

Winston, D., *Philo of Alexandria: The Contemplative Life, The Giants, and Selections* (Mahwah: Paulist Press, 1981).

Wise, M., Abegg, M., and Cook, E. (eds.), *The Dead Sea Scrolls: A New Translation* (London: Harper Collins, 1996).

Wisse, F., 'The nature and purpose of redactional changes in the early Christian texts: the canonical Gospels', in W. L. Petersen (ed.), *Gospel Traditions in the second century* (Notre Dame and London: Notre Dame Press, 1989), 39–53.

Wright, D. F., 'At what ages were people baptized in the early centuries?', *SP* 30 (1997), 389–94.

Wycherley, R. E., *The Athenian Agora*, vol. III, *Literary and Epigraphical Testimonia* (Princeton: American School of Classical Studies at Athens, 1957).

Young, S., 'Being a man: the pursuit of manliness in *The Shepherd of Hermas*', *JECS* 2 (1994), 237–55.

Zaidman, L. Bruit, and Schmitt Pantel, P., *Religion in the Ancient Greek City*, tr. P. Cartledge (Cambridge University Press, 1992).

Zumkeller, A., *Augustine's Ideal of the Religious Life* (New York: Fordham University Press, 1986).

Index